Using TIME MANAGEMENT To Get More Done

Lauren R. Januz

Kim M. Magon

Smith Collins

Publishers and Consultants

Using TIME MANAGEMENT To Get More Done

Lauren R. Januz & Kim M. Magon

EMENT

Cover & book designer: Curt Neitzke

Manufacturing coordinator: O'Collins Corporation

Some of the material in this book originally appeared in the *Execu*time®* newsletter and has been updated for this book.

Publisher's Cataloging in Publication Data

Januz, Lauren R., 1939-
      Using Time Management To Get More Done / by
      Lauren R. Januz and Kim M. Magon.
         p.   cm.
      Includes bibliographical references (p.   ) and index.
      ISBN 0-9623414-5-2

      1. Executives – time management.   2. Time managment.
I. Magon, Kim M., 1962-   II. Title
HF5500.2.J34 1992
658.4'093 dc20   92-72761

Printed in the United States of America

*To all of the grateful friends
of Bill W. and Dr. Bob S., without whose
help, love and friendship this book
never could have been written.*
— Lauren R. Januz

*To my family, especially my
husband Scott, whose love and support
mean the world to me, and my parents,
whose love brought me into the world.*
— Kim M. Magon

using time management to get more done

Table of Contents

part one

INTRODUCTION—HOW YOU CAN USE TIME MANAGEMENT TO GET MORE DONE.

foreword
by
Lauren R. Januz

fifteen years ago I was a very disorganized executive. As the president of a small Chicago-based direct marketing agency and printing company I was continually missing deadlines, losing papers on my desk, and failing to close big deals because I was missing appointments. Phone messages piled up on my desk. I was consistently falling behind in everything that I had to do. I had a dozen people working for me and my shoddy work habits were rubbing off on them.

Employees regularly showed up for work late. They were as disorganized as I was.

We didn't seem to have a sense of direction to our operation.

It seemed (to me, at least) I was doing all the real work, while the people on our payroll were engaged only in "busy work."

I was stressed out. I lived for the three martini lunch and the afternoon commuter train where I could sip a cocktail (or three) and find temporary relief from the pressure. I usually spent my Saturdays and Sundays in the office trying to catch up on the work I hadn't finished during the week.

In short, our office was a mess. I was a mess. I ate too much, drank far too much, got no exercise, got too little sleep and accomplished little during my office time. I was on a path to self-destruction. I decided that something had to be done.

I visited the office of Robert Stone, founder and president of Stone and Adler Inc., a leading direct response agency in Chicago. His business was twenty times the size of mine but I found that the desk he worked from was completely barren. Mine looked somewhat like I envisioned Hiroshima looked like after World War II was over. I asked him how he did it and he told me about some simple time management techniques that he used. Among these techniques were the keeping of a To Do Today list, taking regular inventories of his time use, and a simple "never on Tuesday policy" where he worked at home on Tuesdays. I was fascinated and realized that I, too, must find a solution to managing my time. I found my way into a bookstore in downtown Chicago and saw some books on the subject of time management. I bought one and became fascinated with it. I soon came back and bought some other books on time management. I ordered a Daytimer® pocket secretary and began using its principles to manage my time. The subject of managing my time intrigued me.

Eventually I subscribed to the *Execu*time*® newsletter. I became a serious time management student. In 1980 I bought *Execu*time*® and each month, since 1980, have been researching, writing and publishing material on time management. In late 1991 I sold *Execu*time*® to *Bottom Line Personal* which merged it into *Bottom Line Personal.*

My first book, *Time Management For Executives*, co-authored by Susan K. Jones, former editor of *Execu*time*® became a business book success and brought us hundreds of new subscribers to *Execu*time*®, many of whom have stayed with us all the years we published because they too have found serenity and peace through improving their lifestyles by using good time management techniques.

When I sold *Execu*time*® many of our subscribers wrote to encourage us to publish another book of time management techniques and in 1990 I met Kim M. Magon, a very professional and energetic writer and columnist for many business periodicals. She agreed to undertake the monumental job of sorting through everything I had published since 1980, and the founding of *Execu*time®* in 1977, and assemble it into a logical order for a new book. As Kim became more interested in the subject of time management, she researched hundreds of new articles published on time management in the business press, read dozens of time management books, and interviewed countless business executives.

It is through our combined labors, including virtually every Saturday for a year, that this book is being presented to you now. During the year of work (it's amazing how much we had published in the past decade) we found that few of the successful time management techniques had changed, but sometimes the ways that one accomplished the tasks had. The computer, of course, has had a major impact on the life of every businessperson.

We've tried to present this book in a format that can become an introductory guide to how to get organized, and stay organized and a working guide that you will use for years to come.

Should you wish to comment on any of the material in this, book please write to us at Januz Consultants, 26940 N. Longwood Road, Mettawa-Lake Forest, Illinois 60045-1071. FAX: 708/362-0496.

Acknowledgements

In writing this book on time management I would be remiss if some of the people who have had a part in its creation — and many now no longer are associated with me — did not at least receive some recognition in this book to recognize their contribution to our research on the subject of time management over the years.

To my co-author, Kim M. Magon, for her hours and hours of dedication in weeding through thousands of pages of research, previously published articles and notes over the past dozen years. It has been a joy working with you, Kim. You are an outstanding writer and put organization to a project that I've been wanting to do for years. Kim and I are now working on another time management book, for people who have offices in their home. *Time Management for Home-Based Executives,* is tentatively scheduled for publication during 1993.

To Susan K. Jones, a very successful direct response writer, associate professor at Ferris State College, Big Rapids, Michigan, and the former editor of *Execu*time*®, co-author of my first book, *Time Management for Executives (Scribners 1981)*, author of two books on direct marketing, and delightful person and mother of two fine children, for so much of the original research over nearly five years during the 1980s that has gone into our work.

To Galen R. Meyer, working newspaper editor and the part-time editor of *Execu*time*® for several years, for his contributions to this work.

To Natalie Holmes, Executive Director of the Chicago Association of Direct Marketing for her patience in answering so many of my questions over the past twenty years!

To Charlotte Millman Cohen, Katie Donlon, Ilene Pyster, Bonnie O'Donnell, Paula Gardner Cain, Margaret Haack, all former assistants of mine during my 20 years in the ad agency business.

To Diane Philyaw, my part-time secretary for the past dozen years who is also my cousin's wife, and mother of two lovely teenaged daughters, Ann Marie and Loretta, for her dedicated years of putting up with my quirks and for the fine job she has done.

To George L. Cooper, my boss from 1963-1970 at Transo Envelope Company who taught me more about the printing business than he could ever imagine and to Robert J. "Pierre" Moore, now a senior executive with Philip Morris who was my first real "boss" when I was in college and a lifelong friend.

To James W. Frind, Raymond S. Ihrcke, Joesph R. Kayser, Sheldon Greenberg, Robert Stone, Laurence S. Dunlap and Douglas S. Roberts, seven of the best friends that a man could ever ask for.

To Sonja Peterson, business librarian at the Libertyville (Il) Cook Memorial Library for her assistance more times than I can count on both hands including much help on source material and running a number of data bases for us.

To all the friends of Bill W. and Dr. Bob S. and especially Lynn B., Howard S., Joe P., David R., Bob P., Greg B., Diane H., George M., Russ O., whose friendship means so much to me. And, to Virginia and the rest of the desk staff at Parkside Lodge for their unbelievable confidence, encouragement and support.

To my wife of 29 years, Dorothy, who stuck by me through good times and bad and who is also our part-time circulation manager and bookkeeper.

Kim and I are most grateful to our agent, Lyle Steele, for his continued support, energy, counsel and advice, to Dr. Gary S. Gardiner, Ph.D., our publisher at Smith-Collins, for his friendship, editorial help, and counsel, and to Curt Neitzke, a very talented artist and graphic designer, who has designed our beautiful cover and done all of the design and typesetting for the book using PageMaker for the Macintosh and generally made the book very readable.

Thank you for joining us.   May your time be better spent!

Lauren R. Januz

Note: Mr. Januz is available to provide corporate or association seminars on time management and is available as a keynote speaker for your convention or sales meeting. For further information write Januz Consultants, 26940 N. Longwood Road, Mettawa-Lake Forest, Illinois 60045-1071. FAX: 708/362-0496.

————————

The Serenity Prayer

————————

May God grant me the Serenity

to accept the things that I cannot

change, the Courage to change

the things that I can, and the

Wisdom to know the difference.

————————

PART I

INTRODUCTION—
How You Can Use Time Management To Get More Done.

chapter one

Time Management —
The Benefits,
the Myths

"I wish I could stand on a busy corner, hat in hand, and beg people to throw me all their wasted hours."
Bernard Berenson

each week, millions of people in the corporate world struggle to fit forty-plus hours of work into neat 9-5 slots, Monday through Friday. For many, it's a losing battle and they find themselves still in the office during lunch hours, after hours, and on weekends.

It's a similar battle for the many professionals who race after work to pick up children from day care and come home on Fridays for two fun-filled days of cleaning, grocery shopping, and other chores.

More fortunate people refer to these two days as "the weekend."

While you're off to the dry cleaners, they're the ones jamming up traffic with their bikes on the back of their cars, jogging through a forest preserve, or with golf clubs or tennis racquets in tow. After a recreational break, they're charged up and ready to hit the office on Monday. You're ready for the office too — where you know you'll be able to sit down for a few hours.

The soldiers in this battle, be they CEOs, working parents, or both, have one thing in common. They have all, at one time or another, asked why there are only 24 hours in a day. Most will also tell you on Mondays that their weekends were "too short."

Why are *you* reading this book? Perhaps you're one of those average Americans who spends thirteen hours per weekend on work, shopping, cleaning, errands, and other chores and you'd rather spend them on more fulfilling activities. Or, perhaps your weekends are just fine, thank you, but you feel you could be more effective Monday through Friday if you knew a few time management tricks.

Maybe your doctor advised you to stop working so hard and you don't know any other way. If you don't want to succumb to workaholism, it's time to learn new ways. In Japan, thousands have allegedly died from "Karoshi," meaning they literally worked themselves to death. In addition, more than half of all Americans are dying from heart disease and strokes — many of them preventable. Time management can help reduce stress and improve overall health.

Too many workaholics almost brag about not taking time for personal relaxation and fulfillment. The result is a terrible toll on their health and even their family life — something of unmatched importance to many of today's working parents. The truth is, it's possible to take those 24 hour days, turn them into enough time to get a productive day's work done, and still have time to enjoy a hobby, a walk, a workout, or quality time with your family. By working smarter, not harder, anyone can enjoy a "26 hour day," leaving time for a more enriched lifestyle and increased effectiveness at work.

Benefits of time management

Effective time management techniques can bring many benefits, in addition to improving your health, increasing your work abilities, and increasing time for other enjoyable tasks.

This book will explain how to use time management to get more done, how to plan and organize time, and tools and techniques for successful time management. It will help you reap the many benefits of time management, including:

Adding fun to your job. According to time management expert Edwin C. Bliss, when you feel in control of your work—not vice-versa—

you enjoy it more. It's fun when you know what your objectives and goals are, and when you can see yourself progressing toward those goals.

Adding fun to your life. By getting in control of your work, you can enjoy your leisure time, knowing you deserve it. It's difficult to take time off and relax without worrying about the unfinished work piling up at the office or at home. Says Bliss, "we all know that dark cloud feeling that engulfs us when we're out playing, but have a huge task that's not doing itself while we're away."

Perhaps you haven't had the time to play a sport you once enjoyed or always thought about learning. Creating a couple extra hours a week will help you have the time to do this, start a work-out routine, or simply take walks or bike rides after work. Or, start a hobby. Broaden your horizons and meet new people by joining a group that shares an interest of yours.

If you have children, do they really know you? Or do they only have an image of someone who looks like you but simply comes home every evening just to head for the den or home computer? Spend some time cultivating their interests or helping with homework.

Take time for some personal reading or daydreaming. Read what you want to read, whether it's literature, mysteries, or magazines, — whatever you've been neglecting in order to keep up on the business reading which you've now learned to handle more effectively. Rent a movie, take some time to daydream and set your business and personal goals. Otherwise, you'll forever be doing what's urgent and not what's constructive for you. Or, gain a feeling of accomplishment by doing the household projects that you've been putting off for months.

Becoming more successful in your career. Learn how to plan for short-, medium-, and long-term projects; organize your time and office; delegate successfully; and deal with others more effectively, including bosses, subordinates, peers, and family members. Later chapters in this book will explain how to take advantage of resources and

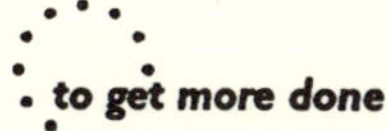

services that can streamline your time use, as well as how to use such time-saving tools as a secretary, the telephone, personal computer, dictating equipment, and other conveniences without being used *by them.*

Improving your physical and mental health. Can time management techniques improve your physical health, lower stress and fatigue levels, and even lengthen your life? We think so. And the workaholics who haven't made it past 55 due to heart attacks or strokes would probably agree. . . if they could.

Principles of time management

We've looked at what time management can do for you, but you may still have one question. What *is* time management? This may best be answered by looking at what it's not. It is not a way to over-organize yourself to the point where you're making too many strategic, impressive-looking plans — and not leaving enough time to complete them. It does not mean organizing the fun out of your life or becoming a robotic model of efficiency that thinks only about work.

Even a former editor of *Execu*Time®*, the newsletter on the effective use of executive time, once confessed: "I still procrastinate. I goof off. I don't always get my work done. My filing piles up. I end up rushing to beat deadlines."

What he does do however, is make time for things that are important to him. "My closets and rooms are more organized. I shuffle paper a lot quicker. And when I do procrastinate, it isn't as hard or as long as it used to be."

There is no single, master theory behind time management. One size doesn't fit all. Everyone has different situations, different needs, and different habits. This book offers many diverse ideas on organizing time. Note those that will fit your style and try them, one at a time, for a trial period. If something doesn't feel comfortable, try something else. Time management is a time-released benefit (no pun intended): eventually the rewards will become greater and it will get easier to save time and become more effective. In other words, it takes time to make time.

As you learn about more time management tools, you may become frustrated because your old systems are "running away with themselves." You see how you could improve them, but it takes all your time just to keep your head above water. What you may need to do is to "bite the bullet" and take time to get organized, once and for all. Take those files in hand. Clean off your desk and get rid of any distracting knick-knacks, pictures, and stacks of folders. Once you've got things organized, it will be much easier to keep them in hand. This is important enough to cut your lunch hour short, or come in early for several days or weeks. Do it now!

According to time management expert Alec Mackenzie, an hour of planning is worth two, three, or four hours of hard work. Yet most executives actively plan only a small part of their working time. By spending a little time planning before you actually start working on a project, you can step up your productivity considerably. Eventually, you'll learn the more you plan, the more you do. Planning for long term projects — things that are weeks, months, even years down the road — will also become easier.

If the subject of time management intrigues you, you need to decide *why* you want to manage your time better before you decide *how*. In other words, don't confuse the means with the ends. What you do with your time is more important than how you save it or even how much time you save. Life is meant to be enjoyed, not endured. Don't focus on saving time because it won't mean much in the end. Instead, focus on improving the quality of time and life, rather than the quantity. Use, not abuse, the time you save.

What's the philosophy behind saving money if it sits in the bank forever? There should be a motive behind saving money, such as traveling, buying a house or automobile, or simply improving the quality of your life. It's easy to become carried away with time management, obsessed with not wasting a second on frivolous activities. But not every minute has to count. Activities you enjoy — listening to music, exercising, sleeping, even watching television — can and should be an end in themselves. Pleasure is what you are working so hard to achieve —

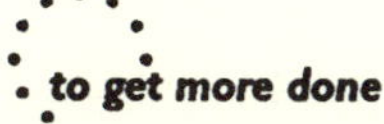

don't manage the fun out of your life. If you have to, include fun time in your appointment book.

Remember too that work and play don't have to be mutually exclusive. Both should give a good measure of pleasure and stimulation. If your work is your play, or vice versa, that's fine too — unless it becomes workaholism. As Alan Laiken put it in *How to Get Control of Your Time and Life,* "Time is life. To waste your time is to waste your life, but to master your time is to master your life and make the most of it."

Time managment consultant and author Dr. Alec Mackenzie has studied time management for years. Over time, he's been able to develop an array of time management principles that pull together the various tools to aid time management. Among these principles are three Murphy's Laws and two corollaries:

1. "Nothing is as simple as it seems."
2. "Everything takes longer than you think."
3. "If anything can go wrong, it will."
4. "There is too much month left at the end of my money."
5. "There is too much work left at the end of my day."

What follows are 40 principles — A to Z — of time management, according to Mackenzie.

Acceptance. Managers should seek the courage to change those things that can be changed, the willingness to accept those that can't be changed, and the wisdom to know the difference.

Activity vs. results. Don't lose sight of your short- and long-term goals by confusing motion with accomplishment, or activity with results. Be result-oriented rather than activity-oriented.

Alternatives. Not generating viable alternative solutions in any situation limits the chances of selecting the most effective course of action.

Anticipation. Anticipatory action is often more effective than remedial action. Plan for the unexpected.

Brevity. Economy of words and actions conserves time while pro-

using time management

moting clarity and understanding.

Clarity. Simple, concise language aids understanding and saves time.

Completed staff work. Delegate the complete responsibility and authority needed for subordinates to complete tasks. This frees them for more important work, increases satisfaction, and improves organizational effectiveness.

Concentration. The Pareto Principle or 20/80 Law: A critical few efforts (about 20 percent) usually produce most of the results (about 80 percent). Concentrate on those "critical few tasks" for major results.

Consolidation. Group similar tasks to eliminate repetition and minimize effort.

Crisis management/over-response. Don't underestimate problems, fail to anticipate them, or over-respond by treating all problems as crises, thereby causing undue anxiety, impaired judgement and hasty decisions.

Daily planning. Planning each day with short- and long-term objectives and goals is essential to effective time management.

Deadlines. Managers can overcome indecision and procrastination by imposing and adhering to their own deadlines.

Delegation/decision level. Delegate the authority for a decision to the lowest managerial level possible.

Effectiveness vs. efficiency. Efficiency is doing the job right. Effectiveness is doing the *right* job right. "Effective action produces the maximum results with the minimum expenditure of resources."

Equal distribution. The great paradox of time: "No one has enough time, yet everyone has all there is."

Faulty perception. How managers think they spend their time is often different from how they actually spend it. Managers commonly deceive themselves into thinking time is going where it should rather than where it actually is.

Feedback. Regular feedback about goal-related performance ensures proper progress. Progress reports should identify problems or deviations in time so that they can be corrected.

Flexibility. Be flexible in scheduling time. Leave room for the

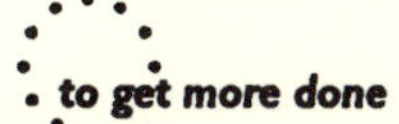

unexpected. Do not over- or under-schedule.

Habit. Managers are often the victims of their own habits and take on the practices of their organizations. Breaking habit patterns is difficult and requires continuous self-discipline.

Implementation and follow-up. Effectively managing time on a daily basis requires implementing time planning and follow-up. Implementing gets it started; follow-up makes sure it gets finished.

Indecision. Many managers hesitate when they have to make a decision. Don't view indecision as a decision not to decide.

Interruption control. Activities should be arranged to minimize the number, impact and duration of interruptions.

Management by exception. Avoid routine details. Managers should only be told of significant and essential problems or successes. Let others do the busy work.

Managerial imperative. Time is the most critical of all managerial resources. It's imperative that managers organize and utilize their time effectively.

Objectives. Pursuing planned objectives is more effective than leaving them up to chance. Management By Objectives (MBO) is based on this idea.

Optimum results. Results tend to be optimized when the greatest benefits are achieved with minimum efforts.

Planned availability. Plan for periods of uninterrupted concentration: a quiet hour, screening of calls and visitors, or hiding away. Open doors invite interruptions.

Planning. Many problems result from action without thought. Every hour spent planning saves three or four in execution — with better results. "By failing to plan, you are planning to fail."

Priority. Budget time for tasks by their priorities. Otherwise, the time you spend on tasks will be inversely related to their importance.

Probability of occurrence. Systematic application of effort increases the probability that the intended event will occur.

Problem analysis. Distinguish between symptoms and causes. Failure to do so means that effort will go toward apparent rather than real problems. Example: If a pipe is leaking, do you clean up the water or plug the leak?

Procrastination. Putting off decisions or actions loses opportunities, increases deadline pressure and generates crises.

Routine/detail. Minimize, consolidate, delegate or eliminate low-value tasks. Divorce yourself from unnecessary detail.

Selective neglect/limited response. Some problems will go away if left alone. Limit your response and effort to what's needed for the problem. But don't ignore those problems that need your action.

Time analysis need. A daily, detailed log of one week's activities is essential to analyze time. Repeat semi-annually to keep bad habits from recurring.

Tyranny of the urgent. Urgent tasks demand instant action, driving the important tasks from our thoughts. Don't neglect the long-term consequences of the more important but less demanding tasks.

Unrealistic time estimates. Managers often underestimate how long they or others will take to complete a task.

Upward delegation. Fostering subordinates to depend upon you for answers — by readily giving solutions or saying "do nothing without checking with me" — encourages upward (reverse) delegation.

Visibility. You'll increase the certainty of doing something if it is kept visible. "You can't do something you can't remember." Calendars and *To Do* lists increase the visibility of tasks, meetings and deadlines.

Work expansion. Parkinson's Law: Work tends to expand to fill the time available.

Putting ideas to work

As you learn about these and other time management principles in this book, you may, in your eagerness to adopt a new lifestyle, find it harder than you thought to incorporate them into your routine. Don't give up. It could be that the day long press and stress of work doesn't allow the time to think out the best ways to tackle tasks. You plunge

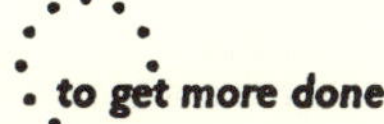

right in and hope to swim. Following old habits is easier than developing new, better ones. In addition, some ideas can be put to use right away while others require time and effort to integrate into your routine — and there just isn't the time. Remember, if you put off implementing new ideas, you'll sacrifice long-term productivity for short-term gains.

The best way to become more effective is to invest a few hours each week on becoming a better time manager. Set aside a regular specific time slot for meetings with yourself, when you can concentrate strictly on self-improvement. Because most people have several habits and ineffective techniques that will show up under regular self-analysis, you'll be able to quickly recoup that time. And those one or two hours gained each day add up to extra weeks over the course of the year. Talk about motivation!

What quality would you most like to improve? Pick an area where you feel you are a little weak, review the subject, develop a strategy and implement it. Weak areas will improve quickly, building enthusiasm and motivation. When you find a good idea that can't be used right away, make a note of it and put it in a time management file or notebook. But the first step is to mark that first meeting on your calendar today — right now. It's the best investment in time that you can make.

Exploding time management myths

"I used to worry that effective use of my time would cut me off from people and make me a cold fish," said the broadcast manager of a television station. "But in practice, I find effectiveness and courtesy go hand in hand. With my time under better control, I feel less resentful of the time I give to others."

There are probably many others who have shyed away from improving their time management effectiveness because they believed myths similar to this one. Another myth is the image of the totally calm executive behind the perfectly clear desk. Some executives have been trying to achieve this image for years. The truth is, nobody can control all of the activities surrounding the way they use time. Managers and supervisors will always need to handle unexpected tasks. Once you stop yearning for complete control, you can begin working toward attain-

using time management

able levels of influence. It may simply be a matter of blocking your time — without interruptions — into 60 or 90 minute sessions to concentrate solely on projects you've decided need your attention.

Here are a few other time management myths. Once you can consider yourself somewhat of an expert, you'll realize these misperceptions are merely excuses to defend an ineffective lifestyle.

"If you want something done right, do it yourself." Not delegating a job that could probably be handled by someone else may have its benefits. You save the time it takes to decide who should handle the job, as well as the time involved in explaining how it should be done. You also sacrifice a few things as well. You're all tied up when something more important comes along — and suddenly it's seen as a crisis — and you're probably making it more difficult for yourself if you're trying to appear indispensable. Not delegating tasks that could be handled by other staff members will not only lead to time management problems, it could also make career advancement difficult.

"Hard work is the key to success." There are probably countless success stories that revolve around this theme. And there are no doubt a few million people who kept their noses to the grindstone throughout their careers — without really fulfilling their dreams. Time management teaches you to work smarter, not harder. According to time management expert Alec Mackenzie, an hour of effective planning saves three to four hours in execution and ensures better results.

"The higher the level at which a decision is made, the better." The higher you go for a decision, the more it costs. Decisions made by those most familiar with the issues usually show the best judgement. According to Mackenzie, some managers waste much of their power making the same kinds of decisions they made in previous positions.

"If you need a project done quickly, give it to the busiest worker." If such people are successfully churning out a great deal of work, it may not be due to their efficiency. Rather, it is their effectiveness that gets the job done. These people have probably learned, whether they know it or not, how to work smarter, not harder. They have learned to take on the right tasks and gain the best results by using available resources, such as time, effectively.

"Time flies." Austin Dobson dispelled this myth best: "Time goes, you say? Ah no! Alas, time stays, we go."

The belief that we don't have enough time may be rooted in the way we use time. Not knowing exactly how long a project will take, not being able to say "no," trying to accomplish too much in too little time, and missing deadlines by not handling priority items first are all methods of mismanaging time. Alec Mackenzie says that time is the enemy to those constantly falling behind, fighting crises and missing deadlines — even though they are often their own worst enemy. "Time is on our side the moment we organize it."

Chapter 1: Summary

■ **By managing our time better we reap many benefits, including increased effectiveness at work and increased time for other areas that are important in our lives. And, because time management helps reduce stress and tension, it can even improve overall health.**

■ **Time management is time released: the longer we work at it, the greater the rewards become.**

■ **An hour of planning is worth two to four hours of hard work, states time management expert Alec Mackenzie. No wonder that studies show the more you plan ... the more you do!**

using time management

chapter two

Evaluating Your Management Style

"The impossible is often the untried."
Jim Goodwin

Consciously or not, we all appreciate personal heroes and role models. Look at the popularity of personality profiles in newspapers and magazines. Consider the success of such best selling autobiographies as Lee A. Iacocca and Donald Trump. We want to know how the movers and shakers became successful. What keeps them motivated? How many hours do they work? What do they do in their spare time? How do they manage their time? And what philosophies have they patterned their lives after?

Even when we were young we tried to find at least one person to emulate. And we probably learned more from that person than we realize. That same modeling process can be used today. For example, one manager identified others in his firm who seemed exceptionally effective. He studied them and looked at what they did and didn't do. Then he patterned some of his management behavior after his chosen "role models." As he adopted more and more of their techniques, he found himself growing in overall effectiveness.

Another successful executive, Don Burnham, former chairman of

Westinghouse Electric, credited his time management techniques to Hi Romnes, once head of Western Electric and later AT&T. "I saw how he had his desk organized and I organized mine the same way," said Burnham. That organization method consisted of filing all correspondence and notes for each project into its own transparent envelope. Each morning, Burnham would stack a few such envelopes on his desk in order of importance and hammer away at them — one at a time — behind a nearly impenetrable secretarial wall. "This daily priority system is absolutely a necessity," he said. "Without it, there would be just too many other people and projects competing for my time."

Successful people seem to share a few common characteristics, including being good time managers. If they spend a lot of time at their jobs, it's because they enjoy their work and not because they can't limit the week to 40 hours. Roger Enrico, president and CEO of Pepsi-Cola USA, arrives at his office at 8:30 a.m. and regularly puts in 12-hour days. Surveys show that higher level executives work close to 60 hours per week on average, compared to 35 hours for most other employees. When asked what they would do differently if they had to relive their careers, most would change very little.

"You must love what you are doing. You do it all your life," suggests Alan Dershowitz, who, by the way, fits quite a bit into his lifestyle. A full-time Harvard law professor, part-time litigator, full-time writer, part-time speaker, and a single parent, Dershowitz says the idea of working for vacations is preposterous and not the way to lead your life.

Habits of the rich and famous

The day begins early for most successful executives, usually around 6 a.m. or sooner. They use alarm clocks to get the day started on time and wake up ready to go. Most need less sleep than the typical eight hours per night. And, because they are generally very healthy and always on the go, they don't seem to miss the extra hours of sleep.

Surveys also show that many managers work their best before and after usual business hours. Almost half of the executives polled in one survey prefer to work early, while 22 percent say they are more productive at the end of the day.

using time management

Other traits of successful time managers include a positive attitude, the ability to concentrate well, and the ability to focus on the big picture rather than excessive details. Typical employees, on the other hand, waste an average of 18 percent of the day procrastinating and another two and a half weeks per year preparing to start and stop work. According to a survey taken by the executive search firm Robert Half & Co. of personnel managers, employees take 8.6 minutes to get started in the morning, 3.3 minutes to prepare for lunch, 3.7 minutes to get going after lunch and 6.7 minutes to prepare for the end of the day.

Upper management, too, has several obstacles to effectiveness that must be overcome. These include interruptions to socialize, unnecessary meetings, and ambiguous priorities. Effective executives, on the other hand, know how their time is spent. They make a habit of logging their time, stopping unproductive, low-priority activities and devoting more of their time to high priorities.

They also keep on top of progress in the various plans they are managing and watch for progress blocks. They teach subordinates to handle assignments or routine tasks, rather than trying to take on an entire job solo. Subordinates are also allowed to handle the work in their own ways, provided they achieve desired results. This may take some getting used to, particularly if you were always taught, "If you want something done right, do it yourself." Explains Enrico, "I was a very hands-on guy and was involved in every detail. I had to learn to back off and have a lot of confidence in the people around me." Confidence, incidentally, means you need only stay in touch with your staff — not on top of them. "Your people can never take enough responsibility," says Enrico. "You almost want to make them take more and more. If you allow people to take more risks, they work harder and come up with more ideas."

Even delegating household jobs such as mowing the lawn, wallpapering, or cleaning the house can buy a lot of time, which can then be spent on valuable leisure time or making more money doing what you do best.

Managing time to work in leisure-time activities is another common goal for successful executives. According to a nationwide

Accountemps study, 45 percent of the leading executives surveyed said that participating in sports is their favorite way of spending their leisure hours. Reading was the choice of 27 percent, while ten percent chose to attend concerts or the theatre. Their favorite sport is golf, followed by jogging and tennis. The study also showed that sports-active executives earn measurably more than their sedentary colleagues.

Creative positions, including managers who do a lot of business writing, may require different time management methods. Rene Gnám, a direct response copywriter, claims it is foolish to try to "write by the clock." Instead, Gnám prefers to write at home, on a park bench, after a nap or shower. He also tries not to limit the time available for creative writing, preferring to have the whole day in front of him. If your firm can't seem to allow you the freedom to create this way, you may be forced to look for an environment where the creative process is better understood, says Gnám.

Managers who have to manage and write need to compartmentalize their work — it's impossible to deal with day-to-day crises and em-ployee problems or questions while writing anything of substance. Try scheduling days for managing and days for writing, with the writing days "off site" at home, a library, or somewhere else quiet and remote.

Effective executives judge themselves by results, rather than by time or effort expended, according to Peter Drucker, quoted in *Working Smart.* "They always start out by asking themselves, 'What's expected of me?' rather than worrying about the techniques or tools they'll need to get there." They also build on their strengths, as well as the strengths of people they work with, according to Drucker. When there's a staffing problem or deficiency, they focus on the opportunity it presents, rather than the problem. And, when personnel do not perform up to stan-dards, they are quick to let them go.

Concentrating on priorities means finding what areas offer poten-tial for the best results. Set priorities and stick with them by doing first things first and letting others stay put so they don't compete for your attention. This makes it easier to devote quality time to a project.

Making effective decisions is another important characteristic. A winning manager can make a decision quickly and stick with it. If it's wrong, they learn from the mistake but don't waste time dwelling on it. Other traits of effective time managers include:

Spending leisure time actively. A contradiction in terms? Perhaps. But most winning managers are uncomfortable just lying around. They spend leisure time on active sports or exercise, reading trade magazines, etc.

Conquering failure. To cultivate the desire to win, it's imperative you conquer any fears of failure, now matter how small. Concentrating on such thoughts as "what if they don't like my ideas" can waste time that could be otherwise spent improving those ideas.

Retaining peace of mind by staying organized. Anchorwoman Connie Chung starts off each day with two lists of things to do — one for herself and one for her assistant. She also relies on her assistant for everything from phone calls and correspondence to chores and shopping.

Discouraging meetings. Many executives dislike typical forms of bureaucracy, such as structured staff meetings. The meetings waste too much time on rhetoric, argue time managers who prefer to use the phone or meet briefly and informally with co-workers.

Scheduling meetings with yourself, however, is an idea that's encouraged by time management experts. "My calendar was so full I had no time alone for projects that needed to be done," complained a field officer of the American Red Cross. "Part of the problem was the numerous meetings for which I was scheduled. So I got the idea to schedule meetings with myself for those necessary but neglected projects. When an interruption threatens, I can honestly say, `Sorry, I'm scheduled for a meeting.'

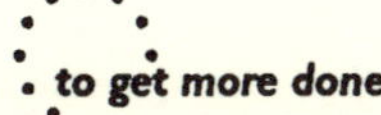

Your management style and personal behavior patterns

Professional athletes have the opportunity to watch themselves on tape, observe their mistakes, and take steps to correct them. A golfer, for example, can watch a video of his swing and realize a narrow stance was affecting his performance. Similarly, we all need to evaluate our management styles periodically. A close look at how we manage our jobs and our time can help pinpoint problem areas.

Although everyone has different management styles, many managers share similar time management problems. Often these problems are a result of a conflict between a manager's personal style and the corporate environment. For example, people who consider themselves "night people" — meaning they are more productive from noon to 8 p.m., for example — may have difficulty being effective in a department run by "morning people." Try to schedule difficult and important tasks for the times when *you* are at your peak.

Just as there are morning and night people, there are also "task-oriented" and "people-oriented" types. The latter prefer talking to people over studying problems on paper. Task oriented people generally rank personnel meetings or sales calls as their least favorite activity. Again, try scheduling uncomfortable tasks for times when you are at your prime.

Other management styles include the diffusion and focused styles. Diffusion style managers prefer to have a lot of projects going simultaneously. When they feel stifled or bored on a project, they turn to another and make a little progress there. This can be an effective style if you try to start new projects as they are "ripe" for action. Make a step-by-step plan for each, then delegate as much of the dirty work as possible. Set a monitoring schedule for each project. This way, you'll be free to pursue other interests.

Focused style managers concentrate all their time, thought, and energy on a single, tightly-focused project. They too can profit from this characteristic by starting with the project that offers the best return on their invested time. If this sounds like your style, make a plan and stick to it. Then make sure other projects are delegated so your staff won't suffer a crisis from neglected problems. Work as hard as you can, as long as you can, until you're finished with the project.

Finally, determine if you are an A or B type person. A-types are compulsive workers who find fulfillment in activity, while B-types are quieter, calculating, and enjoy relationships and self-reflection more than outgoing activities. Whether you're an A or B type, you need rigid self control, suggests management consultant Charles Hamman. A types, who frequently have problems with doing too much, need to avoid doing everything at once. "Work only on your most important activities and let the rest go: delegate work you've been doing yourself; come late or not at all to low priority appointments, hold on before you return that phone call and make all your calls at once; say "no" routinely to requests for your time," says Hamman.

B-types, on the other hand, have problems with delays and frivolous downtime. They need to make an effort to keep working when something "more important" comes along. "Overcome procrastination with firm deadlines for the start, mid-points, and conclusion of a project," says Hamman. He suggests B-types refuse, delegate, or limit paperwork time; use quiet times and self-discipline to reduce time-wasting conversations; schedule 60 to 80 percent of everything they do; and refuse to deviate unless it's for an emergency.

Establishing new behaviors

Once you've recognized tendencies that contribute to poor time management, it becomes easier to take steps to correct those patterns. Some of those tendencies will be behaviors we need to avoid. Further analysis may also reveal the characteristics we lack but that could help us improve time management styles.

It's hard to adopt new behaviors, particularly when the old ones have become routine. Day after day, our lives, actions and results are directed by an automatic pilot. Sometimes it gets you where you want to go, but many times it doesn't. Making a conscious effort to improve one's management style a little bit at a time can pay off by bringing us closer to our ultimate goals.

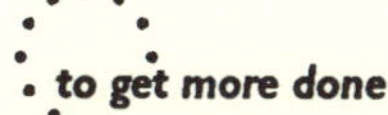

Habits can be time-savers in that they allow us to do things without having to think. But as demands on your time change, the old habits become ineffective. They need to be changed to suit the new demands.

Much of what we do is interconnected. One stimulus leads to a certain habit, one routine invokes another. A little analysis can point out these connections, such as smoking while on the phone and procrastinating on big projects. Habits are difficult to change because they are related to other people, our work, and our environment. Think of your morning routine, for instance. Most of us use the same similar patterns to begin each day. A cup of coffee while chatting with coworkers, then open the mail. After a while, we start the real work of the day.

Psychologist Will James developed a few basic steps to tackle the difficult task of changing behavior patterns. They are:

Desire the change. Unless there is a desire to change, there will be no change. The new habit will fit about as well as clothes two sizes too small. Desire is the key. The greater the want, the more likely it will be successful.

Pinpoint what you want to change. What exactly is the behavior that you want to stop doing? Being late? Overeating? Be precise.

You'll have to closely analyze routine behavior which isn't always easy because it's in the background. Use a time log to note your habits, when and where they occur, and what sets them off. (Time logs are discussed in more detail in Chapter 3.)

Look beyond the physical aspects of your routines in the mental underpinnings. What assumption or reasoning holds you back from achieving what it is that you want? Is it something you or someone else tried before but were stymied by? The more you know about why you do something, the easier it is to change.

Clearly define the new habit. The new behavior must be a better way. If it doesn't seem easier or more effective, it won't be around very long. Be specific about what it is. On a sheet of paper, write the new

using time management

and old habits atop two columns. List and compare the pros and cons. Your new ideas should stand up a lot stronger to the old habit.

Many people are too easygoing in initiating a new habit, thinking it will come quickly. As a result, they don't define it clearly enough. They have only a vague notion of overcoming lateness or stopping procrastination. But the more detailed the habit, the more of a chance it has to succeed.

Be careful not to design the new behavior so that it is so difficult, unwieldy, or out of sync with your personality that it is doomed before you even start. Not all time management methods appeal to all people.

Launch the new habit with great strength and commitment. Do anything you can to make it stand out from the old. Tell friends and coworkers what you plan to do and how you plan to do it. They can offer support and also correct you if you start to slide. Maybe they've been through it before. Groups such as Weight Watchers or Alcoholics Anonymous are successful in helping people change habits for this very reason. Telling others will also help strengthen your resolve. You won't want to fail in front of the others. It's easier to let yourself down but harder if there are others involved.

Start the new behavior as early as possible. Right now is best. Don't wait until the next month to start losing weight, for example. You'll eat your way through the state and lose a lot of enthusiasm and momentum.

Don't deviate from the new behavior until it has taken root in displacing the old. This is the most critical part of changing habits. The more quickly and firmly it is installed, the more likely it is to permanently stick. Any lapse will decrease momentum from the new drive, making it easier to fall back into the old ways. You'd have to start over, which is often harder than starting the first time. And, you may end up doubting your ability and competence to win. If never fed again, your old desires will fade surprisingly easily.

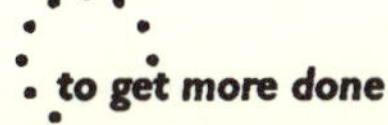

You may often be tempted to go back to old habits because they seem easier, quicker, or less of a hassle. The new ways don't yet feel natural. Or you rationalize by saying, "This one time won't matter." The truth is, it matters a great deal. If you give in to temptation, you'll have to start all over again. Remember too, the hardest time to keep a new behavior is during a crisis. Most people lapse into the habits that are the most comfortable. That's why it's important to continue establishing new habits until they're as comfortable and automatic as the old.

Practice new habits at every opportunity. The new behavior means little — despite all your commitment and good intentions — until you actually use it. Go out of your way to practice the new habits. It's the practice and the success of that practice that counts the most. Arrange your schedule so that you will have to use the new behavior more than before.

How long does a new behavior take to root? It depends on your personality and the difficulty of what you are trying to accomplish. But if you can be consistent in the new behavior for about three to seven weeks, you will likely have grown yourself a new habit. You'll also help your self discipline if you change your environment, especially if the old environment contained cues that initiated your behavior.

Adapting new habits: Dos and Don'ts

To start off on the right track toward adapting new behavior patterns, let's look at what experts refer to as good time management habits. These include keeping a To Do list; saying "no" to others when their goals and needs interfere with yours; and asking, "what's the best use of my time right now?"; tackling important tasks before urgent, or hard tasks before easy ones; and constantly developing new, good habits.

The ability to master a two-letter, one syllable word can amount to considerable time savings. That word is "NO." Even invisible agreements to tolerate interruptions, do projects instead of manage or delegate them, live with problems rather than solve them can use up a lot of quality time, according to Robert Rutherford, a time management consultant. "Break your invisible agreements wherever you find them, and you'll get back to a higher level of effectiveness by refusing to accept others' problems."

A CEO of a large agricultural organization uses two techniques to successfully say "no" to outside demands. The first is to say, "I'm sorry, but I don't have the five hours I'd need to do your project justice." If that doesn't work, he comes back with: "I'll do what you ask if you do something for me in return." Then he makes a comparable request for the caller's time and effort. "I've only had one person accept," he confides. "The rest of my time, I'm home free."

Another method is what a hospital manager calls the Pleasure/Pain Principle. "If it will cause more pain than pleasure, I don't do it. Even the most unpleasant tasks . . . are put into perspective. I don't lose time griping or looking for a way out — I just don't do it!"

Author Somerset Maugham once said, "The unfortunate thing about this world is that good habits are so much easier to give up than bad ones." Nevertheless, here are a few that should be shaken: endless paper shuffling, procrastination and perfectionism, being diverted by interruptions, and not keeping deadlines.

Many executives believe they can do work better than others, and rightfully so. Because they don't delegate, they try to do too much too perfectly and get caught in details others should handle. Meanwhile, some important tasks are done poorly or not at all. The best tasks to delegate are chores that others can readily assume. It may take some time to start, and there will be mistakes. But a manager can control the outcome and avoid errors by keeping the final say.

Procrastination is a common problem. We've probably all wasted time on less important or unnecessary jobs in order to put off doing undesirable tasks. Reduce the harmful effects of procrastination by remembering two principles: "Do it now" and "The only way to get started is to start." Tackle high priority tasks before less important ones, otherwise you'll get off track. Try to handle each matter only once — don't drop it and then come back. Finally, break hard or unpleasant tasks into small steps, with deadlines for each, to make the project seem less overwhelming. ◗

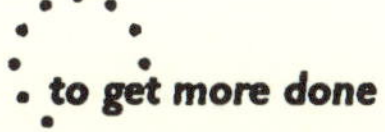

Chapter 2: Summary

■ Successful time managers have several characteristics in common, including a positive attitude, good concentration skills, and a knack for focusing on "the big picture."

■ The typical employee wastes nearly a fifth of the day procrastinating and two and half weeks per year preparing to start and stop work. Try to reduce this wasted time by "compartmentalizing" your work and doing like tasks together.

■ To leave time for long term planning, organizing files, or completing the details on a major project, consider scheduling a meeting with yourself.

chapter three
Getting Organized

think about the people who stand out in your mind as model organizers. They put in a full day's work, never miss a deadline, travel to Atlanta for a four-day meeting and return by Friday to plan a weekend party. No matter how busy they are, they still have time to remember your birthday, or ask how things are going at home. Can these people really be working with the same 24-hour days and seven-day weeks dealt to the rest of us?

Here's the good news: if they can do it, so can you. They have simply applied the idea of working smarter, rather than harder — the old quality, not quantity principle — to every phase of their lives. From getting dressed in the morning and managing their homes to using the telephone, conducting a meeting, traveling, writing and dictating, these people have used the tools and techniques of time management to become success stories.

Many of these tools and techniques, like time itself, are available to everyone. Everyone, no matter how intelligent or ignorant, how accomplished or unskilled, has the same 24 hours a day, 365 days a year.

In that respect, time is one of the few things in life that is free. The only expense involved in time is how it is spent.

Can you imagine winning $3 million in the state lottery and tossing it away? Of course, you don't worry about losing it because it didn't cost you anything, right? If you think about it, you'll realize that time also offers a lot of value, just like money. How much value? An executive making $56,000 a year can easily estimate the cost of his or her time at over $280 an hour. To calculate the actual cost of your time, try this method suggested by Dr. Merrill E. Douglass of the Time Management Center, Marietta, Georgia:

Your annual salary	($56,000)	__________
Plus 100% for overhead	($56,000)	__________
Plus 40% for fringes	($22,000)	__________
Support staff salaries	($36,000)	__________
Plus 140% of their wages for overhead and fringes	($50,400)	__________
TOTAL	($220,800)	__________
Divide total by 52 weeks	($4,246)	__________

If you spend one-third of your normal business week, say 15 hours, at key responsibilities, divide the weekly cost of your time by 15 hours. The hourly cost of that time is $283. Still think time is free?

Once you realize how valuable your time really is, you may be more motivated to plan and organize your days more effectively. Take a look at your daily activity style. If you see areas that need a few changes, perhaps in the way your office is set up or the way in which your day is structured, take the time to organize them once and for all. If this is important to you, it's worth setting aside the excuses.

"But I've never been an organized person — I work better under pressure," yousay? Let's look at the characteristics of an organized person. According to Merrill Douglass, such people are efficient, productive, timely, disciplined, goal oriented, successful, predictable, task oriented, and leadership oriented.

They're good at developing their staffs, delegating, being in control, setting objectives, planning and scheduling, and getting more out of others. If this doesn't sound like you, try making a list of the qualities you lack and incorporating them one by one.

Perhaps you don't even have the time to start getting organized. Your image Monday through Friday is something like that of the white rabbit in Alice In Wonderland who was always scurrying about, muttering "late, late for a very important date." If necessary, come in early a few mornings, work through a couple lunch hours, or take the time one Saturday morning to really organize everything in a way that will help you throughout the week.

The less time you have available, the more important it is to plan and keep a good schedule. Each minute becomes more valuable, and your time must be spent effectively. Even a little bit of disorganization during the day can cause a lot of little problems. And those little problems can turn into big, time-wasting problems — as you probably know. If that one disorganized day ends up spoiling and wasting other days or even weeks in the future, it all becomes part of a vicious, time-consuming circle. It pays to keep the day organized and nip those problems in the bud, just as it pays to keep your desk in order and your mind clear of confusing static.

Some people fear that scheduling their time will box them in and stifle their creativity. In reality, a schedule frees them up to do even more. If you don't write down an upcoming project or event, you'll keep reminding yourself of it. And that mental reminder will keep nagging and popping up at all times, causing the static that interferes with the flow of ideas. Adopt a habit of looking at your schedule regularly and staying up to date with commitments. That way they won't haphazardly wander in and out of your mind.

Some executives find every day an adventure. They have a vague idea of what is going to be happening and what tasks need to be done,

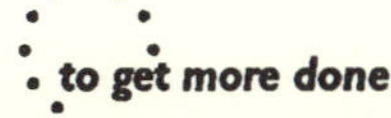

but are often surprised by a last-minute deadline or assignment. Others spend a good part of their days finishing many tasks but find they have overlooked a high-priority item that deserved more attention. Getting organized will help solve these problems. Aids such as "To Do" lists, pocket secretaries, scheduling software, and an office arranged for better productivity will help you begin. Start becoming a better time manager by developing a time management notebook or folder. If you currently have various reminders written on scraps of paper scattered in your briefcase, purse, desk, or car, a master file will be a definite time saver. In it you can jot down ideas you'd like to try — gradually — and a master list of all the projects you need to tackle, whether they're daily mundane activities like opening the mail or long-term projects. Eventually this notebook will act as "control central" as you begin transferring each project to daily or weekly "To Do" lists, or delegating smaller tasks to others.

Let's cut to the core of your organization style: you. How do you begin your day? Is it with a leisurely breakfast and a trip to the closet to don clothes that were carefully picked out the night before? Or is it more reminiscent of Dagwood Bumstead? He slept through his alarm, ate breakfast while he showered, and ran to the door to catch the bus as his wife Blondie held his pants out like a lion trainer holding a hoop. If mornings are a frenzied routine, stop and look at what's causing the tension. Is it lost keys, the second cup of coffee, or last minute dressing or ironing? Perhaps getting up 15 minutes earlier or doing a few things in the evening would reduce the problems. I smile at the latter suggestion because it reminds me of a lady we know. Every night she would set up things needed for the next morning's breakfast. On a tray on the kitchen counter would be a box of cereal, two bowls, two spoons, a pitcher for milk, and loaf of bread. Sometimes we laughed at the compulsiveness with which this ritual was done. (She also packs one month ahead for vacations.) But to this day I've never seen her show one little sign of stress or tension.

Another time-saver and stress-reducer is to set your watch ahead a few minutes. When it looks like you're going to be late for an appointment, you'll suddenly remember the added cushion of time you gave

using time management

yourself. You can also start the day prepared by including a few essential weapons for the day's adventure. Change for tolls and phones, a good pen, accurate watch, business cards, and a little cash are things many people waste valuable time searching for later in the day.

Organizing your office

We'll discuss this in detail later but you can start becoming a more organized person today by making a few simple adjustments at your work space. First, a little streamlining. Conversation pieces such as artwork, photographs, or knick-knacks can personalize an office but they can also contribute to poor time management. In addition to being distracting, such items encourage visitors to comment on the extras, rather than get to the point of their visit. Try substituting the artwork with a framed copy of your company's mission statement. Looking at items relating to company or personal goals will reduce the time spent daydreaming and will offer visitors more incentive to focus on the work at hand.

Within your office, try setting up a specific location for different tasks. Sort mail from your desk, dictate by a window chair, write your To Do list from your side chair, for instance. By creating the right atmosphere for each task, your mind will be able to concentrate better on each matter. If you grow accustomed to dictating by a window, you'll be less likely to distract yourself by glancing at other project files on your desk.

Other tasks can be handled simultaneously. If you need to spend a few minutes on a simple phone call (or worse, waiting on "hold"), try writing a few notes, signing some letters, or reading the mail to fill the empty time. Listen to cassettes while driving or having lunch. Lump similar tasks together such as filing or making copies.

Another method of organizing your desk is that suggested by Don Burnham, one-time chairman of the board at Westinghouse. He files all correspondence and notes for each project into a single transparent envelope. Each morning, he stacks a few of the envelopes on his desk in order of priority. He spends one hour in the morning free from phone calls and other interruptions, and uses that time to concentrate

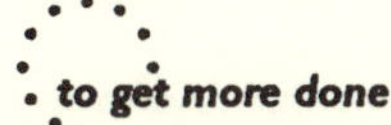

on the first project, second project, and, if time allows, moves on to the third project. "The daily priority system is absolutely a necessity," he says. "Without it, there would just be too many other people and projects competing for my time."

The job of organizing your days and weeks can also be simplified by working within your "prime time." This is the time of day when you have peak energy, concentration, and efficiency. Organizing your schedule to focus on your prime time will help you complete more tasks — and handle them more efficiently.

Prime time differs from person to person, and may even shift due to changes in lifestyle and work habits. Some folks get charged up first thing in the morning, while others can't figure out how to sharpen a pencil until the afternoon. Determine when you're mentally at peak productivity. Then make that time, whether it's 4 to 6 o'clock p.m. or the first hour in the morning, and use it to take on the toughest tasks. Many people are freshest in the morning, yet waste that time on trivial tasks such as opening mail or skimming through in-baskets. Prime time also changes according to the tasks. If something requires concentration and solitude, schedule it for the time of day when you concentrate the best. If something requires involving others, schedule it for when you feel most sociable.

Allot from half an hour to three hours for your prime time activities every day. Experiment to see how long you can maintain a high level of concentration. Schedule this time into your appointment book and note what special tasks you have for each day. Don't waste prime time looking for something to do.

According to Stephanie Wilson, author of *The Organized Executive*, there are two ways of organizing the day's schedule. The first, backward scheduling, makes you determine first what time you'd like to leave the office, forcing you to set priorities and schedule activities accordingly. This "fluid" approach works well for people in creative professions or those who must respond to fast-breaking events. The second method is precise scheduling. Determine ahead of time what you'll be doing each hour or block of the day. This strict approach works best for those who prefer to plan their time precisely and whose administrative duties don't give them a lot of unscheduled people contacts.

How to avoid "over-organizing"

Too much organization can defeat the purpose. People who go overboard can occupy 90 percent of their time planning and organizing — and very little time doing. Avoid scheduling systems that overlap. You are likely to lose track of multiple listings kept in calendars, To Do Today lists, notebooks, and pocket organizers. Keep your schedule simple and in as few places as possible. The goal is to create a definite control system for your time, not a several-part system that causes more indecision than help. People who keep important notes in both a pocket organizer and a computer file may find they're wasting time over-organizing, or have trouble keeping track of in which system they stored an important reminder.

Don't organize the fun out of life. Time management expert Alan Laiken warns that some folks let their time organization habits lead them too far into super-organization and even obsession. Advance planning is important to get your life under control — but don't go overboard. No matter how hard they try, managers cannot control every activity surrounding the way they use time, nor should they have to. Over-organization can also cause people to get irritated by minor developments and lead to feelings of burnout and fatigue.

Keep some flexibility in your schedule — life is full of surprises. The best way to deal with those surprises is to set aside time for them. If you keep a tightly knit schedule, it will fall apart when one thing goes wrong. Schedule a "fudge factor" of 10 to 25 percent in everything you do. If you think a meeting will take an hour, schedule it for an hour and 15 minutes. If a task is totally unfamiliar, you may even want to budget in more time.

In your zest to get organized, remember to block out time for fun and relaxation. This may sound like an odd suggestion — how fun can it be if you have to schedule it? But notice how many hard-charging people cease to function away from work, fearing that fun is wasted time and will hinder effectiveness. In reality, it does just the opposite. The harder, more stressful the work, the greater the need for fun and relaxation. Schedule in breaks; they'll improve your effectiveness and probably your attitude.

Effectiveness requires time off in proportion to time on. Experiment with different combinations of work and play time until you find a pattern that lets you sustain maximum effort for months on end. Cultivate a number of interests. Multi-interest people are more likely to have effective time-management skills because they are motivated to find time for all their activities. Bring your life into balance by setting aside an adequate amount of energy or pleasure breaks. Try setting aside 15 minutes or a half-hour each day for some type of self-improvement break, whether it's learning to play the piano, painting, exercising, or enjoying some activity with your family. Invest the time you've saved through time management techniques to improve yourself a little bit each day.

Benefiting from time logs

Before you can decide how to better spend your time, you need to know how it's being spent now. For many people, time habits have become so routine that they don't even realize how much is wasted on paperwork, unnecessary phone calls, etc. A time log (Figure 3.1) will point out where time is wasted, what activities take up most of your day, who causes the most problems, and whether you spend as much time on high-priority work as you think you do.

Some people are put off by the idea of logging their time because they feel it will take too much effort. But a basic time log is very simple, and its use is only temporary — an occasional diagnostic technique when your effectiveness seems to be slipping. Time logs lead most of their users to two revelations: first, they cannot believe how much time they spend on trivial items and second, they're excited by the opportunity for increased effectiveness revealed. One city administrator found the time log so useful for keeping track of his time, he decided to use it in reverse. "I plan out my schedule to the minute, or at least a day ahead of time, leaving 20 percent unscheduled for flexibility. Then as I go through the day, I check every 30 minutes or so to see if I'm on time. If I'm not, I speed up or move to the next item to get back on track. If

Figure 3.1 Time Log

name _______________________________   date ___________

projects/activities

hours		comments
a.m. 7		
8		
9		
10		
11		
noon		
1		
2		
3		
4		
5		
6		
7		
8		
9		
10		

time summary

Instructions: In each 5, 10, or 15 minute interval (by the clock), place a ✓ in the column that best describes your activity.   © Januz Consultants 1991

to get more done

I am, I pat myself on the back and keep plugging. At the end of the day, I've done everything I planned to do, and sometimes quite a bit more."

There are two methods for keeping time logs, the interval-oriented time log and the task-oriented time log. An interval-oriented time log takes a "snapshot" of what you are doing at 15-or 30-minute segments during the day. It includes two listings, activity and function. The activity column notes what you were doing during those segments, such as calls, meetings, and correspondence. The function column notes why you are doing the activity. At each interval, put a check mark in the column that best describes what you've been doing. (See the sample time log on page 37.) Some time periods may be spent on more than one activity. Don't try to log every event, just concentrate on the most important or longest-lasting tasks. It's not necessary to record every minute to get an accurate picture of your days. A third optional column is a comments and suggestions column for future improvements.

The task-oriented time log keeps track of each and every activity from start to finish. Mark the time you started and finished. Keep the same activity and function columns. Make an entry every time you switch tasks, take a break, receive a phone call, etc. This format is a good idea if you feel you're being swamped by trivial pursuits.

A note of caution: do not wait until the end of the day to fill in the logs, as they will not be as accurate. And don't try to make yourself look good, you'll only be fooling yourself and wasting more time. Also, make specific comments on each activity or function. Descriptions that are too vague make it hard to identify the activity's priority, which makes later analysis more difficult. Rather than writing "talked to John," note "answered John's questions about Project A."

Keep logging your time each day until you have a representative sample of your time use. This may be anywhere from four days to four weeks, although two to three weeks will usually suffice. When you feel the time log is an accurate record of your time use, it's time for a little analysis. Look for patterns and habits in how your time is spent. Compare quality time versus quantity time, urgent versus important. Here are a few questions you may want to ask yourself:

1. Is the majority of your day spent on important, high-payoff activities?

2. What went wrong today, and why?

3. What went right today, and why?

4. Did you have a plan for the day with clear priorities? How long did it take to follow the plan?

5. Were you doing the right job at the right time?

6. Are you happy with the amount of personal, travel, and idle time?

7. What tendencies and habits are apparent from your time log?

8. What is the most productive time of day? Why?

9. What is the least productive time of day? Why?

10. Who or what accounted for most of the interruptions? What were the reasons? How can they be controlled?

11. Can you delegate some activities?

12. Do you spend time in areas that bring maximum benefit in terms of personal and organizational goals?

13. Are low-payoff tasks or low-paying clients monopolizing your time?

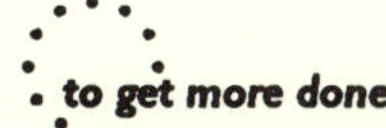

14. Are you spending more time in meetings than you thought? How can this be reduced?

15. Starting tomorrow, how can you make better use of your time?

After asking these and other questions, you may realize that you had little idea where your time went. Our memories are unreliable because they focus on the highlights and overlook poorly used time — the item you want to identify. You may also discover that you spend very little time on high-priority tasks like planning or working toward major goals.

After you've adopted new habits to improve your time use, remember that there's always room for time management improvement. Keep a time log at least once a year, or more if your activities are seasonal. If you have a new job or new conditions, you may want to log time again as a checkup. ●

Chapter 3: Summary

■ The more filled up your day is, the more valuable each minute becomes. Because a little disorganization can lead to big problems, planning and keeping a schedule is vital.

■ Try outfitting your office by reducing distracting knick knacks and setting up different locations for various tasks, such as dictating by the window.

■ Prioritize daily tasks with an A, B or C — then see to it that the A and the B items get done before taking on less important work. Schedule more challenging jobs for the time when your energy is at its peak.

■ Remember that too much organization can defeat the purpose. You'll leave little time for flexibility, leisure, or actually doing the things you planned on.

chapter four

Increasing Time Management Effectiveness

*"It isn't that they can't see the solution.
It is that they can't see the problem."*
G.K. Chesterton

"**I** work better under pressure."
"When I feel like working, I just lie down until the feeling goes away."
"I don't know where to begin."
Sound familiar? For people who procrastinate, these are common excuses, even facts of life. And while they may very well work better under pressure, procrastination usually leads only to slipped productivity.

It's a matter of pacing yourself, just as if you were on a long bike ride. You could ride for half the day at a steady 10 miles per hour, and feel refreshed and ready to start again the next day. Or you could goof around, ride at about 5 miles per hour for a couple hours, waste some more time wondering how far you've yet to go, then panic and sprint for an hour. You may get to your destination eventually but it will cost a lot more energy. And motivation to begin the next day will probably be low as well.

To learn how to stop procrastinating, we need to know why we procrastinate. Is it because we don't like the work we're doing? Or because we don't feel competent? Perhaps by waiting long enough, someone will come along and do it for us.

Procrastinators are not necessarily lazy managers. They're often hard working perfectionists, many of them entrepreneurs, who are afraid a job may not be done right, and therefore don't attempt it at all. Or, they're overwhelmed by an onslaught of things to do and forget to take everything one bit at a time.

Procrastinators are also not easy to spot. Rather than doing nothing, they may look busy doing low-priority projects or simple tasks that should be delegated. It's a common problem — but that doesn't make it okay. Procrastination tends to breed more procrastination. Rather than having a do-it-now attitude, a procrastinator will start putting more and more things off, creating a vicious circle.

If you think you're a procrastinator — but you don't have time to really decide for sure — see if any of the following procrastination models sound familiar.

The escape from reality type. This person believes it is much easier to fill the days with known, easy-to-solve trivia than to tackle a large overwhelming problem. As Olin Miller put it, "If you want to make an easy job seem mighty hard, just keep putting it off."

In addition to getting out of overwhelming tasks, escapees also procrastinate on unpleasant tasks. Rather than starting an urgent but unwelcome project, they'll devote their time to something more pleasant that needs to be done six months down the road.

The get someone else to do it type. Actor Bill Cosby once said that fathers often appear very stupid around the house. They don't know where to put the laundry away, can't start the dishwasher, can't find the dog's leash. Really they're very smart, he explains, because eventually other people — mostly mothers — will tire from their lack of initiative, sigh, and mutter the famous line, "Never mind, *I'll* do it." Which was really the intended goal in the first place. Delegating a job at the start, however, is a much quicker way to hand work off to another person.

The failure fearer. Some managers, usually perfectionists by nature, put off starting a project because they're afraid they might fail or make a mistake.

Isaac Newton's law of inertia works for people as well as objects: a body at rest tends to remain at rest and a body in motion tends to remain in motion. The trick with beating procrastination is to just get going, to build some momentum. The hardest part is getting started. And the longer the delay, the harder it gets.

To build momentum, first admit that you procrastinate and that it is a frustrating and futile way of life. Rationalizing or denying the habit won't help anyone to change it. Second, divide larger projects into starting points and other small segments of 5-, 10-or 30-minute lengths. Add the smaller tasks to your To Do list — in the order to be performed, and do a few pieces every day. Gradually they'll come together, giving you the momentum needed to finish the job. Henry Ford's assembly line started with the realization, "Nothing is particularly hard if you divide it into small jobs."

Remember, perfectionists can't finish a job because they're never satisfied. As a result, they end up not starting a job that they can't finish. Instead of shooting for perfectionism, set realistic performance standards. Once that standard is achieved, further improvements become insignificant, and it becomes easier to move on to the next task. Consider the costs of procrastination. When you feel yourself starting to procrastinate, ask yourself what other problems you will create by putting this off.

Often, unpleasant tasks are not as bad as anticipated. Either way, you need to simply face up to the task and bite the bullet. By procrastinating, you're simply compounding your workload and creating unnecessary feelings of pressure. Try setting aside 10 to 15 minutes for an unpleasant task. It's easier to take things in small doses. Quit when the time is up and continue later for another 15 minutes.

Here are a few additional tips to conquer procrastination:

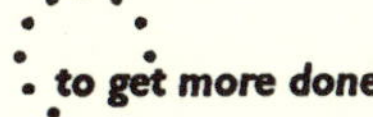

- *Get warmed up with a primer task. A little action may help you get started. Need to write a report? Sketch a quick outline of points you'd like to make. The more important the job, the more time and energy it should receive.*

- *Start the project in small bits -- break it into manageable portions -- if you're working on a long report, for example, start working on one little section of it -- and, perhaps even the easiest part of the report, and get the one little section completed -- then move on to another, and another, and so on.*

- *Make a balance sheet. This is an effective exercise in self-humiliation. On one side of a sheet of paper, list the wonderful things that will result if you do the task now. On the other side, list the reasons why you're putting the task off. Any concrete reasons for postponing the work will show up clearly. But if you are procrastinating, the reasons will look pretty silly when compared to the benefits of completing the work.*

- *Get a partner in procrastination. Make a commitment or wager with someone. You'll be more likely to finish if other people are involved. Commitments to ourselves are easy to break.*

- *Set deadlines. Completion of a task is hard to visualize unless it has a time frame. Deadlines help motivate you to finish the work. If there is no deadline, the work will likely not be completed. Make sure the deadline is realistic, and post it where it will be seen.*

- *Give yourself a reward. A positive solution. Find an important goal or task that you've been putting off, then determine a fitting award for achieving it. The reward will help you get started. Make sure the awards are commensurate with the task. If you haven't earned the reward, don't accept it.*

- *Continually ask yourself, "what's the best use of my time right now?" to ensure that you are tackling the most urgent and important tasks at the right time. Analyze your procrastination habits.*
  - What things do you put off most often?
  - What things are you now putting off?
  - How do you know when you are procrastinating?
  - Are there certain things you like to do when putting off work?
  - What happens when you procrastinate?
  - Are the results mostly good or bad?
  - What causes you to procrastinate? Is there a specific cause or reason?
  - What can you do to overcome this? List specific solutions, set deadlines, and get going.

- *Get someone to do the work. Buy yourself a reprieve. A good tactic if the procrastination is caused by an unpleasant task. It's well worth the cost.*

- *Take advantage of your moods. A common excuse for putting work off is, "I'm not in the mood for it." Don't wait for your mood to fit the task —fit the task to your moods. There is usually some aspect of work that will fit your current mood. If you don't feel like writing a report, you may feel like collecting the facts or doing more research.*

- *Get more information. Procrastination often results from not having enough information. The more you know, the more interested you'll be, and the more you'll want to work on it. Read a book or talk to people in the know about your task.*

- *Develop a do-it-now attitude. Make things happen. Set a schedule and live by it. You may have to play all kinds of mental games to overcome the habit. Whatever it takes, the effort will be worth it.*

- *Use the guilt. If you must procrastinate, at least "waste" your time on work that is somewhat productive. You won't be able to procrastinate on this later.*

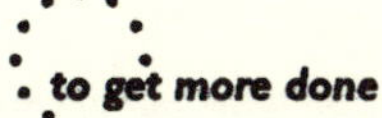

Time wasting habit #2: perfectionism

Perfectionism is another common problem among today's managers. According to *USA Today*, about one person in three is a perfectionist, which often makes that person less effective. Many see perfectionism as a good trait, but the truth is it can backfire on you.

Effects of perfectionism include procrastination, low self-esteem, problem-filled relationships, even anorexia and bulimia. Trade-offs are made in the never-ending search for perfection. They include not knowing when to quit; not allowing room for mistakes and thus denying the opportunity for growth; focusing on mistakes or flaws and not taking into account what's been done well; and not being able to distinguish between perfectionism and the healthy pursuit of excellence.

According to psychologist Debra White, perfectionists deny themselves the feeling of satisfaction. "It's like following the North Star and being upset because you never get there. There is a difference between having dreams and goals and being a perfectionist."

Perfectionists also have a hard time completing projects, making decisions, and admitting errors. They waste time by covering up an error or documenting why they made the mistake, rather than acknowledging and correcting it. Decisions are difficult because each one, no matter how minor, must be perfect. To make a decision or complete a project, perfectionists require all the facts first, no matter what the cost. Or they'll postpone things entirely because they know they can't do it perfectly.

It's a tendency that can be corrected, but it may take a little adjusting to. If you feel you may be falling into the perfectionist trap, make an effort to ease up on yourself. It really will help you manage your work — and your time — more effectively. Here are a few tips to conquer this time waster.

- *Dare to be average. Perfection is an impossible goal, according to author David Burns. "It's really the world's greatest con game."*

- *Don't try to be perfect on things that aren't important.*

- *Be wary of your internal critic — the voice that says, "This isn't good. People won't like it."*

- *List perfectionism's pros and cons. "Once you understand that it does not help in any way, you'll be much more likely to give it up," says Burns.*

- *Every day, deliberately do an unimportant task imperfectly.*

- *Estimate how much time a project is worth and stick to that estimate.*

- *Look forward to the satisfaction of completing a task, rather than finding the most perfect way to finish it.*

- *Be willing to experience anxiety about "loose ends." It will pass if you let some things slide.*

Improving your productivity

We've talked about using time logs and To Do lists to help organize our days and become more productive. New technology continually releases such ideas as facsimile machines, speed dial phones, and more efficient computer programs to make life easier. Is this why the average office worker productively uses only 4.4 hours a day? How can slipped productivity be stopped?

The answer may be "work force management," according to management consultant Mark Marcussen. His system has allowed companies throughout the country to increase the output of both management and staff by as much as 25 percent.

Work force management simply involves developing more efficient work flows in the office, just as is done on the production line. Even though some managers complain about "slow production workers," studies show that timewise, their productivity level is substantially higher than that of white-collar managers.

The key ingredient in this effort is to retrain managers so they can schedule, assign, and coordinate work most efficiently. You can apply the techniques of work force management to your own organization

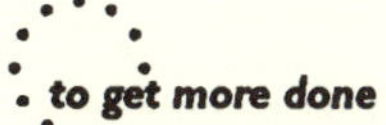

using the steps outlined below.

The first step is to define and document the tasks that need to be done. This is an important starting point, and it will offer some interesting surprises. First, you'll find a considerable number of tasks that overlap. Second, you will find managers spend a great deal of time on needless and pointless endeavors. And third, you'll find that many managers and staffers have entirely different perceptions of what you need done than you do.

As companies grow, it seems the necessary tasks and priorities change to conform to changing external requirements. But somehow, the traditional ways of doing things linger on. You can shave considerable wasted time simply by getting people to concentrate on what really needs to be done.

Once you have defined the needed tasks, you must find out how many people you need to get the work done most efficiently, and what information, tools, and materials they need. A common mistake is to guess or to rely solely on historical data or tradition. The science of work force management will help you develop reasonable task standards rather quickly.

Get your managers involved in this process as early as possible. This way, you'll have assurances that no one winds up with exaggerated or restricted task standards. When everyone agrees on the jointly developed task standard, your managers will be more likely to adhere to it.

Thirdly, train your managers in the need for management controls on the normal flow of work. This may sound obvious but the truth is, many management level people are lax in their exercise of basic management controls. Scheduling tightly, assigning work carefully, and coordinating the work of several people puts a severe strain on their capabilities. Often they simply won't do it. The result is periods of time when little or no work is available, needed information or approval is not available, more people than needed are assigned to a project, or office staffers have no clear idea of what management expects of them.

The fourth step is to adjust your organization and procedures as necessary for your new definitions of tasks and task standards. This may mean reorganizing people, assignments, information, and work flow,

using time management

even reporting relationships. Before you make anything permanent, give the new system a test run for a time.

Remember, these initial standards and definitions are like estimates. They were developed by work sampling, analysis, and self-reporting techniques. You may well have to modify your new standards to conform to day-to-day operating realities. If you maintain an effective reporting system, you can usually fine tune your standards as you go.

Finally, create a system to evaluate performance on the jobs and projects your managers undertake. Make this system flexible, however, so you can also monitor and critique planning and scheduling processes. Your organization will change in the future as it has in the past, and you will continually need to sharpen your system to cope with current situations.

The process of increasing managerial productivity demands attention. Effective planning, estimating, scheduling, assigning, and controlling should reflect the interdependence of these elements. That way, one manager's output becomes the input to the next.

And don't worry about resistance from managers. It's been found that managers are more comfortable with efficient work flows and objective standards. And, the resulting 15-25 percent productivity boosts benefit everyone.

Additional tips to improve productivity include: emptying the "in box" at least once a day; using quick phone calls, memos, or a fax instead of lengthy meetings; implementing a "quiet hour"; and adhering to the four D's — do it now, delegate it, delay it, or dump it. Thinking positively is another way to improve productivity and reduce stress at the same time. As you glance at the items on your To Do list, say to yourself, "Here's what I have to do today and I'm perfectly capable of doing it," rather than "holy cow, how can I possibly get everything done?"

On Fridays, try not to give in to the "TGIF" (thank God it's Friday) syndrome. Otherwise, you and your staff could lose a valuable half day or even more. In an issue of *Supervisory Management*, Jeffrey Davidson of IMR Corporation suggested one low-key and informal approach to help increase productivity without appearing authoritarian or demor-

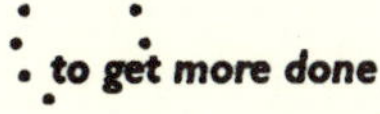

alizing. It's a method that involves organizing files, holding informal meetings, rearranging schedules, and managing attitudes.

Davidson suggests using Friday afternoons to make sure personal and common files are in order, cleared of unnecessary papers, and catalogued or indexed. Suggest to staff members that they do the same. If your firm is trying to reduce its paper flow, Friday afternoons are a good, low-pressure time to examine paper files and decide what can be thrown away. It's also a good time to handle time and expense logs, insurance and medical forms, and miscellaneous forms. This is routine work that doesn't require heavy thought and is suitable for times when we're easily distracted.

Consider making yourself informally available the last two hours of every Friday to staffers who wish to talk. They may be more likely to open up and discuss problems or improvements at this time. Encourage project managers to informally meet with their team members on Friday afternoons so that everyone is prepared to get going first thing Monday morning.

While it may sometimes be difficult to begin a new task late Friday afternoon, it may be feasible to undertake a small task that would later serve as part of a more important project. For example, develop ideas and outline the steps needed to solve a productivity problem. Or, delegate this task to a subordinate. Later on, expand the outline into a formal report.

Finally, remember how your attitude can influence the way your staff approaches their tasks. Do not let your guard down and accept lower productivity.

Stronger concentration

Stronger concentration skills can also improve effectiveness. Using the proper tools, getting rid of disturbances, setting goals, and improving your actual ability to concentrate can all help strengthen this skill. Your present ability to concentrate depends on many things. Most people can concentrate longer when not interrupted or when doing urgent and challenging tasks. But many people have a tough time concentrating on easy or too-difficult tasks without a deadline.

To improve concentration abilities, try thinking with a pencil and paper. The act of putting thoughts on paper automatically focuses attention. Always keep a scratch pad handy, whether you're at a meeting or daydreaming. Jot down ideas as they come — you'll start thinking about and organizing them. The good ideas will easily contrast against the not-so-good ideas.

Learn how to slow down and stop. A good stop will make it easier to start concentrating again. If you find that you're mentally blocked from solving the problem, make a tactical retreat. Here are some helpful ideas to do this:

End work on a good note. If you quit at a point of satisfaction, the work will seem more gratifying and you'll be eager to return to it. Contrast that with the frustration of ending on a bad or sour note.

Stop at a point of accomplishment.

If you stop while stalled, write down the problem and try to clarify why you can't get any further.

Have a logical starting point where you will resume. The best place is the beginning of a section or a natural breaking point. The worst place, on the other hand, is in the middle of an analytical problem.

In addition, try practicing concentration. Mark the time you start concentrating on a task. When your concentration lifts, note the time. After doing this a few times, you'll get a feel for your present limits. Then strive for longer periods. Note your accomplishments and don't let up easily. One hour is a long time to concentrate without a break, but many executives have learned to concentrate for three hours or more. How? They reward themselves with nights on the town, small gifts, or a day off when they reach new levels of skill.

Also, concentrate your time and tasks. Create blocks of time in your schedule that you can use for concentrating on the tougher tasks. Group

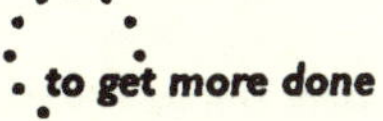

similar tasks together, such as making phone calls or writing letters.

Finally, try to prepare yourself and your surroundings. A quiet office, a clean desk, and a firm commitment all aid your ability to concentrate. As your eyes wander, or side-tracking thoughts come up, gently tug yourself back to the facts and considerations on which you want to concentrate. ◗

Chapter 4: Summary

■ To reduce procrastination, find out why you're procrastinating — do you not enjoy the assignment or are you afraid of doing a less-than-perfect job?

■ Most often, tasks we were dreading turn out better than we thought. Try doing these items a little at a time — say in 10 to 15 minute spurts.

■ Break large or undesirable projects into small, simple tasks.

■ Remember that perfection is an impossible goal.

chapter five

Adopting a Healthy Lifestyle for Better Time Management

"If you watch a game, it's fun. If you play it, it's recreation.
If you work at it, it's golf."
Bob Hope

"When I was forty my doctor advised me that a man in his forties
shouldn't play tennis. I heeded his advice carefully, and could hardly
wait until I reached 50 to start again."
Justice Hugo Black, U.S. Supreme Court

imagine a classified ad that reads —

While the ad sounds a little harsh, and probably a little illegal, being physically fit is often a valuable asset in the job market. An active employee is usually more productive, can work longer hours, presents a better appearance, and is better able to make decisions.

If you're trying to manage your time more effectively, adopting a healthy lifestyle can help. Faced with the challenges of balancing career, family, and other commitments, we all wish at one time or another that our days outnumbered 24 hours. But would you really *want* to spend two more hours at the office? Or would you prefer to take the eight or ten hours you spend there now and get 12 hours worth of work from them? Adding a healthier diet and a little activity to your lifestyle will help you do just that.

A healthy lifestyle will help improve your attitude toward other elements in your life such as your family, stressful situations that arise in the course of the day, even your boss. If you can wake up an hour earlier to walk or work out in the mornings, you'll find you don't even miss that hour of sleep because the six or seven hours left are spent in quality sleep. And, because relaxation is more important than long sleep, it's the quality of sleep, not the quantity, that counts.

If you're trying to figure out how to add more time to your week, you may think adding a few hours of physical activity to your weekly schedule is out of the question. The fact is, it may be just what the doctor ordered. By increasing your physical activity level, you can actually convert the remaining time in your week to quality time.

Signs of health/fitness deficiencies

Take a look at your current diet and exercise regime. Do this even if you've never missed a day of work and always think of yourself as being in the "healthy as a horse" category.

At work, you may be able to read a department's annual progress report and immediately recognize any problems that need correcting. Signs like missed production deadlines, employee turnover, or sales decreases during a normally busy period jump out like red flags. Similarly, there are red flags to look for if your health and fitness level is not what it should be. These may be things that you do that contribute to poor health, such as leading a sedentary lifestyle, or things that signal something is lacking, such as an inability to lose weight.

If your work and lifestyles are mostly sedentary — if you can be termed a "desk potato" — your fitness level is probably below par. Never mind that your weight falls right in the ideal range for your height. You may still face other health problems, especially if a large percentage of that weight is fat.

Do you feel stressed or burned out often? Perhaps you're chalking up too much of this feeling to the "it goes with the job territory" theory. Do you tire easily, perhaps peaking in the morning and becoming practically useless after lunch? While everyone has their "peak operating hours," winding down too early may signal physical problems such as anemia or lack of fitness. Or, you may simply not be eating what you should at lunch. If this sounds like a familiar problem, try eating a better balanced diet, cutting out the sugary snacks between or after meals, and reducing your caffeine intake. If you find you're still having severe energy lapses after altering your diet and activity level, consult a doctor to make sure there are no other problems.

Do you tend to get angry often, blowing up while waiting in traffic or when a staff member makes a minor error? This tendency can greatly increase your chance of having a heart attack. In addition, if you're completely sedentary, your chances of surviving that heart attack are slim. Chronic anger causes the blood pressure to rise, leading to cardio-vascular problems and often death. In a study of doctors and lawyers, more than 15 percent of those at age 25 who had high hostility traits were dead by age 50. Of those with low hostility levels, only 2 percent had died.

If your lifestyle includes smoking, alcohol, or eating out frequently, it can negatively affect your blood pressure, cholesterol and energy levels, even your ability to effectively manage your time.

And, if you've changed your eating habits in an effort to lose weight, you too will benefit by adding a little physical activity to your routine.

Everyone can benefit

Remember your school days, when you were taught that breakfast is the most important meal of the day? Sometimes life's simplest rules are the most helpful. People who want to lose weight decrease their food intake and increase their activity levels. It's that simple. Still, many shun the advice, spending needless time and money looking for an even easier way.

If you want to better manage your time, you too should consider exercising regularly and eating a more balanced diet. And don't listen to what the candy bar makers say. Sure a chocolate bar will pick you up from that afternoon slump but an hour later you'll be feeling less ener-getic than ever. It's a temporary fix. You want a permanent solution: stop falling into the afternoon slump in the first place.

People who exercise regularly gain higher energy levels, enabling them to remain alert longer and work longer hours. And, they're able

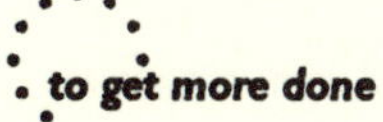

to work more effectively and make better decisions, thus bettering their careers and their company's edge over competition.

Don't wait until Monday. You can take steps right now to improve your health and fitness.

Diet

Start thinking about eating better food as soon as you start your day. Studies show that people who eat breakfast are in better shape than those who don't, even if their daily caloric intake is equal. Spreading the number of calories you eat throughout the day aids weight control. And, a healthy breakfast charges up your metabolism, giving you more energy to start the day. Besides, skipping breakfast will make you more likely to overeat at lunch and lead to that afternoon slump again.

Breakfast doesn't have to be a large meal with pancakes, eggs, and sausage. In fact that may do more harm than good. Instead, opt for high fiber or lean protein breakfasts such as a combination of cereal, fruit, or cottage cheese.

If you really can't fit in five or ten minutes for a light breakfast — perhaps you've already chosen to get up early and take a morning walk or run — take a low-fat muffin or whole wheat bagel (skip the cream cheese) to work. Avoid doughnuts, pastries, or muffins that are high in fat. (One plain doughnut has around 24 times as much fat as four slices of bread with a tablespoon of jam.) Eat on the way, over a morning newspaper, or during your quiet hour as you prepare the day's projects.

It's hard not to fall into the fast food trap at lunch, particularly if you're pressed for time or travel often. Try to limit fast food lunches to one a week. Instead, opt for "power lunches" to give you energy without draining your system in the afternoon. Best bets are grilled fish or chicken, a salad with dressing on the side, or a light sandwich on whole wheat bread — sans mayo. Have it dry or ask for mustard instead.

Many people prefer to have a bigger lunch and lighter dinner, especially if the dinner hour is often 9 p.m. Eating a 1,000 calorie meal soon before retiring makes it harder for your digestive system to work while you're sleeping. If this sounds like you, have a hearty lunch such as pasta with red, not white, sauce, or lean meat with soup and salad.

For a quick dinner, try frozen dinners instead of carry out food. They're not what they used to be. Many companies have introduced healthy, balanced entrees that can be cooked in a microwave in minutes for a light, simple to prepare dinner.

If you're a snack-junkie, opt for a piece of fruit instead of something sweet or from the vending machine. Finally, limit your intake of red meat; fats such as oil, butter, nuts, margarine, and mayonnaise; chocolate; fried and fast foods. Cut down on coffee and alcohol consumption — start drinking six or eight glasses of water each day instead.

Eating out while traveling

The first step to eating better is something few would object to: avoid airline food. Stay away from typically fatty and salty airline meals by calling ahead to order a vegetarian or low-salt meal. Or, skip it altogether and bring fruit, low-fat cheese, and crackers aboard.

In restaurants, always order salad dressing on the side. Then, rather than pouring it on your meal, dip your fork into the dressing before going to your plate for a forkful. At buffets or salad bars, don't just load up everything that catches your eye — build a balanced meal with vegetables, fruit, carbohydrates, and an entree.

Exercise

Many of us literally don't have three hours a week to spend on racquetball or weight training. Others haven't exercised since high school and feel they're too old to start now. The truth is, simply walking two miles a day can improve your effectiveness at work *and* puts your risk of having a heart attack at the same level as those who run over four miles a day. Most people see benefits after exercising just three hours a week. Try varying your workouts with a combination of biking, walking, running, dancing, swimming, or tennis. That way you'll be more likely to stick with an exercise program because you won't grow tired of the same old activity.

Once you start, you'll be more inclined to incorporate activity into your daily routine. Walk, run or bike your way to work in the mornings, or at least to the train or bus stop. Park the car a mile or so from work

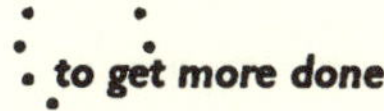

and walk to the office. Walk or run at lunch (or at least *to* lunch). Take the stairs whenever possible. Walk or ride a bike to the store at night for a quick errand. Walk all 18 holes on the golf course.

Adding a little physical activity into your day will help minimize your reaction to stress and help you deal better with customers, other employees, deadlines, and crises. Yoga, a massage, or isometric exercises can also help relieve tension and boost energy levels. These types of activity reward you with lowered tension and stress levels, which helps you to deal more rationally with schedule demands, problems and crisis situations without "blowing the day" due to emotional exhaustion.

Below are a few isometric methods to reduce tension, provided by the stress management counselors at the Management Institute at the University of Wisconsin-Extension, Madison, WI.

- *Rest your hands on your desk with your feet about three to four feet away from the desk. With back and arms straight, do a slow push-up. You'll feel muscle relief in your back, chest, and shoulders.*

- *Clasp your hands in front of your chest with arms parallel to the floor. Push as hard as possible. This is another fine tension reliever.*

- *Grasp the bottom of your chair as you sit. Use both hands, and keep your feet on the floor and your arms and back straight. Lift up — you'll stay seated, but your tension will leave your back and arms.*

- *Squeeze the phone as hard as you can before you hang up after each call. You will rid yourself of harmful muscle tension.*

- *Take a walk to the washroom, for coffee, or around the block. An hour at your desk without a break is the maximum you should expect from yourself except in special, heavy concentration situations. Getting out to "smell the roses" gives you a fresh perspective.*

While sitting in traffic, at your desk, or wherever you begin to feel pressured, try these relaxation techniques:

- *Sit up, back straight: close your eyes and relax. Start to inhale deeply, letting your abdomen rise with each breath; exhale. Visualize a golden light. Imagine you're breathing in that light. Imagine it's refreshing and energizing you. As you exhale, imagine you're expelling all fatigue and stress. Continue for five minutes.*

- *Let your chin sag to your chest. Very slowly let your head drop back; repeat this motion twice as if you were nodding yes. Now gently and slowly roll head clockwise five times around; then counter-clockwise five times. Shrug shoulders, all the way up to your ears. Hold that position, then relax, letting shoulders drop. Repeat three times.*

- *Relax. Place both palms together chest high, elbows out, as if praying. Press hands together hard as you inhale; relax them as you exhale. Repeat five times. Cross arms and press hands against upper arms while inhaling; relax and exhale. Repeat five times.*

Office equipment

Another way to reduce stress at work is to make sure the office equipment you use is not contributing to your aches and pains. If you sit at a desk for as little as four hours a day, you need a chair that will help maximize your physical effectiveness. The wrong chair can impair your time, and cause such problems as back pains, stiff necks, muscle spasms, constipation, headaches, and even phlebitis. Check out the ergonomically-designed chairs at an office supply store. A good chair is firm and offers good back support. Its height should be a little less than the length of your lower leg from knee to foot. The back of the chair should tilt backwards slightly — about seven degrees. The seat length should be no longer than two-thirds the measurement of your thighs.

And, finally, get up, stand, and walk when you can to circulate your blood and relax your muscles. When possible, walk down the hall to drop off a message for a colleague, rather than using the phone. Granted, using the phone would save time, but with the walk you gain a physical lift. Forgo the second or third cup of coffee for a brisk walk around the office. You'll feel refreshed, as well as less nervous for skipping the caffeine. If your concentration lapses and you find yourself staring out the window a bit too long, get up and run in place for a minute to stimulate the circulation and flow of oxygen.

Habits to eliminate

Now that we've talked about what habits you should add to your life, let's mention those that would be best left out of the picture.

Smoking

A reformed smoker often watched a colleague hopelessly try to quit the cigarette habit, only to start again three days, one day, or five hours later.

"I'm having a bad day," he'd explain.

"Well, at least the way you've chosen to deal with your bad day will help eliminate any future days," she answered.

Giving up smoking is a challenge but one that offers so many rewards. Lengthening your life and improving the health of those around you are just two. Better managing your time is another.

Because the carbon monoxide in smoke makes it more difficult for your blood to carry oxygen, smoking can make you lazy. In addition, think of all the time spent searching for ash trays, lighters, and vending machine change, as well as actually lighting and puffing away on each cigarette.

A whopping 83 percent of lung cancer cases are caused by cigarette smoking. Besides being the number one cause of cancer and heart disease, smoking is the most avoidable cause of death and morbidity. Cutting down isn't enough: just two cigarettes a day over a thirty-year period will double the risk of contracting lung cancer. Three will triple that risk, four will quadruple it, etc.

Stop smoking and your lungs will immediately begin the path to recovery. After ten years the added risk of lung cancer is virtually none. And, studies show that just two years after quitting, your chances of a heart attack return to normal.

Alcohol

Alcohol and recreational drugs such as marijuana or cocaine will also lower your energy and motivation levels. If you tend to drink or use more when you're traveling or entertaining clients, switch to club sodas, juice spritzers, or simply a diet Coke with a twist of lime. Or, cut your intake in half by alternating a soda after each mixed drink.

Remember, alcohol is a habit-forming depressant. And 10-12 percent of the American population is so allergic to alcohol that they are destined to become addicted to the beverage if they use it at all. One or two drinks at lunch will cause you to work more slowly in the afternoon and can easily slip into a habit of "a couple before lunch", "a few before dinner" and a "nightcap before bed." Wouldn't you rather slow down when you can enjoy yourself, like on the weekend? ◗

Chapter 5: Summary

■ **A healthy lifestyle can help people become more productive.**

■ **Don't skip breakfast. A light morning meal can boost your energy and metabolism for the rest of the day.**

■ **A little exercise goes a long way. Even walking two miles a day substantially reduces your risk of having a heart attack. It also helps people deal better with the day's crises.**

■ **Avoid smoking, alcohol and recreational drug use for maximum efficiency.**

PART II

Planning and Organizing Your Time

chapter six

Setting Goals

"I have learned this at least by my experiment: that if one advances confidently in the direction of his dreams, and endeavors to live the life which he has imagined, he will meet with a success unexpected in common hours."
Henry David Thoreau

Long term planning has long been a popular subject among entrepreneurial executives. Asked how they achieved success, many business owners will credit their five year plans. Business plans typically outline the company's history, structure, personnel, market, competition, and finances. They also look at what the company's goals and marketing strategy will be over the next one-, three-, and five-year periods.

The key to reaching those goals is to set specific objectives. A manufacturer can decide to increase sales by 25 percent over the next year. Or, it may aim to be among the top three companies in its industry five years down the road.

Individuals can also benefit from setting their own goals, both personal and career-related. A list of well-defined goals, clear objectives, and a daily list of plans to achieve those goals will help any manager improve their chances for success. These too should be specific but realistic. We all want to be millionaires by age thirty but unless we could figure out a way to delay a few birthdays, it may not be a realistic goal. (And if you can learn how to put off birthdays, that discovery alone will bring you fame and fortune.)

Many people shy away from setting long-term or even short-term goals because they don't want to carve them in stone. They feel if they don't reach a goal it will represent failure. The truth is, goals should be dropped, altered, and extended as conditions demand. Keeping out-of-date and unrealistic goals in your plan makes it difficult to focus on a true course in your life.

What's more, goals are personal. Although they should be written down somewhere, nobody but you has to see them. They are for you to shape, work on, evaluate, and change. And that's true about daily, weekly, monthly and long-term goals.

Setting goals is an important element of time management. How we spend time should be continually compared with our goals and plans to reach them. This brings consistency to our efforts and our lives. Some people have listed 100 goals to achieve in their lifetimes, from riding a balloon to climbing Mt. Everest. Your own goals don't have to be as far reaching, although they can be. Consider setting goals related to time management, personal commitments, and career success.

By putting these goals into writing, the odds are greatly increased that they'll eventually be reached. Writing your goals on paper (or computer disk) helps to establish discipline. What would you like to be doing in a month? In five years? Keep them short and clearly stated. Knowing what you want is the first step in getting it. Otherwise, you're just floundering aimlessly. It takes a little time in the beginning to set those goals, but it saves a lot more in the end.

Think about setting both short- and long-term goals. Not every goal has to be set a year or more in the future. Achieving short-term goals creates momentum, a feeling of achievement, and a desire to reach other goals. They also have a direct effect on how you spend and save your time. They increase productivity because you can anticipate problems and concentrate on what's important. Short-term goals point out opportunities and let you head off impending problems before they strike.

Goals can be divided into three general categories: lifetime, intermediate, and daily goals. All three areas should correlate for maximum effectiveness. In other words, the daily objectives should contribute to the achievement of intermediate and lifetime goals. What you do today

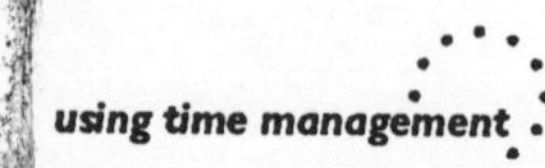

and tomorrow should relate to what you want to do in the next month or year. If the efforts don't match up, you'll start from scratch again.

Lifetime goals can be anything you wish to accomplish or experience in your lifetime. Often, they'll take more than a year to achieve. To determine your lifetime goals, randomly list the personal goals you'd like to accomplish, such as earn a master's degree, learn another language, take a cruise around the world. On another sheet of paper, list your professional goals. Aim for specific jobs or offices, rather than listing "get a promotion."

Combine goals from both lists if anything is related. Pare down and reorganize the list until it represents what you want out of life and what you are willing to work for. It may mean deleting most of the fantasies (but keep one or two just in case). Rather than planning out your entire life in specific details, the list is meant to provide a general but flexible course.

Also, keep your goals specific and measurable. Specific goals provide more direction. Don't say "I'd like to be less bothered at work," when "I'm going to cut down on phone interruptions" will more clearly state the goal. Giving goals shape, dimension, and depth will help you realize when you've achieved those goals. The more clearly you define and understand the goals, the more likely you are to perceive and take steps to achieve them. Conversely, if goals are vague, they can be harder to reach.

Intermediate goals are specific tasks you'd like to accomplish in the next six to 12 months. Prioritize your goals, then answer these questions for each:

Why do you want to achieve this goal?

What will achieving it do for you?

How will achieving this goal contribute to reaching your lifetime goals?

What price will it take to reach this goal? Are you willing to pay it?

What will happen if you fail?

What subgoals are necessary to achieve this goal? List the target dates.

What can you do today that will get you started on this goal?

For daily goals, consult the To Do list we discussed in Chapter 7. A portion of the items on that list should correlate with your intermediate and lifetime goals. Keep those goals in mind every day. Ask yourself, "Is what I'm doing moving me closer to my goals?" If the answer is no, delegate the work or put it off to a better time.

General goal guidelines

Your goals should be your own. While taking suggestions from others can help to trigger a few of your own goals, do not allow your goals to be determined by other people, such as spouses, employers, or children. At work, however, your organization's goals and objectives serve as a general road map for your own goals. The better people understand their company's goals and objectives, the more likely they are to work toward and achieve them.

Keep the goal-setting process realistic. You can simply list the things you'd like to do or make it fancy with timetables and priorities. The effort needed depends on the sorts of goals that you set. If a goal should be at all limited, it should be to what's truly important. Having too many goals dilutes interest, effort, emphasis, and odds of success.

The goals themselves should also be realistic. They should not be so outrageous and far-fetched that they can never be reached, but they also shouldn't be so easy that they become meaningless. Reaching the goals should stretch your abilities. Satisfaction is continually setting challenging but reasonable goals. Unattainable goals are only fantasies.

Consider some of your past goals. Did you reach them? Was the effort worth the outcome? If you have had problems attaining your old goals, especially the short-term ones, try to analyze where the problem lies. Perhaps you aimed too high or were not being realistic about a deadline. Learn from your mistakes and plan accordingly.

What kind of result do you expect from your goals? Do you want perfect results or average results? Now consider the effort needed to reach your goal expectations. Will the time and effort be worth the outcome? If so, fine. If not, downgrade your expectations. This helps give priorities to your goals, just as you attach priorities to your daily, weekly, and long-range tasks. And some goals are definitely more important than others.

using time management

Remember, your goals are only written on paper, not etched in stone. Don't feel you're setting a permanent course for your life. Life is a process that changes constantly. Your goals need to reflect those changes. They should clarify what you want to do, not limit change or growth. "A good plan is like a comfortable shoe. It serves its purpose and flexes to accommodate the needs of the user," says Michael LeBoeuf in *Working Smart.*

Twice a year or so, re-evaluate and rework your goals. They should reflect the current you, not the person who wrote them six months before. The goals can be adapted, changed, and discarded as you need. Re-evaluate or clarify goals when you're undergoing major changes, such as a promotion, job change, or marriage.

While setting goals, you may find that some of them conflict, or prevent another from being achieved. You may want to travel, for instance, yet expand your house that same year. Or, you may want to be the best salesperson in your company, yet spend more time with your family. Look for these inconsistencies when you first plot your goals to save time and frustration.

Finally, set target dates for your goals. A goal isn't a goal until it is committed to a deadline — and a lifetime doesn't count. Target dates, like goals themselves, also need to be realistic. Setting target dates is a major step in increasing motivation and commitment. They also make it easier to break the goals into easily-attainable subgoals with deadlines.

Step two: *attack!*

After you've thought about and listed your goals, you need to determine the best means with which to reach them. Make a chart to illustrate lifetime, intermediate, and daily goals. This helps bring them from the conceptual stage to actual planning. List the high-priority goals at the top and the remaining goals in descending order of importance. Plotting them out should show relationships — goals and subgoals — that you didn't see before. Group them accordingly.

Include any problems or opportunities that you anticipate and strategies for solving the problems and exploiting the opportunities. Make up a checklist of specific steps that are needed to reach a goal.

Target your goals one at a time. Trying to improve every aspect of your life at once will only lead to frustration because it will make the job seem too monumental. Limiting your efforts to one goal at a time will give you a tight focus and make the task less intimidating.

For example, you may want to concentrate on telephone interruptions for a week or longer. Plot out your strategy for relieving this common complaint. Study up on it. Approach your secretary one day to discuss how you'd like to resolve the problem. A few days later, work with your co-workers and assistants. Work on it together until the problem has been eased or resolved.

Reviewing time management goals

Obviously, one of the reasons for reading this book is to fulfill the goal of better time management. Think about the major problems in that area that you'd like to solve. Rank them in order of priority. Consult co-workers, assistants, or your spouse for their input. Perhaps they've noticed some problem areas and can offer solutions.

Over the coming year, try to tackle one problem each month. Study up on solutions and work the corrective actions into your everyday routine. Keep a note card handy that lists solutions to that month's problem. The more you read the card, the more the solutions will stick with you.

While not everybody has the same time management weaknesses, the following schedule may be useful in pinpointing your own time management goals.

January: telephones

Eliminate wasted time on the phone by cutting the chatter. Try to get to the point fast and stay there. End all calls promptly. Have your secretary screen all of your incoming calls and offer help to callers on run-of-the-mill matters. Your secretary can also find the answers on some subjects for return phone calls. Set aside a time for calling and returning calls. Group them together for when the people are most likely to be in — this keeps you from breaking up your day. Finally, know what's happening to your phone use. Keep a record of incoming and outgoing calls and analyze it.

using time management

February: interruptions

Keep them short and to the point. You will never get rid of all interruptions, as they are a part of every job. Don't let them get to you, unless they're all too frequent. Try scheduling a time for interruptions, new developments, and visitors every day into your appointment book. Refer the interruptions to that time, if possible. At other times, close your door to keep people away, or face your desk away from traffic. Don't let visitors sit — they'll never get up. Hold fast, stand-up meetings where you control time. Or, go to the other person's office so you can control when you leave. When asked, "Got a minute?" say "no" if you don't.

March: paperwork

Aim to create as little paperwork as possible. When you pick up a piece of paper, do something with it: route it, toss it, file it, respond or make a decision. Try not to shuffle it or handle the same piece of paper twice. Toss out as much as possible. Most of what you file won't be looked at again. Also, keep writing short, sweet, and simple. Secretaries can help answer routine correspondence, type dictated letters, help edit letters and reports, and preview and compile reading material.

April: "firefighting"

Be prepared for a crisis by anticipating and planning contingency plans. Make sure everyone knows what to do and how to react. If the same type of crisis happens several times, there's an error in the system. Find it and solve the problem. Then you have more time for unique crises. Learn lessons from what caused the crisis so it doesn't happen again. Do the work right the first time, and encourage others to do so. Finally, consider posting a sign in the office that reads, "Procrastination on your part does not constitute an emergency on my part."

May: priorities

Learn to sort out your tasks by priority: high, medium, and low. Prioritize your tasks on your daily To Do list. Update the list at lunch and add new items as needed. Try to tackle high priority tasks during prime time or quiet hour and save low priority tasks for when you are likely to be interrupted.

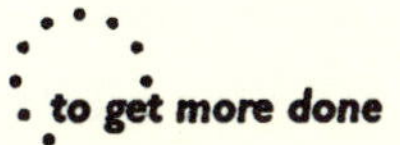

June: artificial deadlines

Deadlines force you to finish earlier than required — you'll start quicker, be prepared for problems and have time to react. Sooner started, sooner finished. If nothing else, you'll feel you have better control over your time. Deadlines force us to face difficult and unpleasant tasks earlier. These tasks often take longer than anticipated. Force yourself to obey early deadlines. Otherwise, they won't do any good.

July: procrastination

Have the courage to face this problem. Ask yourself why you are procrastinating. Is the task too hard? Is the outcome harmful? Do you understand the task? If the task is too big or overwhelming, try to develop some momentum. Break it into manageable pieces and tackle a small, rather easy portion of the task. Reward yourself for beating procrastination. Promise yourself a chocolate sundae if you finish a hard part by a certain time. Punish yourself if you don't meet the deadline.

August: work less

Don't pride yourself on your input — instead, pride yourself on your output. Hard work and long hours do not mean that you are getting more done. Executives must have time to think and confront the future. Yet they spend most of their time solving immediate, short-term problems. Find time for what is most important. Delegate routine or easy work. It's important to be relaxed some of the time in order to do your most innovative and productive work.

September: be organized

Keep your desk clear of everything except what's necessary for the immediate task. Block out your time and concentrate on one item at a time. Know how long tasks will take and plan around that. Be realistic on your To Do today lists. Keep a plan for daily, weekly, monthly, and yearly goals. Don't waste any time. Use those extra five or ten minutes to do small projects. Keep a file of such "quicky tasks" handy.

October: protect your time

Fight for your time. Don't let chatty visitors, poor meetings, or bad seminars take your valuable time. If you don't watch your time, no one else will. Also, respect other people's time and they'll respect yours. Do this by being on time for meetings or interviews, avoiding chit-chat, and not writing overlong reports. Learn to say "no" to work put upon you when you have other work that ranks higher in priority. Finally, lock your door, disappear, or hide out when you have important work to do and can't be interrupted.

November: two things at a time

While driving or commuting, listen to informative or inspirational cassette tapes, dictate letters and messages, or memorize material. Plan the next day while walking the dog, jogging, or doing other mindless tasks. Combine business and pleasure trips. Also, combine trips around town so as not to overlap steps.

December: ask questions

Here are some thought-provoking suggestions from Edward Dayton, author of *Tools for Time Management*.

- Ask why and you may eliminate it.
- Ask where and you may find a better place to do it.
- Ask when and you may find a better schedule.
- Ask who and you are likely to find the most appropriate person to do it.
- Ask what and you may find you are working on the wrong problem.
- Ask how and you may find a better solution.

Setting corporate goals

Once you learn to manage your time more efficiently, it will seem easier to reach personal goals because the process of setting and achieving those goals will also become more efficient.

Corporate goals can also be identified through this process. It's called Management by Objectives (MBO). Very simply, MBO is a method of tying your firm's goals and outcome to a set of objectives

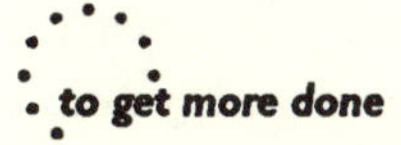

designed especially for each individual. MBO starts at the top and works its way down to every employee. Put in simpler terms: if you know where you're going, you'll get there. Several books have been written on the subject of MBO by university professors Dr. Peter Drucker, Dr. George Odiorne and Dr. Dale D. McConkey and others that you may want to read.

MBO gives your efforts and time a focus. Most everything you do should be with the goals and objectives in mind. Your time and work should revolve around those goals. Excise the extraneous.

While the underlying structure of MBO is pretty simple, overlaying it onto your management structure is often difficult — think of it as a challenge.

The start of a new year is a good time to consider implementing MBO. Or if you have an MBO program that isn't being used properly, consider revitalizing it. MBO can increase efficiency and communication, improve planning, and create an informed, concerned, and trusting work force.

A flexible planning method, MBO can be used by big corporations, smaller operations, or just one person. A survey of *Execu*Time®* readers showed about 55 percent used MBO. Although many lamented that their firms only partially or half-heartedly followed the program, most employees welcomed it. One woman said that her firm did not use MBO, but that she did.

Advantages of MBO

- *MBO encourages employee commitment and involvement because they help to determine their own goals within certain parameters. Success and failure are no longer subjective to whims and personal opinions.*

- *MBO gives each employee "turf." They cannot blame failure on someone else's policies or work. Each person is committed to managing his or her goals.*

- *MBO makes performance reviews easier and more effective. No more subjectivity. Performance is compared to the ability to reach those objectives.*

- *MBO encourages employees to communicate and work as a team. To meet their objectives, employees must know the department's goals. No one should be confused. Everyone has a part.*

- *MBO builds a solid foundation for budgets and funding requests. Planning will show personnel and equipment needs before there is a crisis.*

How MBO works

There are several phases to the MBO process, according to Mitchell Posner in *Executive Essentials.* The first is setting clear, specific, detailed objectives that can be understood by everyone. There are four kinds of objectives, which can be set up for any kind of task:

1. *Organizational* – for the entire firm.
2. *Unit* – for a specific division or department.
3. *Individual* – to complement the first two objectives. The individual is the key to the unit and must know his or her part of the whole plan.
4. *Personal* – the individual determines these on his or her own. They can be for just about anything: achievement, promotion, personal life, etc.

Keep objectives small and tightly focused. Try not to focus on too many at one time.

The second phase is the implementation phase. It's easier to develop and brainstorm the goals than it is to actually achieve them. Your plan for action should be extremely thorough and detailed, while still being flexible. Put the plan, your blueprint toward making those goals, into writing. Both the supervisor and subordinate should keep up-to-date copies of the plan.

A few days after you've finished the plan, go back through it and look for problem areas and flaws. You'll usually find a few, but better to find them now than when the plan is implemented.

Thirdly, review performance. The supervisor and subordinate should occasionally review and evaluate the worker's performance in light of the MBO goals. Don't make these reviews too formal — their intent is to improve performance, not fix blame.

An individual should look at the objectives and appraise the plan every day or once a week. When necessary, modify your objectives. Some people include their MBO goals with their To Do today lists or appointment books for a constant reminder.

Finally, prepare periodic reports that cover points of progress on the plan for action, discuss performance, and re-evaluate objectives. If you're leery of reports, do this verbally in a short meeting, but keep the records. Use them to fine tune your MBO objectives and plans. Develop actions to resolve problems that arise. Remember, MBO is in a constant flux and adapts to the situation. It needs constant feedback so that it can be properly primed and adjusted.

How to implement an effective MBO program

According to Posner, these are requirements for an effective MBO:

Be aware of employee needs. Create a supportive atmosphere to help increase employee competence and ability. The frequent evaluations on performance should be done constructively with the intent of improving — not setting blame.

Make duties clear. No one should have any doubts about their part of the plan or what they have to do.

Management must be committed. If upper management doesn't take MBO seriously, it will fail. Everyone must be committed and willing to take the time.

Establish standards. Everyone should know exactly what is expected of them because different people expect different results. The standards will serve as a visible reference point. The objective should be measurable in some fashion — not a vague description or idea. They don't have to be numerical, however. Detailed definitions will do.

Develop an information network. Information should flow with equal speed and ease up and down the corporate system. Keep records to provide a way of reviewing the objectives and settling any confusion. Don't be too informal.

Objectives should be complementary. The objectives for all departments, managers, and employees should interlock.

Have deadlines. Deadlines always force people to be more efficient and aware.

Objectives and plans should be reasonable, acceptable, and challenging. You should always be striving to improve performance. Involve subordinates when creating the plan for action — and give them the authority to get the jobs done. Ask yourself whether the person has the capability to achieve the task or whether the goals are feasible. Goals that cannot be reached are frustrating and irritating.

Getting started

If you don't have any corporate goals, make them now. Develop a list of short-term goals for this year. Then work those into a five-year plan. Be sure to be realistic and honest. If you approach it correctly and with enthusiasm, MBO can't help but make some noticeable improvements. ◐

Chapter 6: Summary

■ Goals need to be continually modified to reflect current achievements, not to mention reality. The first step toward reaching your goals is to set specific objectives.

■ Keep realistic goals, whether they're daily objectives or lifetime wants. Setting too many goals dilutes the effort that could otherwise be put toward the most important items.

■ Set a course toward achieving time management goals by working on a new area each month. If the telephone wastes a lot of your time, take the first month to reduce unwanted calls and shorten lengthy conversations.

chapter seven
Creating Daily Plans
To Meet Your Goals

"It is nonsense to say there is not enough time to be fully informed . . . Time given to thought is the greatest timesaver of all."
Norman Cousins

"**F**ail to plan, plan to fail." In a survey of 1100 executives, more than 80 percent said they were dissatisfied with their career progress and level of effectiveness. The reason: they lacked the planning skills to aim for and achieve attainable, reasonable goals. Many executives stay away from planning because they think it will take too much time. Often, they're the same movers and shakers that helped create five-year plans to illustrate company objectives. Yet they haven't made the connection that personal goals can also be translated into monthly, weekly, and daily plans.

Starting the day without a plan means the rest of the day will be spent reacting rather than acting. How would you prefer to spend your time — working from the in-basket of petty tasks that others have provided, or taking advantage of opportunities from which you can advance and profit?

While a certain number of crises and unexpected assignments are unavoidable, planning what you can pays off by creating direction, excitement, and motivation. Good planning also increases your ability to manage those around you.

Perhaps misconceptions of what a plan is and what it does have made you shy away from creating your own plans. Planning is not deciding each step and tiny detail in advance and then blindly following through on them. It's also not a loosely conceived and leisurely mental stroll along the path. It's somewhere in between — a means rather than an end.

Advantages of planning

A plan is like a road map. It tells you (and anyone else) where you are, where you want to go and how you intend to get there. It should also say why you want to go there — the motivation behind the plan. And it should show potential roadblocks and problems along the way, with alternate routes outlined. But a plan is better than a road map because it can be improved, altered, and redefined as you follow it.

A plan will also help you determine whether the work is worth the effort and headaches since you can plot the potential outcomes and costs. The job is already half done if you've planned properly.

Planning also increases productivity. A one-week plan can help you get 5-10 percent more done. What's more, with the plan you begin to recognize those minor crises that caught you by surprise when you didn't plan much at all. A one-month plan often increases output by as much as 15 percent. Looking ahead 30 days can help you head off impending crises entirely, as you will recognize them far enough in advance to totally prevent them.

A six-month plan can improve managerial skills by allowing you to recognize new opportunities and help you take advantage of them. In addition, your overall effectiveness is enhanced because you can see which tasks among the many available are most likely to help you reach your long-term goals. Finally, one-, three- and five-year plans can help you take charge of your career and your life and direct the two so that you can achieve the goals that are most important to you. If you have ever considered changing careers, switching companies or making other major changes, you need the leverage that such a long-term plan can provide.

One *Execu*Time*® reader, the purchasing manager of a southeast furniture factory, said he used a simple four-step method for converting distant goals into action steps. "The method helps me make my goals concrete, and has made a tremendous difference in achieving what I hope for," he said. Here is his simple four-step method:

1. Pinpoint intermediate markers to hit;
2. Decide on tangible measures to identify when each marker has been reached;
3. Create a plan to reach those tangible measures;
4. Break the plan down into daily action steps.

A similar way to transform your personal goals into workable plans is with a "planning inventory." First, list five major goals you'd like to achieve in your lifetime. Select the one goal you'd like to achieve first. Next, identify steps you can take toward this goal, in chronological order. Finally, break down the first step into one-day tasks you can accomplish. In chronological order, these are the bases for your daily plans. What you can attain is a matter for your own judgment. But you can make it easier on your judgment by using the planning inventory to reduce your overall goals down to a series of interim targets.

How to plan

At its simplest levels, planning is a linear action. Planning is a process of reasoning, anticipating, and thinking. The more often you plan, the better and more comprehensive you'll become. Your planning efforts should integrate short-, medium- and long-term goals. If the goals don't work together, you'll accomplish little of significance. Use the following process, which details planning at all levels, to bring all your goals together.

Daily planning

Every day, decide and list what tasks you want to accomplish, what the priorities are for each task, and what it will take in terms of time, effort, and materials to complete each task. Then start in on the highest priority task, continuing until you have finished or can't go any further. Then move on to the next highest priority.

Figure 7.1 To Do Today

TO DO TODAY

NAME ____ DATE _______________

PRIORITY	CLIENT/TASK/JOBS	TYPE	DEADLINE	ESTIMATED TIME				✓	PHONE CALLS (name, purpose)

LETTERS/REPORTS TO WRITE

PEOPLE TO SEE/DISCUSSION TOPICS	ACTIVE PROSPECTS	Follow-Up	

LONG RANGE (task, when due)

We've illustrated a simple To Do Today list that we make available. A full year's supply, 6 pads of 50 sheets each, for $39.95 plus $4.50 S/H may be ordered from Desktop Graphics, Inc., 26940 Longwood Road, Lake Forest, IL 60045-0631, check with order please. © Januz Consultants 1991

Leave 25 to 50 percent of your day unscheduled, as needs demand. Many top priority tasks are unplanned or emergencies that can't be scheduled.

Weekly planning

Use the same procedure used above to plan out the week. Once a week (Friday is best), select the goals to achieve the following week and work up a plan for reaching those goals. Break them down into daily sub-goals, and insert these into a daily To Do list. See illustration on page 86.

Monthly planning

Again, use the same procedure. At the end of the month, take an hour to decide what you want to accomplish over the next month. Decide on plans for reaching those goals on a week-to-week basis. Include items from your long-range and professional goals.

Yearly planning

The best way to find time for important but easy-to-delay tasks is to include it in your annual time budget. Start making a yearly plan that includes the long-range projects you'd like to finish. Give each project enough time so you can make steady progress to meet it. Then, assign specific dates so you know when to work on the project, what you will accomplish each time, and how much time you'll need. Mark those dates in your calendar — and don't break them! Keep the plan handy so you can check your progress.

Planning aids

Several aids are available to help track plans, not to mention an abundance of other information as well. These include pocket planning books, electronic planners, computer programs, simple To Do lists, and wall charts. Rather than going overboard and buying the whole nine yards, you'll want to examine each option carefully and choose the one that best fits your work and lifestyle.

Some people are happy with a pocket diary, while others swear by

the newer computerized time management programs. Pick a planner based on your needs. If it didn't work last year, try a different method. Here are a few styles to choose from.

Day-Timers and other pocket planners

Comprehensive wallet notebooks such as those available from Day-Timers (1 Daytimer Plaza, Dept. J, Allentown, PA 18195) or Day-Runner (sold through most better office supply/stationery stores) include a To Do Today list, appointment book, diary and time record, expense and reimbursement record, project file, tickler reminder, and name and address file. See illustrations on pages 90-91.

Incidentally, Day-Timers publishes a 96-page catalog of time management and office necessities and is available free upon request by writing to the address above. Their catalog contains a host of products for the executive interested in better using his/her time.

A good planner should include the following ingredients:

Planner format

Your appointment book is a planning tool, not a diary for the day's events. It should include room for daily, weekly, quarterly, and yearly planning. Last year's calendar and five-year planner are good additions.

Good page format

Good planners divide each hour into quarters; have extra space for luncheon appointments; are simple and easy to read; and allot less space for weekends and nights. Extras include space for notes, expenses/reimbursements, "things to do," and memos/calls received.

Easy access

Information you use most often should be easy to find. The fewer extraneous reference pages the better. Also, look for a double-ribbon bookmark that will mark two pages at the same time.

Time use log

A full-blown time log is too personal and bulky to be included in

using time management

a planner for time management training or research. Try a time log before setting up your planner to locate problem areas.

But, a good time-planner appointment book includes a diary record of what has transpired on a daily basis. While it does not give the detail that a true time log gives it offers a historical record of what you have accomplished daily and is the basis for deciding when it's time to take another true time log inventory.

Space for phone numbers

Some 85 percent of your calls are probably made to 30 or 40 numbers, so it helps to have them handy. Look for a listing of toll-free 800 numbers as well.

Good looks

You will probably be using your planner often in front of other people, so get an impressive-looking planner. Whether you decide on a pocket type (to fit in a man's jacket pocket or in a woman's purse) or a larger notebook style, consider investing in a good cover so that you make a good impression on people when you use it. At all costs avoid the cheap plastic covers that come with the books and, instead, invest in the better leather covers. It should also be bound loose enough to lie flat on a desk without the help of hands.

Personal information page

This lists credit card, bank account, and insurance policy numbers, birthdays, and similar information.

Electronic pocket scheduling devices

Several computer manufacturers have recently come out with a pocket-sized electronic version of the pocket secretary books. About the size of a pocket/purse calculator, the products can store appointments, addresses and phone numbers, expenses, and things to do.

One of the better and most popular of these is the Casio B.O.S.S. with 64K of memory (this is the one Mr. Januz uses) available for about $200 from most computer stores or office supply stores or at Service

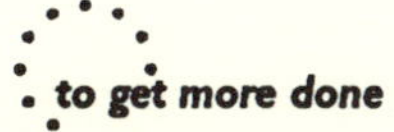

 Day-Timer Formats

Illustration courtesy of Day-Timers Inc., Allentown, PA 18195-1551

Exclusive 5-in-1 Design
Key to Day-Timer Effectiveness

Regardless of format, all Day-Timers feature an orderly, multi-purpose page layout that organizes your day. The exclusive 5-in-1 design combines five functions in one complete system. All five key functions are included in each Day-Timer. Note, however, that the amount of space devoted to each function varies from one format to the next.

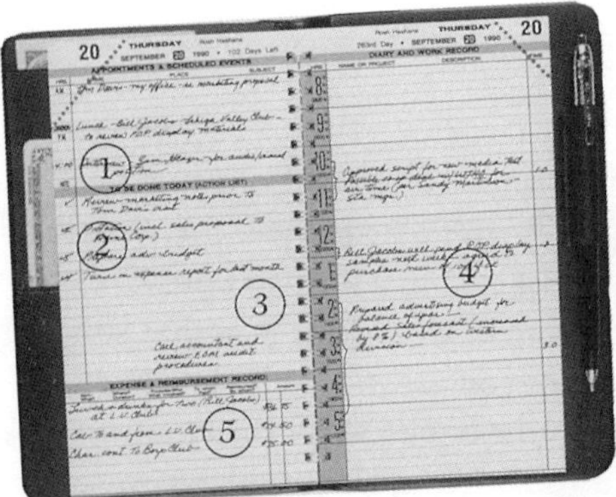

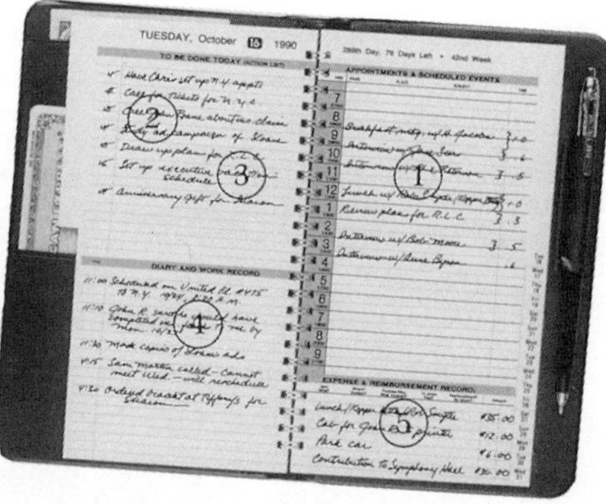

① **Appointment Book** *In this section, list all appointments for conferences, events and activities that have a definite time and place; this prevents schedule conflicts. There's also room to fill in names, locations and subjects for discussion. Enter only time-pegged events in this section. That way, a glance at you Day-Timer lets you know when you have a time/place commitment.*

② **To Be Done Today (Action List)** *Plan your work here. Record projects with deadlines, such as reports and presentations. First thing in the morning, scan the day's schedule. Add any new projects or work that hasn't been completed. Then prioritize your tasks according to their importance. You'll be off to an organized start.*

③ **Tickler Reminder** *Use the "to be done today" section to enter reminders for personal or business matters that will require you attention at a later time. Eliminates the need for a separate tickler file.*

④ **Work Diary & Time Record** *This section acts as you daily log or work accomplished. The same area also can be used to document your time record for client billing.*

⑤ **Expense/Reimbursement Record** *Enter all business-related expenses on the spot. Your notes provide the documentation needed for business reimbursement and tax purposes.*

using time management

Figure 7.3 · Day-Timer Original 2-page Format

Illustration courtesy of Day-Timers Inc., Allentown, PA 18195-1551

2-Page-Per-Day Original Format
An In-Depth Record of Everything You Accomplish

This is the original Day-Timer format. Each day has a two-page spread with plenty of room for exact time records. It's excellent if you have a heavy workload that requires a system with maximum capacity for detail. This version is ideally suited to anyone who works during conventional business hours—8a.m. to 6p.m. Use the left-hand page to list everything to be done each day; appointment hours are open. The right-hand page serves as your record of work accomplished; work diary hours are calibrated so you can keep precise time records. The pages have perforated corners that can be torn off each day so that the current date always shows.

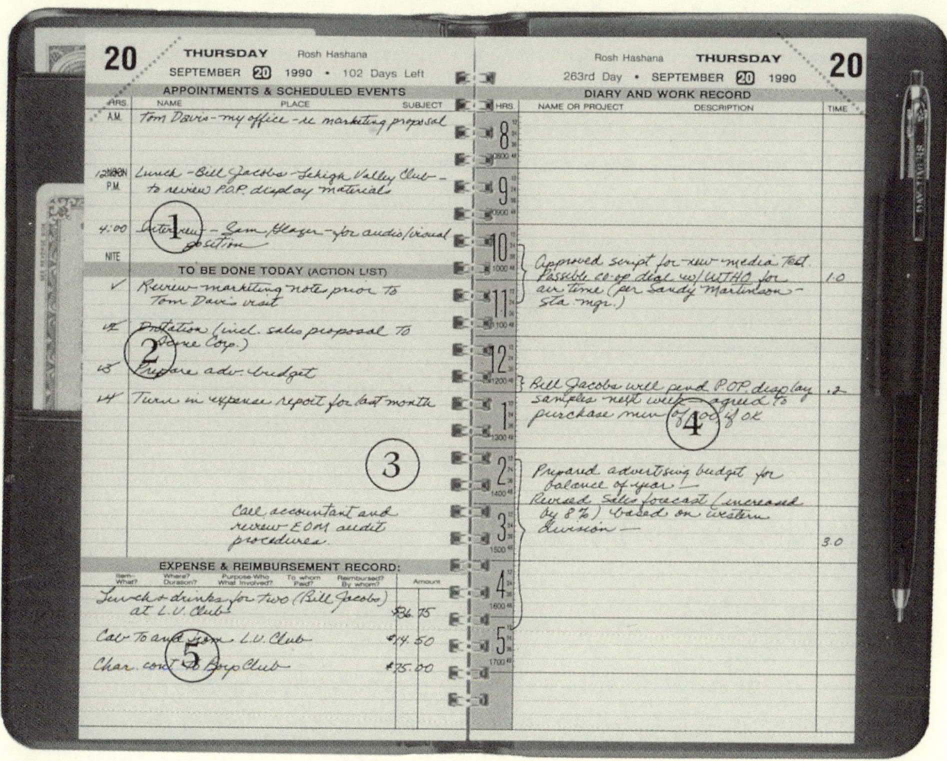

Merchandise Co. Inc. (P. O. Box 25130, Nashville, TN 37202-5130), one of the more popular nationwide catalog showrooms. It is available in both 16k and 32k versions but unless cost is critical we suggest you opt for the 64k version.

The Sharp Wizard is equal to the B.O.S.S. (but slightly more expensive), and it has a wider variety of interchangeable cartridges for more sophisticated functions. Many of these also function as a calculator and address book.

Less and more expensive ones are available with varying memory sizes and features. Beware of those selling in the $20-50 range — while they may do you well as an address book, they are just too limited in features to provide any real planning benefit.

If the majority of your time is spent in the office, however, consider personal computer programs designed to help you organize your time. The absolute best, in our opinion, is OnTime. It can record appointments and projects to handle today, this week, this month or next year. For more information on the OnTime program, see Chapter 21, "Personal Information Management Systems," where we'll illustrate some of the screens in actual use and give you the address of where to order OnTime. OnTime is available in both personal and network versions.

Whatever method you choose to log assignments, there are several ways in which you can make it even more effective. First, make sure the list is maintained. It's easy to get gung-ho over things, buy a fancy notebook, pen in the next month's projects, and then forget the whole thing three weeks later. As your days and weeks progress, add or subtract items according to needs and time available.

Starting a To Do list

A To Do list, whether in a pad, a Daytimer type book or on a computer, is the key component of any time management planning method.

Get in the habit of writing down what you want to accomplish by first making up a list of all the tasks you need to complete in the next week. Prioritize this list with numbers from one to 10 with the most important job getting a number one priority.

Consult your master list of things to do, as well as any other sources, such as a new project that's just been handed to you. A weekly planner lays out your plans for the entire week and allows you to see problem areas and get a grasp of what is ahead. Simply shuffle all your tasks into appropriate morning and afternoon slots. Each Friday, take 15 minutes or so and make up a planning sheet for the next week. Before leaving work each day, transfer completed items to a new To Do list for the next day. A computer program, such as OnTime, will do this automatically for you if you simply remove those items that were completed.

The five or ten minutes spent making out a list will help reap enormous time and productivity benefits. Include several areas to keep you on top of calls to make, people to see, letters and reports, deadlines, assignments, and priorities. The most important area of this form is a list of tasks and assignments that need to be done that day. Include the time the task is due, estimated time it will take to complete and anything else needed to finish the task, such as writing a memo, letter, or abstract. Fill this out first thing in the morning, or at the end of the previous day. Kim finds the latter works even better because she doesn't arrive at work in a panic about what needs to be done. She has already carefully plotted this out prior to leaving the day before. It's a great stress reliever to know if and when everything will be done.

The list can be as detailed or simple, creative or straightforward as its writer desires, although a certain amount of detail will help avoid confusion later. If a list just says "make follow-up call," the person who wrote it may wonder hours later who it was they were supposed to call. Others prefer to write the phone number next to the name of the person they're calling, to save them time looking it up later. Some people prefer writing their list on a pad of paper or steno pad, which can be propped on a desk for constant visibility. Others may opt for preprinted "To Do" forms.

One writer found added motivation by simply writing "Do" at the top of her list rather than "To Do." "Switching from the wimpy infinitive to the action-oriented imperative worked. I made my list, and then I did," she explained.

One note of caution: don't get caught in an activity trap, doing tasks

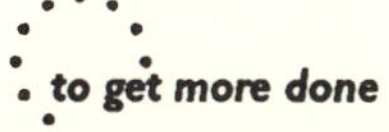

just to keep busy. Schedule in time for some of the creative and intangible tasks that are hard to define: improving your work, planning for the long term, developing creative ideas.

Organizing priorities

Grade each item on a priority scale and then attack the master list bit by bit. Transfer a few priority items to a daily list, delegate any medium- or low-priority items that can be handled elsewhere, and eliminate items that no longer seem important after looking at the grand scheme of things.

Schedule work in blocks of time. The largest chunks of time should go to the important things you must do. Then leave plenty of time for interruptions, emergencies and other tasks. Schedule similar tasks together. Tackling similar tasks at the same time or right after each other also speeds up the process. If you have to make six phone calls, four of which are essential, group those four together. Save the other two calls for when all the high-priority tasks are completed. Unfortunately, most schedules don't allow blocks of time in which to group activities, which is why many people resort to the scatter-shot approach. The "assembly line" process makes it easier when going from one project to the next. You'll have on hand the needed tools, information, and mental focus.

The key to managing time is setting, starting, and then finishing priority tasks. Setting priorities can be as easy as ABC by giving all tasks and activities a priority of A, B, or C. "A" tasks have a high value, meaning they must be completed right away or by day's end. "B" tasks have a medium value. They should be done some time, but not right away. "C" tasks have a low value. It's nice to finish these, but not necessary. They can often be skipped or delegated. According to Pareto's Principle, 80 percent of the value comes from 20 percent of the items. That's why it's important to set priorities and tackle the vital projects. When setting priorities, determine which activities have the greatest effect on profits or success and place them first. Focus on results, not activities. Don't become so involved in finishing tasks or busy work that you lose sight of the real priority — completing high-payoff tasks.

Focus energy and concentration on the most important task at hand. Trying to do too many things at once leads to confusion and a plethora of uncompleted tasks. Rather than finish half of four tasks, finish two whole ones. It takes less time, energy and concentration while increasing momentum and motivation. Eternally hanging onto unfinished tasks can result in feelings of fatigue and defeat. Your mind will work part time on trying to finish them — even while you think you're concentrating on something else. Mark the quick and easy tasks. As the day progresses, there will be time when you have a moment or two to finish a short task, perhaps a quick call or a hand-written note.

Spend most of your time on those items that need the most work — and that yield the most results. Gradually, work your way through the list, checking off or drawing a line through each task you've completed, or noting the results you achieved, such as "delegated to Bob" or "ordered new equipment." One of the side benefits of keeping this type of list is the satisfaction of crossing off each item. Ending the day with a list that has been pretty well crossed off offers quite a spiritual lift of accomplishment. Remember, a simple check mark or line drawn through each item is better than marking it into oblivion. If necessary, you want to be able to read what you've done at a later date. This will help you improve your ability to estimate time for future projects.

In addition to the desktop pad of paper, To Do lists can also be included in an appointment book, a method favored by those who travel or need to keep their list with them at all times. Others may want to consider organizing projects on a wall chart. The two- by-three foot laminated charts, which are available from office supply stores, can help organize days, weeks and months in advance. They also save desk space, as well as the time spent flipping through hand held booklets. Use different colors to block out the portions of the days, weeks, or months you plan to be occupied with various projects. Schedule your most important, most beneficial projects first, then fit the smaller ones in the remaining time. Once they're posted, you can't help but use them, because they'll dominate the wall and make obvious where you should be spending more of your time.

Tackling your To Do list

"There's no time like the present" is an adage that's lasted so long because it's true. Don't sit on something if you can move it. This habit will spur you to action and help you to be aware of how much you can accomplish in a single day, hour or minute. Fight procrastination. The longer the wait, the harder the start. Each week, do one thing you hate yet have to do.

Don't, however, try to take on more than you can accomplish. Keep your list short and allot more time than necessary for most tasks. By continually listing more things than you can accomplish in a day, you'll only set yourself up for frustration when you're unable to finish. Some tasks, particularly high priority items, often take longer than we imagine. Overestimating time on a project by 10 to 25 percent will allow extra time for unexpected interruptions or tasks that take longer than expected.

Break larger tasks into small parts. Tasks that appear large, endless or insurmountable often lead to procrastination because there isn't an obvious place in which to start the effort. Break those mountains into small hills that are easily climbed — and then get going. Include two or three smaller items in your To Do Today list. Rather than noting a big assignment, such as "prepare Johnson report," list the smaller components of the project: "get statistics from Denise," "write first draft of proposal," "make up visual aid." Another technique is breaking the project into "instant" five-minute tasks. Start a planning project with a telephone call to get information. Later, follow up the call with another "instant" project of setting a timetable, etc. Cross off each smaller task as it's completed. Another technique is to divide the large task according to available time. If you have a half hour free each morning, do as much as you can in that time. Or choose tasks that fill the time.

Many people tend to overestimate or underestimate the time it will take to complete a project, which can lead to excess stress. This is the most common scheduling problem. Try to allow more time than you think a project will take. If you finish the work ahead of schedule, reward yourself with a quick break or cup of coffee and get on to the next item. Yet don't overestimate the time it will take either. Find a happy

using time management

medium between the laws of Murphy and Parkinson. According to Parkinson's Law, "Work expands to fill the time available for its completion," meaning if you allow too much time, it might take longer to finish the work. On the other hand, Murphy's Laws say: if anything can go wrong it will, nothing is ever as simple as it seems, and everything takes longer than you expect.

Here are a few additional scheduling tips:

■ *Resist unscheduled activities. Their lure can be very strong. Avoid impulse where possible, yet don't pass up every opportunity that comes along.*

■ *Be appointment savvy. Always make appointments, confirm appointments, and do everything possible to stick to them. Become a stickler for appointments and those around you will do the same.*

■ *Recognize time wasting tasks. If a task is continually carried over from To Do list to the next To Do list without getting done, it probably wasn't important in the first place. Skip it or delegate it. Don't weigh down your schedule or conscience with excess baggage.* ◑

Chapter 7: Summary

■ A good plan is more of a roadmap, not necessarily a step-by-step list of how to achieve your goals.

■ All plans — whether daily, weekly, or monthly — improve productivity. Planning efforts should consist of short-, medium-, and long-term goals.

■ Many products are available to help you keep track of plans and other information. These include planning notebooks, electronic diaries, wall charts, and computer programs.

■ Keeping a list of things to do is vital to any time management program because it helps people set priorities and work toward fulfilling them.

chapter eight

Progress Check — Are You Reaching Your Goals?

"No statue was ever erected to the memory
of a man or woman who thought
it was best to let well enough alone."
Watchman-Examiner

Some people, awed by the success of those who have "reached the top," will marvel and sigh, "Luck is on their side." But managing our time and achieving our goals takes a bit more than luck. It also takes effort, planning, willpower, and time.

Some of that time must be spent examining our own progress every few months or so. It's important not to get so caught up in daily tasks that we forget to do this periodically. It's like taking a long road trip. Imagine you have 600 miles to drive to your destination. You plan an estimated time of arrival before leaving, based on how fast you'll be driving, how many stops for gas or meals, and so forth. If you plan on driving an average of 50 miles per hour, you figure you'll complete the trip within 12 hours. But if you look at your watch to assess your progress after three hours and found you've only gone 100 miles, it's time to rethink your plan. Perhaps your original goal was not realistic, or you're making too many stops along the way.

In the same manner, we need to pull out our list of charted goals every few months or so and see if we are on the right track. Ask yourself what you have done lately to improve your time management skills. Have you picked up a few good habits and concepts? Did you improve some areas for just a couple weeks and then fall back into the old routine? Or have you become worse than ever? (For more self evaluation, consult the time management quiz at the end of this chapter.)

This evaluation process can be done for both short- and long-term goals. Taking a quick assessment smack in the middle of your time frame is best. For example, go through your daily To Do list every day during or after lunch to re-evaluate your activities for the remainder of the afternoon. Straighten out your work area, do some quick filing and information gathering to become mentally prepared for the afternoon. Repeat the process for weekly, monthly, and yearly goals halfway through the time frame. Be honest with yourself. Have you made enough progress in each area to feel confident that you'll achieve the goal in time? Have you improved your time management skills in any way?

Examine in particular any problems you had with telephones, interruptions, paperwork, crisis management, priorities, deadlines, and procrastination. The best way to improve your skills in those areas is to move slowly with one subject at a time. It is too easy to forget about making changes when they're attempted all at once.

Try to eliminate tasks, responsibilities and habits that no longer seem worth doing. To do this, check your master to do list and follow up files. Consider the time you put into each task, the reward you receive, and the relationship between the two. Remember, 80 percent of the rewards come from 20 percent of the projects. Dump a few less valuable tasks and it will free you up to tackle more important goals and challenges.

Once you've taken a close look at the progress you've made in reaching each goal, make a note of your progress near each goal. For example, say two months ago you were aiming to finish a 200-page master's thesis in four months. By now you should have developed a working outline, finished all research, and have a good 50 pages written. Now you either look at that initial goal and snicker or you have 150 pages done and you're wondering when did life get so easy.

After assessing the progress you've made with each goal, you'll need to do one of two things. If you don't feel you're on the right track toward completing that goal, rethink your means of getting there. Or, rethink the goal itself. Perhaps it wasn't really important, or the deadline you set wasn't realistic. Second, if you have achieved your goal, or are pretty close, it's time to set new milestones.

Plotting new means

If we examine a goal and find that it seems too far away from achieving, we need to plot new means for bringing the goal closer to reality. This can be done by adjusting the time period expected to realize a goal, adjusting the goal itself, searching for better methods to reach the goal, or, as a last resort, abandoning the goal altogether.

Another option is to try harder. "If at first you don't succeed, try, try again," is an adage we've probably heard since kindergarten. Most people, with the possible exception of athletes, can usually find an energy reserve from which to draw upon, according to Gilbert Brim, author of *Losing and Winning: the Nature of Ambition in Everyday Life*. But trying harder is not the solution for everybody. Sometimes when we try too hard, we end up ruining the performance, adds Brim. Or, we put in more effort than the value of the goal warrants or spoil the chances of achieving another goal.

Setting additional goals

We respond to personal wins and losses by constantly resetting our goals. That's a process of life. Most people don't lose 40 pounds and say, "That was great. Now I'm done." Most are eager to embark on new goals, such as an exercise plan designed to keep the weight off or promote overall fitness. Landing a new job as a salesperson is an achievement but it can also mark the start of a new goal: to become the company's best salesperson or to become sales manager, for instance.

When we succeed, we raise our hopes for next time. It may mean trying to achieve future goals in less time, or adding different goals altogether. When people succeed at work, their jobs suddenly become easier because they now require less effort and ability. Usually, they move on to other challenges.

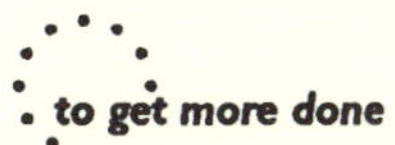

Brim cites a study of successful AT&T executives who had reached middle management by the end of an eight-year study period. Spurred on by their own success, the executives became more work oriented. Less successful employees, on the other hand, had re-focused their goals to center on family, religious, or recreational activities.

Another way to examine our goals and progress is to use the "P.A.C.E." formula. P.A.C.E., which stands for Prioritze/Plan, Action, Celebrate, and Energy, was developed by Doctors Lee Gardenswartz and Anita Rowe, two human resource development trainers in California.

Here's a run-down of how the program works:

Prioritize/Plan

To begin using PACE, start by writing down what you value the most in life. Jot down your personal and professional goals too, as well as the most important of these goals. Break down your selected goal into small steps — the actions necessary to achieve your goal. Then identify the obstacles to your achievement, and list them on paper along with ideas on how to deal with each.

Action

The next phase makes your goal real to you and to others. Fantasize about the fulfillment of your goal, then broadcast what you are planning to do to at least one family member, one friend, and one co-worker. Finally, commit yourself to the goal by listing what price you will have to pay (lost free time, money, etc.) for the achievement of your goal. Remember the old proverb: "You can have anything you want if you are willing to pay for it." Chart your commitment plan step by step.

Celebration

Joy should come not only from the completion of your task, but from the process as well. If you make it part of your goal to transform mundane tasks into reward-oriented achievements, your goals will come faster and easier. Determine ways you can reward yourself along the way, and share your celebrations with others — especially those to whom you have "broadcasted."

using time management

Energy

To step up your energy, evaluate the energizers and drainers in your life. Few people ever stop to think about this, but it's crucial. Also, determine what signals your body and mind give off when they are running on empty. When these signals occur, stop for food, rest, leisure activities, or whatever it is that energizes you. And make sure your priorities are clear!

Increasing willpower

Remember, success is harder than failure. Yet many people give up after one slight failure. Not everyone can succeed regularly, even on routine tasks. To become a good time manager — one who succeeds more often than fails — takes willpower. It's willpower and self-discipline that help us to not be discouraged by everyday failures and faults. And it's the willpower that makes us want to do better next time.

Learn to focus only on success, especially the big victories that mean so much more than the small failures, and to find value and motivation in those failures. How many times have you given up because of a failure? Most diets end after one eating binge. Would-be dieters give up because of a momentary failure, even if they succeeded the rest of the time. Willpower helps people start the diet again and resist temptation.

Willpower is an essential ingredient to becoming a better time manager, says Alan Laiken in *How to Get Control of your Time and your Life*. According to Laiken, willpower is needed every day to:

- plan when you're rushed, overwhelmed, and overworked;
- stay involved and interested in a project that keeps hitting dead ends;
- avoid burying your head in a book or otherwise escaping important but unpleasant priority tasks;
- maintain a positive attitude in spite of failure;
- do something every day that leads to or is part of a lifetime goal;
- overcome fears, real or imagined, at work or at home;
- resist doing a very easy and unimportant task when there's a more important and unpleasant project waiting.

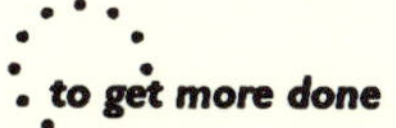

It's important to develop your own resources of willpower to face and overcome everyday problems, says Laiken. While some people have more willpower than others, that can change. It is possible to develop willpower so that you can do almost anything you want, so that it's there when you need it the most.

You probably exercise a little willpower everyday without even realizing it. Getting out of bed earlier than you want to, ordering a light salad instead of a cheeseburger for lunch, struggling to finish a report at work, skipping your favorite TV show to attend a PTA meeting, and passing up a bowl of ice cream are all instances that we deal with in everyday life.

We can use these instances to build our willpower gradually, just as you don't start a running program by racing in a marathon. Instead, you should gradually work yourself into better shape. Build momentum by accomplishing easy tasks. Too many people set their goals too high at the start, and don't have enough willpower to succeed.

To increase willpower, start practicing and using it in easy situations. Then gradually apply it to more difficult situations. Normally, people test their willpower only when they need it, only to fail because the tasks are often very difficult. The key is to proceed in gradual stages.

Willpower is needed when we decide to do one thing, but are pulled by the desire to do something else. You may decide to clean the house early one Saturday, but would rather stay in bed. Or you may decide to stay late to finish a report when you'd rather give up and go home. Sometimes sticking with your original and conscious decision can be very difficult.

The next time you are turning against a conscious decision, go ahead and give in. But make a mental note that you decided to stay in bed, for example. Take credit for the decision. You may have not have had much control over the decision — it may have been as much a compulsion as a choice. But remember: you did make a decision and it did lead to action.

Start exercising some willpower at home, by reading, going through files, playing with the kids — anything but watching television, if that's your vice. After demonstrating and improving your willpower against simple things, turn gradually to more difficult tasks.

If you confront a difficult task, don't be concerned with conquering it, Laiken says. Be satisfied that you would put up a better fight than you could have earlier. "When you develop willpower, time is on your side if you improve just a little every day," according to Laiken. Most importantly, willpower helps us develop the self-discipline to make better use of our time.

Self evaluation: questions on time

This is a quick self-quiz that will help you to grade and evaluate your own time and people management skills, habits, and practices. Take this quiz once or twice a year — twice a year if you don't do so well the first time. Being continually vigilant on time management more than pays for the effort.

When finished with the first part of the quiz, take some time to evaluate each of your "no" answers. These are areas where improvement is needed — study up on them or focus on doing better. The more "yes" answers, the better a time manager you are. But don't be dismayed if you have many "no" answers — we all could use improvement. Take the criticism constructively.

The second part of the quiz is made up of questions that are meant for more open answers and reflection.

Yes   No

☐ ☐ 1. Is this quiz keeping you from doing more important activities? (If so, then put this down and come back to it later!)

☐ ☐ 2. Do you have a clearly defined set of lifetime goals in writing?

☐ ☐ 3. Do you have a similar set of goals for the next few years?

☐ ☐ 4. Do you have a similar set of goals for the next few months?

☐ ☐ 5. Do you have a good idea of what you want to accomplish this week?

☐ ☐ 6. Do you know your purpose or mission in life?

☐ ☐ 7. Do you regularly ask Laiken's question, "What is the best use of my time right now?

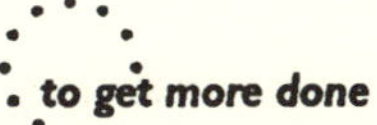

Yes **No**

☐ ☐ 8. Do you regularly force yourself to plan?

☐ ☐ 9. Did you work today on something that is related to your long-term goals?

☐ ☐ 10. Do you work on highest-priority tasks first?

☐ ☐ 11. Do you focus on results (what you are getting done) rather than the amount of activity (what you are doing)?

☐ ☐ 12. Do you try to do your most important tasks during quiet hour or prime time?

☐ ☐ 13. Do you know what you are doing next?

☐ ☐ 14. Do you set priorities according to importance rather than urgency?

☐ ☐ 15. Do you delegate as much as possible?

☐ ☐ 16. Do you delegate challenging jobs along with routine?

☐ ☐ 17. Do you delegate authority as well as responsibility?

☐ ☐ 18. Do you prevent subordinates from delegating upward decisions or tasks they find difficult or touchy?

☐ ☐ 19. Are you doing things for others (not necessarily subordinates) that they should be doing themselves?

☐ ☐ 21. Do you mark priorities on your To Do Today list?

☐ ☐ 22. Are there usually items on your To Do Today list that aren't worth doing at all?

☐ ☐ 23. Do you use a time log periodically to determine whether you are slipping into unproductive habits?

☐ ☐ 24. Do you tend to put off so much work for tomorrow that you can't even get it done then?

☐ ☐ 25. Do you do things that others can do better or faster?

☐ ☐ 26. Do you set deadlines for yourself and strictly enforce them?

☐ ☐ 27. Do you set deadlines for subordinates?

☐ ☐ 28. Do you use subordinates to help yourself get better control of time usage?

☐ ☐ 29. Do you keep in mind the dollar value of your time?

using time management

Yes   No

☐ ☐ 30. Have you taken steps to keep information and publications from reaching you unscreened by others?

☐ ☐ 31. Does a secretary, receptionist or assistant screen visitors and telephone calls before they reach you?

☐ ☐ 32. Do your secretaries and assistants offer to help others before coming to you with their requests? And do they have the authority?

☐ ☐ 33. Do you handle a piece of paper only once, deciding right away whether to read, file, assign, or toss it?

☐ ☐ 34. Do you regularly make minor decisions quickly?

☐ ☐ 35. Do you try to live in the present by avoiding the habit of rehashing previous failures and successes?

☐ ☐ 36. Do you allow "open" time in your schedule for contingencies?

☐ ☐ 37. Do you know when to quit working on a task, or do you keep at it until it is perfect?

☐ ☐ 38. Do you have people who can manage your office in your absence?

☐ ☐ 39. Do you regularly have a written agenda for meetings that is distributed to all participants beforehand?

☐ ☐ 40. Do your meetings stick to that agenda?

☐ ☐ 41. At the end of meetings, do you quickly review all decisions?

☐ ☐ 42. Do you take steps to examine recurring crises and make sure they won't happen again?

☐ ☐ 43. Do you constantly try to establish habits that make you a better and more efficient manager of time?

☐ ☐ 44. Do you ask, "Is this really needed?" when thinking of an activity, traveling, writing a report, or calling a meeting?

☐ ☐ 45. Do you use a computer, or dictate letters and other paperwork rather than writing it out by hand?

☐ ☐ 46. Do you occasionally keep a log of interruptions to see if there are any trends or recurring causes?

☐ ☐ 47. Do you put a date on every piece of paper you handle?

☐ ☐ 48. Do you give your undivided attention to people speaking to you?

☐ ☐ 49. Do you control your time or do circumstances or other people's priorities determine your actions?

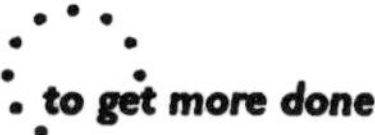

Not all of the important questions on your management of time and people fit into this strict yes or no category. Here are other open-ended questions you may want to consider. If it is helpful, write the answer on a sheet of paper and contemplate your answers.

1. What are your unfulfilled aspirations?
2. If you were to have only one goal, what would that be?
3. If you could do only one thing today, what would that be?
4. What tasks or activities are you doing that you can completely eliminate? How about those you assign to others?
5. How much time did you waste today and how did you waste it? Does this happen regularly? ●

■ **Every few months or so, consult your personal list of goals to make sure you're on the right track, or to see if adjustments should be made.**

■ **Be wary of diving head first into a new routine, then falling back on the old habits a few weeks later.**

■ **Remember P.A.C.E.: Prioritize/Plan, Action, Celebration, and Energy.**

chapter nine

Dealing With Interruptions & Crises

*"Common sense in an uncommon degree
is what the world calls wisdom."*
Samuel Taylor Coleridge

got a minute?

Whether it's a phone call or a drop-in visitor, the average manager is interrupted every eight minutes. For managers in high tech fields who supervise a large staff, the interruption rate increases to every five minutes.

It doesn't take long for "got a minute?" to add up to half a day wasted. In addition to the time spent dealing with the interruption, it takes some time to return our concentration to the task at hand before the interruption.

It's a constant contradiction. Working with people requires interacting with people. This is necessary to stay informed and maintain a good working relationship with co-workers. Working on your own tasks requires solitude, quiet, and concentration. The dilemma is one of the top time management problems for executives.

The best method of dealing with interruptions and crises is to plan for them, at least to the extent possible. Reserve two portions of your day — one for working quietly on high priority projects, the other for meeting with co-workers. While there will always be the occasional crisis that cannot be scheduled for a later time, sticking to this schedule as much as possible will be a boon to your effectiveness and mental attitude.

What time of day do you feel most sociable? Use this time to schedule interviews, reports from subordinates, or "office hours" when staff members are welcome to discuss what's on their mind. The next time you hear, "Got a minute?" turn it into a time saver by answering directly, "No, I'm busy now. Can it wait until 1:00?" Most likely, one of two things will happen. One, the person will have solved the problem — or forgotten about it — by the time 1:00 rolls around. Or two, they'll come back at 1:00 and you'll be able to deal with the situation more effectively.

Perhaps you're bothered by outside interruptions — a client who calls constantly with simple questions. Can you tell a client you're too busy to speak with them? Probably not. But you can minimize the effect of these interruptions by scheduling regular phone calls or meetings with the client. If they know they'll speak to you every Thursday afternoon, they'll be more likely to save up routine questions and needs for that conversation. Of course, occasional emergencies may surface between meetings, but the draining away of your time by inconsequential matters could be cut back this way.

Think ahead to others' demands. Get a feel for your client's or supervisor's needs and be prepared so a regular need does not become a last minute demand. If in October your client asks for some figures for a monthly meeting at his corporate headquarters, ask if such figures will be needed every month. If so, schedule them into your regular plan; do not wait to be asked in November.

Additional ways to handle interruptions are to seclude yourself for an hour or even a day, discourage office visitors, or reroute minor interruptions. Preventing crises and calmly handling those that can't be avoided are also great time savers.

Discouraging office visitors. Discourage interruptions in your office by not volunteering to hold meetings in your office and not keeping extra chairs on hand to accommodate visitors.

Eliminate unscheduled visits from outside salespeople or vendors by asking them to make appointments or drop in only at specific times when you'll receive visitors. Even if your job is in the purchasing department, you're being unfair to yourself if you allow salespeople to drop in whenever they are "in the neighborhood." Simply explain that you prefer not to see people without an appointment. Or, have a receptionist or secretary screen unwelcome visitors.

Rerouting minor interruptions. "I used to be swamped with phone calls, letters, and even drop-in visitors seeking information and answers right now. There was not enough time in the day to handle them all," writes one *Execu*Time® reader. After realizing that at least half of the interruptions didn't really need his attention anyway, this manager developed a system for rerouting the inquiries — without even having to handle them personally.

"I developed a guidebook to the company for my secretary," says the customer service manager. "It lists just about every sort of inquiry, and notes the person I think can best handle it. Now my secretary reroutes nearly all those misdirected inquiries, and I have the time I need to adequately handle the complaints that belong in my department."

Take a day off. If interruptions have really progressed beyond a manageable level, spend an entire day in a conference room, library, motel room, or other quiet place. Spend the whole day out of touch with your usual routine to use it to concentrate on something more important. You will get a surprising amount accomplished, perhaps more than you could in a week of routine coping. If you hesitate to do this because you fear the office will be in chaos when you return, you may be too indispensable. Make sure your office and staff are set up for maximum effectiveness.

The quiet hour

An underrated, often overlooked idea, the quiet hour may be your best chance to get control of your work load. The basic rules of a quiet

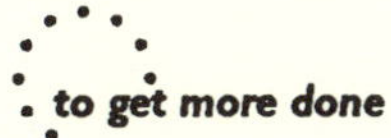

to get more done

hour are simple: no phone calls or visitors, no unnecessary talking or moving around. It's a simple idea, but one that offers exciting advantages.

The basic idea is to provide a quiet work period when interruptions are totally shut off, so management teams can concentrate. The result is almost always tremendous enthusiasm and a big jump in management output.

In addition, the quiet hour builds your working momentum and eliminates your loss of time and energy from unwanted interruptions. There are no slow-downs and start-ups, you just keep forging ahead. By the end of the quiet hour, you're in overdrive, accomplishing more per minute than you could in almost any other context. Once you get used to the quiet, you can really make time.

Many executives report being able to get two hours of work or more done in that one quiet hour. If possible, schedule the quiet hour for the beginning of the day. "I get so much done that first hour," says one quiet hour devotee, "I almost don't care about the rest of the day. I'm well ahead of the game by 10:00!" Another long-time reader of *Execu***Time*® suggests that the quiet hour works best for her between 10 a.m. and

Please Come Back at

_____ **:** _____

using time management

11:00 and, because it is so close to lunch break she frequently gets an extra hour of quiet even after she opens her office door because people have forgotten that she isn't available between 11:00 and 12:00.

You'll have to determine the best time for your own quiet hour. The quiet hour leads naturally to other effective practices: making phone calls all at one sitting, running errands through the building in one trip, etc.

Implementing a quiet hour involves garnering full support of your co-workers and subordinates. Do this by making them aware of the benefits and taking a vote on when would be the time to hold a quiet hour. Install a three month trial period to derail objections and give people a chance to benefit. Encourage managers to plan, get organized, dream up new projects or new solutions to problems. They can also concentrate on their most important project that day. More often than not, this is the work that suffers most from normal interruptions and office interaction. Have support staff use the time to put things in order, catch up on overdue paperwork, and intercept stray phone calls or visitors.

But alternatives to the program outlined above can certainly be just as effective. If yours is a service business, for example, consider having quiet hour for a few key personnel rather than the whole company. Have a quiet hour once or twice a week, rather than daily. Determine what time you have the fewest contacts with customers, or make it a flexible meeting date. Or, schedule it for one or two departments at a time.

It's true not every business can feasibly install a quiet hour. But every individual executive can institute his/her own quiet hour by simply closing the office door and hanging a sign on it "do not disturb—quiet hour." And the advantage of a "solo" quiet hour is that you can pick the time you want the quiet hour to be.

If your organization refuses to begin a quiet hour, try using the idea for yourself and your staff. You can institute your own personal quiet hour by coming in an hour early, working from noon to one and taking a late lunch, or hiding out in a conference room, library or vacant office for an hour if the sign on your office door doesn't work out.

Preventing crises

Similar to the guidebook set up by the manager mentioned above, crises can also be handled by setting forth a few alternative plans in advance. For recurring crises, catalog a set of routine remedies, just as they do in a hospital emergency room. You'll be surprised to learn there really is such thing as a routine emergency. Handle these with a step-by-step procedure prepared in advance.

Delegate responsibility for various crises by identifying the strengths and weaknesses of your staff. Assign different emergencies to the person most apt to handle them. Another solution is to learn why the same crises keep recurring, and find a way to fix them permanently.

Responding to crises should be done without over- or underreacting. When a staff member flies into your office with what appears to be an emergency, try evaluating the situation for five minutes. Is this really a crisis? Is there anything you can do at this point? If not, why stop doing other work? You cannot afford the luxury of worrying over something that can't be helped. If there is something you can do, stop and look at your to do today list. Is this enough of a crisis to bump something off the list of priorities? Even if it is, it may not become your most important job. Try not to react to the pressure of the situation rather than to the importance of the question.

Before dealing with any crisis, think back to any similar situations you may have faced in the past. What worked then? What didn't work? Use your company's history and your own experience to shed light on the current problem.

Try also not to blame another co-worker for the situation. Alienating someone in this way will add to the problem and waste even more time. Instead, try planning a step-by-step program to resolve the crisis, giving each staff member a plan of action. Keep out of the detail work; it's your job to stay in touch with the big picture. Then, when everything is over, quietly and rationally evaluate the cause for the crisis.

When crises can't be avoided

A certain number of interruptions and crises are unavoidable. One way to avoid some of the time wasted by those interruptions is to take a few seconds before you stop for the interruption and jot a brief reminder of what you're thinking, doing, or about to say. Learning to pick up where you left off as quickly as possible can save hours every month.

According to Dr. Robert Riley, of the University of Cincinnati, interruptions have three distinct parts: initial socializing, the reason for the interruption, and final socializing. You can dramatically lower the time spent on the interruption by trying to eliminate the socializing and cut to the core of the problem, says Riley. First, quickly and directly ask for the reason behind the interruption. Then handle the problem in your usual effective manner. Finally, cut through the final socializing with a comment like, "I'm glad we settled that. Now I can concentrate on the other work I've got to do."

If you enjoy the social aspect, or if your co-worker feels it's important to discuss the situation after it's over, why not turn your lunch hour into a working lunch and reserve the socializing for then?

Some crises can be avoided completely if they can be caught in the "simmering stage." The way to do this is to learn to recognize the symptoms that precede full-blown crises. Are there any procedures or systems in your organization that are too laid back for comfort? Would a few more checks and balances keep the problem from recurring?

Crises are usually caused by lack of planning, incorrect time estimates, and sweeping things under the rug. Some people almost enjoy crises, and will do very little to avoid them. Remind them that fire fighters also make a living out of responding to emergencies, but they also promote preventing the emergency in the first place.

Sweeping a potential crisis under the rug by holding back the facts or denying the problem will not make the problem go away. Don't be afraid to let management know when a potential crisis occurs; it usually takes less time to solve the problem before it reaches a full-blown crisis stage.

If you're the type of person who starts projects too close to the deadline, try setting a personal deadline three or four days earlier than the actual date the project is needed. That way you have time to accommodate unplanned emergencies. And completing a project early will impress supervisors and leave a feeling of personal satisfaction. ◕

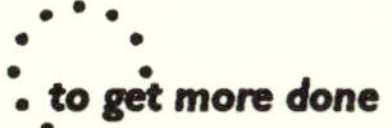

Chapter 9: Summary

■ **The best way to deal with interruptions and crises is to schedule part of the day for priority tasks and the other part for interaction with staff members.**

■ **Allow one hour per day for quiet, uninterrupted concentration.**

■ **Delegate different types of crises to various staff members. If the same problem occurs over and over, find out why and develop a permanent solution.**

■ **Some crises can be reduced by creating deadlines for the various stages of a project — i.e., initial outline, research, rough draft, and revision.**

using time management

chapter ten

Don't Worry, Be Happy —
Dealing With Office-Based Stress

"I've been on a calendar, but never on time."
Marilyn Monroe

the problem:

- *Industry loses nearly $137 million every day due to absenteeism and medical expenses relating to headaches alone, says the book, On An Average Day. Annually, stress-related problems and mental illness cost businesses $150 billion in health insurance and disability claims, lost productivity, and other expenses.*

- *The American Medical Association reports that 80 percent of hospital beds in the U.S. are filled by people with stress-related diseases.*

- *Problems associated with stress include headaches; high blood pressure; wrinkles; depression; muscle tension; neck, back and shoulder pain; irritability and mood changes; indigestion; blurred vision; a lowered immune system; and even cancer. Prolonged stress can result in skin problems, muscle twitches, baldness, angina attacks, and sexual problems.*

While stress will always be part of our lives, it is our mental reaction to stress that can cause problems. This is known as the "fight or flight" response. When a person does not respond properly to pressures and challenges, the result is negative stress. Feeling too anxious over a problem, for example, can lead to insomnia and an inability to concentrate. Some people may turn to such substances as drugs, alcohol, coffee, or cigarettes to relieve the pressure. While these may appear to provide temporary relief, they do not confront the real problem. In fact, they add a host of other problems.

Studies show that the majority of our country's managers experience too much stress. For some, stress and depression levels are severe enough to affect job performance. Even if you love your job, working 12 hours a day at it can be stressful.

The causes

Despite all the publicity, the problem is getting worse, particularly for baby boomers and middle managers. Problems such as too much work, lack of control, limited job opportunities, non-supportive management or co-workers, and job insecurity can all trigger feelings of stress and depression. Corporate mergers and buy-outs compound the problem.

Today's baby boomers are hardest hit because they don't have the outside support their parents relied on to cope with stress. Instead, they tend to marry later in life, have fewer children, be less religious, and more mobile.

Why are we stressed? We've discussed ten common causes below. If these sound like familiar problems, you've already made some progress in reducing your stress level. Identifying the stressor is the first step toward dealing with the problem. The second is to read on to the list of solutions later in this chapter.

"Top Ten Causes of Everyday Stress"

1. **This speedy society in which we live.** Were you under the impression that these high-tech aids such as the personal computer,

overnight mail, and facsimile machine were designed to make our lives easier? Me too. But the tools have an effect we didn't count on. Because they can do things in an instant, it seems we too are expected to act immediately, which only frees us up for more work. Often, there is no time to delegate or think how the task could be handled best if given a little time. In addition, we tend to become too dependent on these tools. If they break down, so do we.

2. Fear of not "keeping up with the Joneses." With all the new technology and information we're given constantly, there's often tremendous pressure to keep on top of it all. It's difficult to know which magazines or newspapers to read, programs to watch, or seminars to attend to keep informed.

3. "Mergack-phobia": fear of mergers and acquisitions. The wave of corporate mergers and acquisitions in the past decade or so has resulted in a lot of insecurity among all levels of employees. Even high level executives, who previously felt their performance would warrant permanent positions, can be given the pink slip at a moment's notice.

4. The two D's: meeting deadlines and "doing more with less." Although the concept of setting a deadline to complete a project can help ensure that project gets done, working too closely to the deadline — or trying to meet several in a short period of time — can bring on high levels of stress. Also, as companies try to improve their revenue-per-employee ratios, streamlined staffs are forced to do more with less. Those who have discovered time management techniques and other methods to increase effectiveness are meeting the challenge.

5. The un-supervisor. A common complaint among workers is that middle managers and other supervisors lack the skills needed to perform their jobs effectively. They're used to doing, not managing. This results in stress for both supervisors, who don't understand what they're doing wrong, and staff, who feel their responsibilities are not really their own.

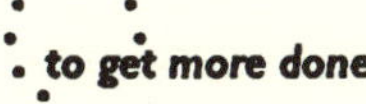

6. Unhealthy work environments. The news on "sick building syndrome" — offices with bacteria-laden air systems, asbestos fibers, cigarette smoke, and possible harm from laser printers and photocopiers — is that these types of environments can result in stress and physical ailments. Work environments that lack human factors engineering can also cause physical problems such as neck pain and carpal tunnel syndrome, as well as decreased morale and productivity.

7. The Superparent syndrome. Parents who wish they could be in two places at once, i.e., with the kids after school but still at the office all day, often experience frustration, guilt, and yes, stress.

8. Just say no! Not saying no to projects you know you can't or shouldn't take on can bring on feelings of pressure and stress once you stop to think about how you really are going to handle everything. It can also negate all the time management efforts you've worked so hard to implement.

9. Working too long. Consistently putting in 50, 60, or more hours at the office all week leaves little time for the outside activities that help reduce stress. It also depletes valuable energy that could otherwise be spent on family, work, or other commitments.

10. Bringing work home. You say you only put in 45 hours at the office — but take home enough paperwork to fill up a couple hours each evening and all day Saturday? Sorry, that still falls under the "working too long" category.

The solutions

Fortunately, there are cures for the above ailments. The key is to take charge of stress before it affects morale and job performance. Maintaining a healthier diet and managing time better are two widely encouraged solutions. Another is to identify the stressor and adjust your attitude toward it.

using time management

Sally Scobey, a motivational speaker and former NBC-TV regional news anchor, believes people can reduce life-threatening stresses by redefining them. She cites a favorite quote from Eleanor Roosevelt: "No one can make you feel inferior without your consent." In other words, no stressor has the power to threaten your body if you don't let that stressor get to you.

Stress is a lot like that bully you knew in grade school: if you let it bother you, it will. But if you learn to deal with it positively, it suddenly becomes an ally. Positive stress can be motivating, inspiring, and invigorating, which may be why some people insist "they work better under pressure."

"What we have to do is dig deep, past what we think is expected of us," says Scobey. "Are you stressed out because you are not doing what you truly want to do? If so, life is made of choices."

If it means you'll be happier and less stressed in another type of job, the choice may be to leave your current position. Or, you can stick with the job and work on changing your view of a stressful situation.

Often, this change in perspective is all you need to get back on track and reduce the accompanying stress. Is that person worth the potential health risk that stress can cause? Are you going to let this individual shorten your life span?

A phrase that can be helpful to memorize in a stressful situation, suggests Scobey, is to say: "This person/situation is not worth the stress I'm putting myself through. This is sapping my energy from more important people and issues in my life. I refuse to let them have that much control over me!"

Solutions to stress can be as simple as laughter, gardening, reading or taking a "decompression break." Some people may prefer more unusual or expensive answers like taking a Club Med vacation. Adjustments in attitude can also relieve stress. Exercise, however, is often prescribed by doctors because it lowers the heart rate and helps reduce the muscle tension which leads to stress and irritability.

There's no excuse not to exercise — even walking is found to be very beneficial. It lowers blood pressure, improves circulation, helps bones retain calcium, and even promotes weight loss by redirecting the blood flow away from the digestive tract to the muscles.

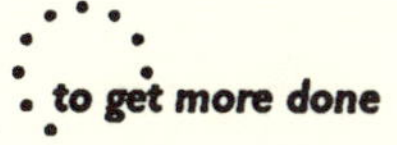

The next time you're depressed about something, try exercise. Even if you're not up to it at first, your attitude will adjust beautifully after a workout. There's a theory that endorphins, a chemical the body produces, kick in to give you a natural high. No matter what the problem is, it will bother you less after a jog or trip to the health club.

Three of the "top ten causes" listed earlier are common enough to warrant some extra advice on solving the problems. These include working too many hours, taking too much work home, and not saying "no" to time-consuming and low priority projects.

Shortening long hours.

For a few precious executives, 40 hours is all it takes — or all they want to spend — to finish their work. But many managers regularly log in 50 to 60 hours a week in the office. If this brings on severe conflicts with your family and personal life, it can result in stress for both you and your family.

In addition, working long hours is no guarantee of promotion, success, or even satisfaction. "Many organizations use people up and burn them out with no intention of promoting them, although they hold out promotion as a reward," reported Jerry Harvey of George Washington University in *USA Today*. "Working long hours when you don't enjoy doing so is a symptom of compulsive, obsessive illness," Harvey adds.

Betty Lehan Harragan, also a writer for *USA Today*, agrees, noting that working long hours can even be a hazard to your career. "If the standard in your office is that everyone pays attention to regular hours and you stay late, the boss may decide you're in over your head, you can't do the job in the time allotted, and you look incompetent," she says.

Often, managers who work excessive hours are wasting a third or more of that time. Why? Because they lack time management, delegation, and organizational skills.

Taking too much work home.

Occasionally taking work home is a price most executives expect to pay. After all, what else is a briefcase for if not to bring home work —

using time management

except to carry a lunch, newspaper, and calculator?

Continually bringing home a briefcase bulging with work, however, is a sign that something is wrong. Especially if the work brought home is the type of work that should be done at the office during regular hours. Too much "homework" can hurt performance and attitudes by leading to burnout, laxness, and resentment of responsibilities and supervisors. In addition, it can strain a family's relationship. Family members often view time at home as "their time." Taking this away can create bad feelings and resentment about your work.

If you bring work home on a regular basis, is it because of poor time management or delegation skills? Or could it be because you suffer from a "martyr complex" — trying to impress the boss, co-workers or family with how hard you work, or trying to appear indispensable.

Not saying "NO!"

Time management success is dependent upon some skills which have to do with self-esteem, assertiveness, and an overall attitude toward oneself and others. One of the saddest time management "hang ups" comes when people are afraid to say that simple little, two-letter word – *NO* – and make it stick.

There are ways to say no without feeling guilty. Manuel J. Smith, Ph.D., is an assertiveness trainer whose advice on how to say no has been read by thousands of people in search of this important type of inner strength. He starts each person's training with a personal "Bill of Rights," which helps the non-assertive type to "steel" himself or herself against the outside "shoulds" of others without giving in to the pressure. Some highlights from this "Bill of Rights" are as follows:

1. You are the judge of your own behavior.

2. You don't owe a "because" with every answer.

3. You can decide if you're going to help others find solutions to their problems.

4. You have the right to change your mind without going into all the reasons.

5. It is your right to make mistakes.

6. You are allowed to say "I don't know."

7. It's not necessary for you to have the "good opinion" of everyone.

8. You have the right to be illogical.

9. You can say "I don't understand" and "I don't care."

Another way to solve problems of stress is to find a confidante and bring any anxieties into the open. Having a spouse, friend, or co-worker who can objectively listen to your concerns is a big help. And often, when you articulate your fears and concerns, they seem less worrisome than they did in your mind.

Or, release penned-up anxieties by confiding in a journal. Writing can help put "our problems into a more manageable form, which can make them more understandable and perhaps even a little easier to solve," says James Pennebaker, Ph.D. and author of *Opening Up: The Healing Powers of Confiding in Others*. Pennebaker suggests setting a specific place and time limit for writing, such as 20 minutes — although it's not necessary to write every day.

It's also important to take action, rather than becoming paralyzed with fear when a problem presents itself. Try to assess the situation for a moment, then take the first step toward correcting it. If possible, ease your mind by delegating some tasks to others. Depending on the situation, a co-worker, spouse, or outside service may be able to lighten the workload.

If you're a worrier, try to use the habit constructively, rather than obsessively. "Don't Worry, Be Happy" is a popular song that propelled Bobby McPheron to fame and fortune with its simple message. To rid yourself of worry and indecisiveness, ask yourself, "What's the worst thing that can happen?" If you can deal with the worst, you can deal with anything in between. In most cases, the worst is not likely to occur anyway.

According to *P.S. Professional Secretaries*, there are two kinds of worriers in the world, constructive worriers and destructive worriers. If you think you fit in the latter category of worriers, take a look at these ideas on handling your problems and perhaps even using them constructively.

First, accept the fact that everybody worries. Since childhood we've been taught to anticipate future problems — if only the consequences of eating too much candy or missing the school bus. After a while this caution turns to worry, even though most of our parents' and teachers' advice was "for our own good." Recognize that worry is a needed part of life, but obsession with worry is not.

Actually, worry can be beneficial. The person who insists on projecting a sunny, Pollyanna image even when negative situations are on the horizon is doing himself or herself a disservice. If you are concerned about your health, act on that concern and visit a doctor. If you are worried about getting behind at work, take the opportunity to review your time management basics and look for the time drains. Turning your worries into the basis for constructive action is the most effective way to deal with them.

The more you dwell on your worries, the more you are liable to blow them out of proportion. What's more, you can waste a lot of time putting unnecessary weight on imagined slights from your boss or associates. Don't let yourself wallow in the "what ifs" and past mistakes. Simply promise yourself that you'll learn from the mistake and then get on with your life.

Find constructive new ways to worry. This may mean taking control of your imagination if it tends to go off on its own tangents, and scolding yourself for indulging in fantasy worries. Do it out loud if it works best.

Not all solutions work for all people. A grade school teacher who looks forward to meditating after dealing with thirty 10-year-olds all day may insist that her friend, a newspaper reporter stressed out by deadlines, try meditation also. But the reporter laughs at the idea of sitting yoga-style and chanting all afternoon so he instead takes up jogging 10 miles a week. Just as people's reactions to stressful situations differ, so do their solutions.

Here are a few additional suggestions to handle stress. These are called "action breaks" or "decompression breaks" because they are short, simple methods of taking a break from a busy and stressful lifestyle.

It's important to include these in your routine both at work and at

home. At the office, try taking a mental break with short walks around the office, a ride on an exercise bike or a friendly phone call to unwind when things seem out of control. It's equally important to unwind with a decompression break at home. Working out, taking a walk or even a quick shower can minimize any stress from the workday and help turn time spent at home and with the family into quality time.

Chapter 10: Summary

■ **We can't eliminate stress from our lives, but we can improve the way we react to it.**

■ **If you allow stress to bother you, it will. But if you deal with it positively, it can motivate and inspire.**

■ **Spend time reading, exercising, relaxing, or working on a hobby.**

■ **Learn to say "no" to time-consuming requests or tasks that you really shouldn't take on.**

using time management

PART III
Techniques For Successful Time Management

Office Interaction

"It's nice to be important, but it's more important to be nice."
John Cassis

time management doesn't have to be a route you go alone. Assistants and co-workers can help you capitalize from various techniques. And, if you've found time management principles helpful in your own job, you may want to encourage the rest of the office to adopt their own methods. But we'll discuss that later in Chapter 15, Time Management for More Efficient Personnel.

For now, let's look at how your own time management efforts can be enhanced through secretaries, assistants, and colleagues. It's best to start an overall program with a few small projects than to launch a comprehensive, wide-ranging program. Small projects generate the enthusiasm and energy needed to sustain changes, while a large program can get bogged down and lose all momentum and interest.

Pick an area where improvement is urgently needed. But instead of attacking the whole goal, start in on a sub-goal that can be done in a few weeks. These are called "breakthrough projects" because they improve performance and develop managerial skill and confidence — making a long-term success. A good way to assure success is to involve people who can make a project succeed, and can provide practical and stimulating ideas.

Encourage staff suggestions

Try to encourage others' input in your time management program. Perhaps you have a few habits, such as calling too many meetings or asking for detailed progress reports, that actually slow them down. Encourage other employees to tell you how you may be wasting their time. This type of "give and take" discussion offers two benefits. First, it can help improve your own time management style, and second, it may eventually allow you to share your views about other time wasting procedures in the office.

Along this same line, consider installing a time-saving suggestion box. Perhaps the best ideas can be shared on a regular basis in staff meetings, or passed along in memos that can be filed in a special binder, eventually comprising the company's own time management handbook.

Suggestion box systems yield new ideas and improve staff morale. Statistics vary, but research devoted to the study of suggestion systems says that for every dollar spent on programs to solicit employee suggestions, about $30 to $100 worth of practical ideas is generated. Here are a few guidelines to help you put a time-savers suggestion plan into practice:

- *Offer monetary rewards. Offer incentives to contribute to the suggestion box, such as extra time off or a small bonus or gift certificate. Or compensate the idea-giver on a scale that varies according to the long-term value of his or her idea.*

- *Don't expect 100 percent participation. Studies show you will involve about one in five of your employees. Of the suggestions received, one third will be practical.*

- *Get the legal rights to the ideas. Once employees receive their rewards, have them sign over the legal rights to the idea to avoid future conflicts.*

using time management

Encourage employee input with regard to deadlines, decisions, and priorities as well. Often, they may hesitate to jump right into a project because they resent having deadlines chosen by managers who haven't taken the time to assess the performance required from the employee's point of view. If possible, discuss projects and deadlines with employees to get their views and set realistic priorities. This can help foster a consensus that allows teamwork toward a mutual goal.

Working with secretaries and assistants

Secretaries and assistants can be of invaluable help in maintaining your own time management habits. For example, if you think the idea of a quiet hour would help you get more productivity out of each day, ask your secretary to help enforce the idea by shielding all your calls and rerouting visitors. In appreciation, perhaps you can offer to answer the phones or reroute the calls later in the day so your assistant can have his or her own quiet hour.

Maintaining a good working relationship with secretaries and assistants is an excellent way to maximize time management effectiveness. With many secretarial jobs going begging today because of a lack of qualified secretaries, keeping good relations with your secretary can be vital.

According to *P.S. for Professional Secretaries*, the relationship between managers and secretaries could easily be improved by making a few adjustments in attitude. These include:

Recognizing that the secretary is an important part of the management team, and that he or she can should work *with* the boss toward a common goal.

Helping secretaries to administer management plans by making sure they have an understanding of the boss's job, goals and objectives, and are kept informed of these as they change.

Allowing secretaries to participate in administration policy and procedure — once again with working toward common objectives as a goal.

to get more done

Acting positively toward the secretarial position and encouraging secretaries to hone their skills with internal and external training sessions and continuing education.

Not letting secretaries feel they have reached a "dead end" in terms of salary, promotions, or responsibility. Give rewards based on contributions to the firm, education, and attitude, rather than on the basis of a rigid set of standards.

Developing subordinates you can trust means they need to trust you, too. How do your people relate to you? Do they seem afraid or ill-at-ease in your presence? If so, perhaps you come across as too intimidating or overbearing. Smile more, and take time to say a few personal words to each person each day. It could work wonders.

If your subordinates hesitate to take even the slightest action without your approval or guidance, perhaps you should examine the way you deal with them. Try not to encourage this attitude by hovering over them or by punishing their moves toward independence if they make even a slight error.

Also, try to provide an atmosphere of team spirit. With more cooperation and less back-biting and gossip, you will accomplish more, both individually and together.

Remember the old Abbott and Costello shows when they needed to move a trunk or piece of furniture? How often did we watch them struggle with a simple job because Abbott was pushing the item in one direction and Costello was pulling it in another? If you and your secretary are also working in different directions, that can be a time waster. The National Secretaries Association has developed a prototype secretarial job description. Reading this over from time to time can help to make sure you are both striving for the same objectives. You may never wish to have your secretary take over all of the functions described, but this optimum plan serves as a valuable guideline.

1. Relieves executive of various administrative details.

2. Coordinates and maintains effective office procedures and efficient work flow.

3. Implements policies and procedures set by employer.

4. Establishes and maintains harmonious working relationships with supervisors, co-workers, subordinates, clients, and suppliers.

5. Schedules appointments and maintains calendar.

6. Receives and assists visitors and telephone callers and refers them to executive or other appropriate person as circumstances warrant.

7. Arranges business itineraries and coordinates executive's travel.

8. Takes action authorized during executive's absence and uses initiative and judgement to see that matters requiring attention are referred to delegated authority or handled in a manner so as to minimize effect of employer's absence.

9. Takes manual shorthand and transcribes from it or transcribes from machine dictation.

10. Types material from longhand or rough copy.

11. Sorts, reads, and annotates incoming mail and documents and attaches appropriate files to facilitate necessary action.

12. Determines routing, signatures required, and maintains follow-up.

13. Composes correspondence and reports for own or executive's signature.

14. Prepares communication outlined by executive in oral or written directions.

15. Researches and abstracts information and supporting data in preparation for meetings, work projects, and reports.

16. Correlates and edits materials submitted by others.

17. Organizes material which may be presented to executive in draft form.

18. Maintains filing and records management system and other office flow procedures.

19. Makes arrangements for and coordinates conferences and meetings. May serve as recorder of minutes with responsibility for transcription and distribution to participants.

to get more done

20. May supervise or hire other employees; select and/or make recommendations for purchase of supplies or equipment; maintain budget and expense account records, financial records, and confidential files.
21. Maintain up-to-date procedures manual for specific duties handled on the job.
22. Performs other duties as assigned or as judgement or necessity dictates.

If trained to help you, your subordinates can be your greatest allies in improving your time use. You may even be able to lighten the load for helpful assistants by clearing out unnecessary and repetitive clerical work and freeing them up to take on more interesting and challenging work.

Some companies claim their offices are more efficient without secretaries, arguing that a majority of the functions they perform consist of neatly typed but relatively unimportant letters, inter-office memos, and routine reports. In other words, work that often is unnecessary.

As an alternative, these firms have switched to speed memos, handwritten memos, and phone calls for short, simple items. This alone has cut 90 percent of the time used for typing letters and inter-office mail. They also recommend using one-page summaries, outlines, briefings, and graphic reports whenever possible. This makes it easier to read and prepare a lengthy report, as it reduces 90 percent of report typing and re-typing. By eliminating much of the typing, as well as the filing, sorting, stacking and copying that accompanies it, these firms have freed up a gold-mine of administrative time and talent.

Administrative assistants

One way to use this talent would be to train an employee already familiar with the business as an executive assistant. Executive or administrative assistants can be a valuable time saver by helping you to get more done without working longer hours. Many executives have an administrative assistant in addition to a secretary.

Administrative assistants are generally fully involved, responsible members of a management team. They know how you operate, what

using time management

jobs you do, and with whom you communicate. More than a secretary, administrative assistants acquire vertical knowledge about a job. In other words, they can take an important project from start to finish, whereas horizontal knowledge would limit them to a few specific areas of a project.

As your assistant learns more about your position and organization, he or she can help with such time management tasks as making out your To Do list, handling routine correspondence, reading trade publications and reports, and researching needed information. Eventually, assistants can give reports or attend meetings in your place, help solve problems, schedule travel and other arrangements, and delegate work to other employees.

Here are a few nuts-and-bolts ideas designed to increase the efficiency of both secretaries and assistants:

Taking phone messages. Encourage secretaries and assistants to take comprehensive phone messages. The key is to get as much information as possible from the caller so that the call can be handled without your getting involved. If you must return the call, have the assistant furnish the necessary files and other support material along with the message.

Says the financial vice president of a discount chain, "When I call and the party is out, I insist on leaving a message with the secretary. I make sure they write down my name and phone number, the purpose of my call, and the type of response I desire — yes or no, if possible. In most cases, I can instruct my own secretary to relay my message and get my answer for me. Then if I call again and the party is out again, I can at least get the information I need."

Using a job jar. Try the technique used in the Blondie comic strip to get Dagwood to do some work around the house. Jobs at the office that never seem to get done, such as filing samples or other material and organizing drawers for greater efficiency, can help fill up occasional free time. The luck of the draw adds a bit of excitement to the concept of catching up on overdue support work.

Using part-time or temporary help. Employees who are unable or unwilling to put in overtime will appreciate the opportunity to delegate time-consuming jobs to a part-time or temporary worker. This can be especially helpful during a company's busy season or times of crisis, as it allows the full-time staffers to handle more important priorities.

Keeping variety in the job. Offer varying and challenging assignments that promote learning and growth. From time to time, shift your people from assignment to assignment. And don't save all the plum assignments for yourself if a secretary or assistant can handle them.

Personnel expert Angelo Fortuna, of ARA Services, says one way to get the most from each employee's time is to have different expectations based on that individual's strengths and weaknesses. For example, say you have two clerk/typists in your office. The stated goal for them is to keep up with filing and to be able to type 60 words per minute. But one typist can easily type 80 words per minute. The other, although barely a 60 word-per-minute typist, has a flair for composing letters. Smart managers let each employee know that they recognize these strengths and help develop them. The faster typist may be encouraged to develop steno skills in preparation for an executive secretarial job. The "writer" could be asked to help his or her boss with correspondence, and would learn the purpose of the correspondence and its significance for sales, company policy, etc.

By grooming the employees according to individual strengths, an employee whose boss has high expectations can rise to the occasion much better than the employee who has been managed "by the book," says Fortuna.

Dealing with superiors and peers

When the tables are turned and it's your supervisor's job to dictate how projects should be assigned and organized, it's not always easy to make that person understand your commitment to time management. One way to handle unexpected changes in plans that you have no way of avoiding is to leave a margin of about 20 percent unscheduled time in your day.

First and foremost, try to educate your boss and colleagues about your efforts in time management and what you have done — or can do — to improve department performance. If you've implemented a quiet hour, learned to concentrate longer, or have developed a step-by-step plan to meet a certain objective, let your boss know of your progress. This may also set the stage for tactful suggestions when you see a way your boss or co-workers might improve their time use. Consider a good time management book as a birthday or holiday gift to your boss.

Second, keep your priority and To Do lists visible. When your boss hands you a new assignment, pull out the priority list and go over it together. That way you can both decide how — and where — to fit the new project into your list. You should not be obligated to squeeze it all in as if the new assignment were just an additional job to be completed in the same time frame.

Another thing to ask when handed a new assignment is how long the job will take to complete. Then keep careful records on the actual time involved. If your boss has been underestimating the time it takes to do various jobs, you'll be better able to improve future estimates.

To maintain a smooth working relationship with your boss, according to management consultant Christopher Hegarty, is to strive for synergy. "You can work in harmony with your boss by searching out things you could take over for him or her, and doing them in such a way that the `team' of the two of you becomes effective for the boss. For instance, say your boss dislikes attending meetings and you see the meetings as a way to learn and become visible to management. It benefits your `team' if you start attending some of the meetings for your boss, assuming he or she is agreeable."

Also, use time spent waiting for bosses or co-workers effectively. Say the boss calls a meeting, you hustle to complete what you're working on to attend the meeting, and the boss shows up twenty to thirty minutes late. To save your sanity and your schedule, try taking some portable work with you to the meeting. That way, he or she will see that you can get things done in any setting.

Years ago, the purchasing director of a metal-working company suggested this method to use waiting time effectively:

> "I was bugged by people who never showed, or who showed up late, for appointments with me. I'd stop work and be sitting for ten, fifteen, twenty minutes or longer. I finally decided that I couldn't afford the wasted time, so now I do a few things to minimize the loss. First, I keep right on working as though the appointment does not exist; this eliminates my stopping work early and idly waiting. Second, I always have some quick reading material at hand, or other short pieces of work I can pick up and put down at a moment's notice. Then, when I do finish up a meeting or other large piece of work in time for an appointment, I can keep busy until the other person actually shows up.
>
> "Finally, I observe a general rule: the person who wants more from the other should be the pursuer. This means if I want something from someone else, I'll call, write, and otherwise pursue it to make sure the appointment happens as scheduled. But if the other guy wants something from me, then I'll sit tight and keep working, and wait for him to make contact with me."

Remember that you are only human and have limitations. Remind your boss of this fact — tactfully — when it's clear he or she expects you to pile on assignment after assignment, increasing your workweek to 50, 60, or even 70 hours. If you honestly can't take on an assignment, learn to say no effectively. One way to do this, suggests Hegarty, is to acknowledge that it is an important issue, but one that you do not have the time to do justice to, or one that somebody else may be better qualified to handle. Then suggest alternative ways to get the work done, such as bringing in a consultant or assigning the job to another employee. ◕

Chapter 11: Summary

■ **Learn how secretaries and assistants can help you improve your time management skills.**

■ **Consider using part-time or temporary help during busy periods, or when a large project requires more time than available.**

■ **Let your boss and co-workers know about your time management efforts and how they've improved, or can improve, department performance.**

chapter twelve
Communication Tips

*"Time is a sort of river of passing events, and strong is its current;
no sooner is a thing brought to sight than it is swept by and
another takes its place, and this too will be swept away."*
Marcus Aurelius

how can we manage our time better through effective
communication skills? Two areas can zap large chunks of our time: conversations and paperwork. Of course, that's not to say we should simply
eliminate all conversations and paperwork. That would certainly introduce
a host of other problems. What we can do, however, is focus on clearer
communications — getting to the point sooner, and reducing the time-
wasting elements of office conversations and paperwork.

More effective conversations

If we can learn to communicate clearly the first time around, eliminate the "fat" from our conversations, and learn to use feedback effectively, we can save time with more effective conversations.

In conversations, learn to communicate more effectively both on
the phone and in person. This way, you'll leave each meeting or phone
call with a specific, mutual understanding of what went on and what is
to be done. The following tips for better communication can be applied
to conversations with subordinates, peers, and clients.

Try to organize your conversations as you would a written report. Think about the differences between the typical conversation and the written report. In writing a memo or a letter, for instance, we learn it has three components: the introduction, the body, and the conclusion. Yet in business conversations, we tend to ramble and jump from topic to topic. Mentioning one idea sparks a story from another person and soon the entire meeting is off on a different tangent before the original topic is resolved.

Even in everyday conversations this happens frequently, usually to be brought back on track when someone says, "How did we get on this subject, anyway?" While this can be fun at a small gathering of friends, at work it only takes valuable time out of a short eight-hour day.

To avoid this time waster, steer the conversation to the matter at hand. Use devices such as summarizing, listing, and identifying individual responsibilities to keep things on course. If you recognize a few people who frequently jump from topic to topic, try to take the reins and organize the discussion. Prepare for the conversation by outlining what you plan to get out of it. Keep the outline in front of you and don't let the conversation end before you are able to make sure that all of your points have been sufficiently covered. Otherwise, you can end a long conversation with a "rambler" like this without yielding even one concrete decision.

On occasion, a free-flowing conversation can be helpful. Brainstorming and planning sessions are one example where conversations needn't be limited. You needn't make every encounter with an employee strictly business. In fact, it's crucial that you know what's going on around the office. Make sure you do take some time to talk informally with your peers and subordinates so you know what people are thinking. That way, you can spot problems and opportunities in advance.

One of the best ways to impress upon others the importance you attach to your conversations with them is to follow up with a memo that covers the points and decisions. For the most dramatic effect, take out your dictating machine while you're still with the person and record the important concepts for the record. Doing so emphasizes your agreement as to what is to be done, by whom, and when. Your associates can't plead "failure to communicate" when the agreement is both spoken and written down on paper.

It's also important to communicate your position so that others react appropriately. As a manager, you must keep your attitude managerial even when you're talking informally with co-workers. That way, when the time comes for you to speak authoritatively and give assignments and specific orders, those who work for you will be conditioned to react positively to your "commanding" attitude.

Studies show that employees want to respect the person they work for — not feel like he or she is more of a buddy. If you must choose between being "one of the crowd" or a respected manager, work on the area of respect. Ways to do this include exhibiting confidence, proving yourself trustworthy, and being fair, conclude studies by the Research Institute of America.

Try to control the open door policy. You may need to be accessible, but not to the point of overexposure. To communicate, you must be available, but you must not sacrifice your hard won "quiet hour" time or your To Do schedule to give the impression of accessibility. Instead, work on being accessible by scheduling communication times for mutual convenience. This allows you to control your day and also shows your respect for the other person's time. And the scheduling of the communication period will formalize the occasion so it will be easier to cut down on small talk.

It's unfair to your subordinates if you waiver from "frivolous friend" to "no-nonsense boss." Be disciplined about your business conversations, even when they're informal. You must not allow yourself to waste someone else's time just because you've decided you deserve a bit of pleasant conversation. Save the rambling chatter for definite social occasions. That way, when you get down to business with an organized, goal-oriented conversation, people will know what to expect from you and how to react.

Time wasted in conversations is a common problem. According to one analysis of 18 "typical" executives in 14 different companies, an average of 5-1/2 hours per day was spent in meetings, dictation, phone calls, and other forms of conversation. Yet each executive wasted about

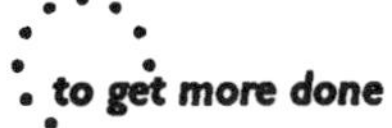

two of those hours in "conversational fat" — stories about last night's ball game, personal accounts of the weekend, and other tidbits taken too far.

According to Charles H. Ford, a consultant on organizational behavior, conversational fat breaks down into four categories: completely extraneous conversation, non-essential background data, tangential conversation, and conclusion supporting information.

The first of these areas, extraneous conversation, bears no relationship to any business matter. These are the examples mentioned above — weekend golf scores, office gossip, and the "story" that starts off a meeting. While some of this may be necessary to grease the path of human contact, it shouldn't be as much as what we put up with.

Non-essential background data is conversation thrown in about he history and development of current facts. Generally, the background data doesn't involve the person speaking, but details what other people have or have not done regarding the information you seek. It may be interesting and informative, but it's hardly necessary. In many cases, you've heard the story already.

The third form of wasted conversation is tangential conversation. This is what happens when we lose control of the discussion and watch topics sail off sequentially into remote fields. You start a planning session on employee benefits, which turns to a conversation about the high cost of health insurance. Soon another employee is talking about how much her sister paid to remove an ingrown toenail, and that leads to wondering how much money a podiatrist makes in a year. Unless tightly controlled, these conversations can stretch a 2-3 second answer into an hour of pointless discussion.

Conclusion supporting information, explains Ford, is aimed at documenting the time and effort expended to arrive at the basic conclusion. This is similar in form to non-essential background data, but usually concentrates on the speaker's own activities, rather than those of other people. It may be material you should know, but in the wrong place and time it's conversational fat.

To reduce conversational fat, make a point to be aware of your own communication — what you say and what you hear. You'll probably be amazed at how much of what's said will never be missed once you learn to trim it. And you don't have to be impolite or inhuman to do this.

Before you can trim the fat, however, you have to train yourself to notice it as it comes at you. The amount of fat in any one conversation will vary from minute to minute, just as the fat will vary from one conversation to another. You have to stay on the alert as much as possible for unwanted fat, and be ready to react quickly when you hear it. The greatest gains against conversational fat come only when you attack it over long periods of time.

Even more sinister is that people tend to accept a certain level of conversational fat, and each organization has a "fat level" that's considered "normal." You won't get it to drop below this level without serious, positive action from you and others you can enlist in your cause.

As you build awareness of the problem and the time stakes involved, you can attack the four categories of fat directly and immediately. For example, point out completely extraneous conversation to the perpetrator. When one executive hears this type of fat, he simply suggests: "I'd like to hear that, but I've got to leave in a few minutes for an important appointment. Can we save that for later after we wind this up?" Usually, later almost never comes.

Non-essential background data is more insidious since it tends to be more interesting and gossipy. Still, you can prevent much of it. A good line goes like this: "I know a lot of work and aggravation went into developing this report, but can you tell me the status as of right now?" The other person, now aware you're appreciating all the background work, is more comfortable giving you the short answer you need.

You can trim tangential conversation by adhering strictly to a recognized target. The chief executive of a machine tool company, for example, prints the subject on a small desk-top easel everyone can see. When conversation begins to leave the subject, he gently taps the easel with a pointer. As time passes, he has had to tap less and less. He says the resulting concentration on a single subject makes his meetings more productive than ever.

Finally, it's perfectly natural and tempting for people to build up their roles with conclusion supporting information. For example, your sales manager will have trouble summing up his months of work in the

single sales projection figure you ask him to give you. So he begins supporting his conclusion with reams of unnecessary information. You can de-fat many such conversations by giving credit up front. For example: "John, I know you've personally put a lot of work into this item. As this is your baby, what's your bottom line estimate of how many widgets we'll sell next year?" This double-barrelled emphasis on the conclusion you want, and your prior recognition of the other person's efforts, will scale down the conversational fat to a manageable level.

Cutting fat and jargon

It's important to watch not only what you say but how you say it. Did you know that conversations laced with jargon can dampen a company's productivity? And the bigger the company, the worse the problem.

Eliminating jargon is the key to communicating effectively, reported Roderick Wilkinson in *Administrative Management.* Jargon dehumanizes the company, adds to confusion and reduces loyalty and morale. It makes it more difficult for employees to take an interest in or enjoy their work, and to maintain good relations.

Employees would rather be referred to in a personal way, without cold and impersonal jargon. Some are more frightened of high sounding, large words and phrases than they admit. Words such as "evaluate" rather than "judge," "promulgate" rather than "putting a notice on a board," "industrial action" rather than "strike," and "compensated" rather than "paid" tend to make people feel like cogs in the machine. "They feel programmed to do just their simple tasks — and they want more than that," says Wilkinson.

Examples of bad jargon

Instead of:	Use:
Compensated	*Paid*
Evaluate	*Judge*
Hired	*Employed*
Industrial action	*Strike*

Instead of:	Use:
Promulgate	*Put a notice on the board*
Requisition	*Request*
Visitation	*Talk*

In addition, jargon diffuses communication, increasing the odds of screw-ups due to misinterpretation and confusion. But don't go overboard and over-simplify all phrases or business stationery. Just don't let the words clutter actions or commands.

Using feedback

To make sure you're understood the first time — and save time otherwise spent repeating yourself — try getting some feedback. There's no use in trying to "save time" by cutting off communications before both parties are well understood. In fact, it's a notorious time waster, because you and the other person could well be spinning your wheels until the misunderstandings are uncovered and cleared up.

The feedback technique can help you make sure you leave a meeting in accord. The following are suggestions on giving and getting constructive feedback, according to the Atlanta Consulting Group.

How to give feedback

1. Make sure you intend to be helpful. No subtle digs allowed.
2. Ask the person if s/he is open to feedback, if you are not asked for it.
3. Be as specific as possible — don't generalize, as it's too easy to agree in principle and not agree on the form for carrying it out.
4. Describe another's behavior, but do not "color" that description to turn it into an evaluation.
5. If your feedback is negative, or if the person you're speaking with disbelieves it, be generous about inviting him/her to check with others for a "second opinion."

How to receive feedback

1. Be specific when requesting feedback. If you ask too general a question, you will hear "what you want to hear."
2. Do your best to avoid defensiveness. It's better not to ask for feedback than to receive it with a chip on your shoulder.
3. Summarize what you've heard to make sure true communication is taking place.
4. Give feedback on the feedback — let the communicator know how you feel about what you've been told. Do this in a descriptive way, without evaluating the feedback. In other words, stay detached a bit — don't let personalities get involved.

How to get started with feedback

Experiment with the following questions:
Is there anything I do that puzzles you?
What was your first impression of the XYZ plan?
What is your current impression of the plan?
What are the stronger/weaker points of the program we've just put together?

Body language and conversations

Interpreting people's body language can also save time spent getting and receiving messages. Both John Baird Jr. and Gretchen Weiting have researched non-verbal communication as it applies to business. When having a discussion with a colleague, they suggest paying attention to proximity, posture, gestures, facial expressions, and tone of voice.

For example, how far does your boss seat you from himself or herself? How far do you seat guests from your desk? The further distance, the greater the implied "status gulf." Try sitting closer to guests and you'll find you can get down to specifics faster, as a feeling of warmth is easier to establish and maintain.

Try to lean forward to indicate acceptance and liking for your guest. Keep arms open rather than folded. Folding arms and leaning back indicates dislike and hostility, and lessen the chance for effective communication.

Look for frequent gestures, as these are a positive sign. Wide, open-palm, gestures are more friendly than closed-fist movements or stiff, gestureless talks. The latter tends to encourage visitors to clam up.

When you can recognize these traits in the people you deal with, you can interpret messages quickly and on a better basis. Use body language yourself to encourage faster communication and confidence between yourself and others.

The written word

While the suggestions above deal primarily with oral conversations, written communication can also be made more effective. Of course, the easiest way to save time handling written memos and other paperwork is not to deal with them at all, but this may not be possible if you want to stay employed long.

Instead, try to handle each piece of paper only once. As you open your mail, dictate your answers to the correspondence. Another way to save time writing reports and memos is to dictate into a recorder while waiting or traveling. If somebody writes you a letter requesting simple information, make a photocopy of the letter and write your answer on that copy. Stamp on the letter "we have kept a copy" so correspondents know you're not dismissing their ideas.

When possible, use the telephone rather than writing a memo or letter — it saves time and money. It also gives a chance to ask questions to ensure understanding. If you need to document something, ask yourself what's the worst thing that can happen if you fail to do so. If the answer isn't too bad, don't write it down.

Cut writing time with clarity

For reports and letters that simply can't be avoided, the goal is to get them done in less time and ensure that people will indeed read and act upon your work.

Studies show that the most appealing items in a stack are read first. For most people, short, snappy reading material is most appealing. Set up reports and letters with lots of spaces, bold type, short paragraphs,

and short sentences. If you must write a long report, attach a cover page with a short summary or introduction.

When sending a letter, take a tip from the direct-mail industry to gain quick readership. Have your letters folded with the head out so no one wastes time unfolding your letter to get your ideas.

Avoid writing the same letters or reports more than once by keeping copies of your best memos, letters, and reports. Rather than starting from scratch when a new writing occasion comes up, simply modify these favorites to suit the situation. Keep this file of starter memos, letters, and the like in two identical loose-leaf notebooks — one for your reference and one for your typist's. Organize the notebooks by topic and number individual paragraphs, as well as entire letters and reports, so they can be easily identified. This way, you can simply refer to the paragraph or letter number you want to use, and dictate any additional comments you need to make. Let your typist take it from there, creating a new letter from your verbal cut-and-paste job.

In addition, if you have literature to distribute, or cost information or other facts that are sent out repeatedly, make sure that as much as possible is pre-printed so that you can avoid repetitive typing.

For letters that you write often, such as instructions to a supplier, make up a checklist of all the items you need to mention. That way you won't find yourself writing additional letters to add forgotten points or clarify vaguely stated expectations.

If you do not feel confident creating your own book of letters, consider borrowing items from a book of standard letters. One book that might be helpful is L.W. Frailey's *Handbook of Business Letters*, which offers 761 indexed letters for every purpose from appreciation to credit and collections.

Consider writing letters in memo format. These feature the traditional "To," "From," and "Subject" heading at the top. The short reference to the subject of the memo helps put the reader in the right frame of mind. Memos are usually one page in length; if they must be longer than this, consider adding a one-paragraph summary at the beginning of the letter. One paragraph, or even one sentence, summaries are also helpful at the top of a lengthy report.

On occasion, we all face personal battles with writer's block. A sales manager in an electronics manufacturing company gives this advice for those who cannot get started with their writing:

"Writing was a chore for me until I found an easy six-step approach: (1) *think* about what you want the finished piece to look like; (2) *prime yourself* with the facts, ideas, and benefits you want to use; (3) *write* a paragraph or a page on each major point and keep them all on separate sheets of paper; (4) *shuffle* them around until the arrangement makes sense; (5) *write* any introductions or bridge-building material you need to link the major pieces together; (6) *proofread* aloud. Now my writing is a pleasure, and it seems to be much more effective than before."

Tips for more effective business communications

Finally, extend your dedication to effective time management to your business stationery. In addition to listing your complete address, zip code, area code and phone number on your letterhead and business cards, print the hours you accept and return telephone calls. List the hours during which you will accept appointments also.

If your location is not well known, add a small vicinity map and/or directions on your letterhead or the back of your card. If you move, send your change of address on ready-made Rolodex® cards. Do the same when sending an introductory note to a prospective client. ◖

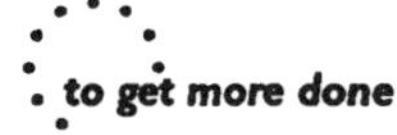

Chapter 12: Summary

■ **Organize conversations like a written report, with an introduction, body, and conclusion. Keep conversations on track by leaving free-flowing, directionless talk for brainstorming sessions.**

■ **If you must choose between being "one of the crowd" and being a respected manager, go for respect.**

■ **Make an effort to improve conversational effectiveness by giving and receiving feedback.**

■ **Improve written material by writing clearly and concisely, and save time by using form letters whenever possible.**

using time management

Reading & Speed Reading

"All my possessions for a moment of time."
Last words of Queen Elizabeth I

No time to read? While technical manuals, business books, and magazines abound, most people are hard pressed to keep up with it all. Even I've ordered several books of interest to writers in my field, yet they usually sit on shelves in my office until my next plane trip or vacation.

How long has it been since you've read a book on a subject important to your field of business? If it's been a while, you may feel that you don't have the time to devote to books — especially technical ones. Yet even reading for 15 minutes a day can stir up benefits, according to marketing and time management expert Ron Davis. For one, setting aside this time each day will allow you to read (or at least scan) up to 50 books per year! That alone could put you on top of worthwhile reading in your field.

There is no argument that making the time to read will offer valuable benefits. Reading helps reduce tension and stimulate ideas. Davis found another benefit from the knowledge he had picked up through reading: he began writing columns for trade publications in his field. As a columnist, he was even able to trade his writings for free advertising space, as well as monthly fees.

Finding the time to read

Now that you're convinced that finding the time to read will pay off, how can you manage your schedule to fit that reading time? Basically there are three ways to accommodate reading time. The first is to reduce the amount of reading you need to do. The second is to learn to retain more of what you read. And finally, you can fit more reading into your schedule if you learn to read faster.

Eliminate unnecessary reading

If it offers nothing to gain, don't read it. If it's a newspaper or interesting magazine that benefits readers by increasing their knowledge in a certain area, read it if you'd like. At the same time, however, you probably have subscriptions to newspapers or magazines that would be nice to read, but rarely can you find the time. Instead, they sit in a stack somewhere in your office or living room. They collect dust, they waste space, and they waste trees. If you receive reports from people at work that don't apply to you, ask them to cross your name off their list. You may also wish to do this with much of the direct mail you receive at home.

Check the file of things at work that you've been meaning to read. Do they still seem important? Chances are, there are a few items that are no longer relevant or interesting. Toss them out before you waste any more time wondering when you can get to them all.

Learn to be selective about what you read. Encourage subordinates to include summaries of their reports at the front. That way you can determine in advance if this is truly something you need to read. Do the same with books; read the jacket copy and table of contents before deciding to read it in its entirety. Check the beginning and end of each section, including introductions and chapter summaries, before reading the middle.

How to delegate reading tasks

One way to save time deciding what should be read is to have a secretary or assistant make a copy of the contents page and have you highlight items of interest. The person can then photocopy only those stories and file them in a "reading/research" folder. This saves time leafing through a lengthy journal to find what applies to you. It also makes it easier to carry reading material with you to appointments, lunch, business trips, etc.

An executive from a computer manufacturing firm gave us this advice for pre-screening reading: "I save time by getting my secretary to pre-screen all my reading. I've taught her to give me mail, journals, memos, and anything else on paper in one of four categories: (a) requires immediate action or decision; (b) useful information for background or future use; (c) routine or optional reading; and (d) applies to an ongoing project, specified. She handles everything else that comes in. I read only what's important and useful — a tremendous time-saver."

You can also reduce the amount of material to read by delegating some reading to an assistant or even to a paid reader. Have the person summarize or outline important facts from relevant works. This will not only save you time, it will help staff members learn more about their field or industry. Don't have an assistant to delegate to? How about starting a "cooperative reading program." Split trade publications and other journals up among your colleagues, then meet for a half hour each week to discuss the highlights of what everyone has read.

Newsletters also provide helpful summaries of relevant news and other information. *Bottom Line Personal* and *Communication Briefings* are two helpful publications. Consult the trade associations or the local library for newsletters that serve your particular field.

Here are a few additional ideas to help you get the most benefits from your reading time:

- *Read while you walk. A Spokane, Washington, consultant combines his walking break with a reading period for material of immediate interest that comes in each morning. After a morning's concentration, he loads his pockets with reading material and walks*

to the local park. He skims the material on the way, then reads important items in-depth once he reaches a park bench. The break provides fresh air, exercise, a new perspective, and valuable time to read.

■ *Get a quick overview.* Need to write a report about an unfamiliar subject? Or, perhaps a new product is in the development stage and you want to learn about the raw materials that go into it. If the topic is not one you are used to working with, you could spend endless hours searching out the simple, basic information you need. Instead, try the children's or junior's department of your library or bookstore. Children's books are almost as well researched as those for adults, but leave out the long-winded verbiage that keeps you from getting the point fast.

■ *Retain information through repetition.* Suggests one Execu*Time® reader, "While many items of information need only one or two readings, I have found that worthwhile items often require repetition. But this need not be a time-waster. For example, I mark in the margins of Execu*Time® ideas especially pertinent to me. Months later, I quickly review to check my memory and increase the benefits I get from the material. I also ready very important items into my cassette recorder, and listen to the tapes while driving, shaving, dressing, etc. I may spend 10 percent more time on an item this way, but I get 80 percent more benefit than I would from a quick reading and subsequent forgetting."

■ *Make notes on reports.* Similarly, when you read a long report, note main points, ideas, and analysis in the margins. Ask your secretary to type them up and staple the paper to the front of your report before it's filed. This way you'll have an instant review to read if you should call for the report again.

- *Request short reports. Keep writing and reading to a minimum by demanding that each item fit on one double-spaced page. You can always look up the detailed background or data if necessary.*

How/when to use speed reading techniques

Although they can't be used for all types of reading material, one way to reduce reading time is to learn a few speed reading techniques. According to Walter B. Pitkin, most reading material can be broken into four categories:

- Light reading, such as newspapers and simple fiction. This can usually be read at 5 to 6 words per second.

- Average reading, such as serious news articles and trade journals. These should be read at four words per second.

- Solid reading, or technical material not in your own field, needs to be read at only three words per second.

- Heavy reading is reserved for new subjects that must be mastered to prepare for technical discussions. This type of reading should be paced at 6,000 words per hour.

One speed reading course can help peel hours off the time you spend on light to average reading. Check your local college or university to find out about upcoming speed reading courses or seminars. Well-known organizations such as Evelyn Wood Reading Dynamics (800/447-READ) or PACE Group (214/644-2135) offer public seminars and corporate courses.

Just about everyone can benefit from a speed reading course because we all learned to read out loud and, perhaps subconsciously, we continue to carefully pronounce each word in our minds. Some people even move their lips when they read. To eliminate this habit, practice reading simple newspaper articles while saying something else, such as the numbers one through four or the first few words of a familiar poem, suggests

speed-reading expert Judith F. Larson. While comprehension will initially be low, eventually you'll learn to read without the lip movements.

When we silently vocalize what we read, we end up reading at about the same speed that we talk, which is only a half to a fourth of the speed at which we're capable of reading. Evelyn Wood courses, for example, teach students to move their hands down the page, allowing the eye to focus on bigger blocks of text, rather than one word at a time.

Finally, several companies have recently come out with speed reading software to help people improve their reading speeds and comprehension levels. Here is an overview of the programs we found available:

Smart Eyes. This program includes exercises to help people read faster and smarter. Students can choose the speed at which they'd like to read, in words per minute, and record their scores to track improvement levels. The package also includes a manual with seven lesson plans, all of which can be finished in 15 minutes a day in a six-week period. (Addison-Wesley Publishing Co. Inc., One Jacob Way, Reading, MA 01867; 617/944-3700.)

The Evelyn Wood Dynamic Reader. This program includes eye exercises to improve reading speed, as well as drills that emphasize comprehension and retention. Students have the option of reading material in full-screen displays or one line at a time, which prohibits them from re-reading material. The program also includes a comprehensive manual. (Timeworks Inc., 444 Lake Cook Rd., Deerfield, IL 60015; 800/323-9755 or 708/948-9200.)

Speed Reading Tutor IV. Designed by the Georgia Institute of Technology, this program features an introductory session and eight lessons that cover exercises in eye span, word and phrase recognition, and overall speed. And, it can store records for up to eight people. (Simon & Schuster, 212/373-8000.)

Speed Reading Tutor II. Both Speed Reading Tutor II and IV offer alternative ways to speed reading than the hand movements emphasized by the Evelyn Wood courses. Instead, students work with zigzag eye exercises, in which text appears in different parts of the screen. This is a four to eight week program that includes both adult and children's versions. (Davidson, 213/534-4070.) ●

Chapter 13: Summary

■ **Reading reduces tension and stimulates ideas. Setting aside just 15 minutes a day to read can allow you to read several books and trade journals per year.**

■ **Don't waste time reading items that offer no benefit, whether personal or professional.**

■ **Use speed reading techniques whenever possible.**

chapter fourteen
Filing Techniques

"All that I know I learned after I was thirty."
Georges Clemenceau

it may not be the most popular task for office-based executives, but it is a very necessary one. The right filing system is essential when you need to find the minutes of last month's meeting, statistics for an upcoming report, or receipts for this week's expense report. Yet how much time do we waste each day looking for those very items?

Filing systems in this country accumulate new paper at the rate of one million pages per minute. And sometimes it seems as if every one of those pieces crosses *your* desk. Whether the paper you deal with is a one-page plan for a billion dollar project or 1000 memos on basic nuts and bolts, nearly everything you do starts and stops on paper.

Yet research shows that most executives have only primitive understandings of how to cope effectively with that much paper. Around the beginning of the year or so, many managers will attempt to organize things with a new filing system, only to fall behind in maintaining the system and give in to old habits of hiding everything in a credenza or secret "catch-all."

Think of a filing system as you think of your finances. You wouldn't toss a checking deposit slip with your savings account, or record the same check twice because you couldn't find the first entry, would you? While there are exceptions, most people understand the need for accurate banking records. They appreciate having everything spelled out neatly in little passbooks: checks entered, dates, amounts, numbers, withdrawals, etc. An organized filing system can offer the same peace of mind.

The system we describe in this chapter is called the Executive Information System. It is one model that helps create a place for everything and needs minimum effort to maintain. It includes six sections: a time file, project file, reading/research file, ideas and plans file, trip files, and alphabetical storage files.

To get a clear picture of what files you need to keep handy, try keeping a file log for three to five days or so. (Figure 3.1, page 37) Each time you turn to your files, or send your secretary to retrieve certain information, record what you need and why. Use abbreviations, initials, codes, and numbers to make it easier to record repetitive trips to the file cabinets.

Count the number of times you log each kind and category of paper. Look for two patterns: first, the files you call for most often; and second, what groupings or categories would best fit your information demands. If you can learn to file according to these two patterns, you'll have the best information system possible. The closer you can come, the more satisfied you're going to be, and the more time and effort you're going to save.

The "holding" or "on-going project" file

We liken this file to the pile of papers on your desk. We keep ours in a file drawer in our desks where it is the most convenient — it is a series of hanging file folders, each labeled for a pending task or ongoing project. Instead of having all these folders in one big pile on our desks or credenzas, each project has its own hanging folder. A hanging folder may be labeled something such as "Directory Advertising" or "1993 Budgets" and have a series of manila folders in it. This file is typically used to hold data that is part of an ongoing or never-ending project —

using time management

a project that regularly resurfaces and needs add on work but does not have a specific resurfacing date.

It is probably our most used of all files. We still have one pile of pending papers on our desk — but only one — and that can best be labeled — "projects not yet assigned" or "incoming reading". That becomes the one and only pile of papers on our desks — everything else on our desks fits a category of a telephone, stapler, desk pen set, memo pad holder, pencil caddie, etc. The "holding" or "on-going project" file is one we're in and out of several times a day to retrieve needed information for a current project.

If your workspace has been overcome with endless piles of paper, the project file is the answer. The project file provides room to categorize, group, and store current working papers, as well as ideas and plans you're initiating or completing. It can also store most of your day-to-day working papers.

Give each project a name that covers it completely in your mind. If necessary, create "sub-project" folders to divide the information into smaller, cohesive units. For example, the "Collier" project might include in one folder all the paperwork regarding your dealings with Abigail Collier. But the "Hoover" project might contain hundreds of folders, each with a fairly separate sheaf of papers on planning, building, and maintaining a giant hydro-electric facility. If an item definitely has relevance to two or more folders, cross-reference it.

File the project folders in strict alphabetic order in a special group by themselves. Create new project folders as often as necessary, and keep all working papers in these folders and off your desk — except the one you're working on.

Use folders labeled Priority One, Priority Two, and Priority Three to hold all your incidental but important tasks that don't warrant project folders of their own. These are not merely places to store pointless tasks. Priority One is absolutely vital — work on immediately. Priority Two contains tasks to work on as soon as possible. Priority Three holds items to schedule now and do when appropriate.

Store these folders in your project file, and leave notes about the priority items in your time file. Keep a folder labeled "To Finish Today"

for all the little items you want to recall and complete before leaving the office. Instead of having a cluttered desk, you can stuff the clutter into this folder. Get in the habit of checking the folder for items to do several times during the day. This folder is a great place for single call-backs, routine replies, short and quick questions you want to attend to later in the day.

The Time File, "To Do Today", "follow-up" or "tickler" file

This file consists of 43 file folders, one for each day of the current month plus one for each month of the coming year. It probably belongs in the other drawer in your desk or certainly in your credenza.

This is an automatic memory for short and simple items such as notes, memos, and material you may want to look at in more detail later. You can place whole folders in here if you want to be sure to find them on, say, the 13th of the month. If you've never worked with a time file, you're in for a time management treat.

This file automatically brings back to your attention projects that are temporarily put on hold but for which you have a definite deadline.

To create a time file, label a set of hanging file folders one through 31, for each day of the month, as well as one for every month. Load the time file with everything you can't handle today, such as notes, memos, and actual paperwork. If the item lacks a built-in follow up date, such as "please call me back on the 26th," assign it a place in the time file on your own initiative.

Keep the time file handy, as it will soon become one of your most useful items. Let the time file take care of simple memory items: jot a note for everything you're supposed to remember and put it somewhere in the file. The file can track items such as simple reminders for things one week ahead and follow-up items for two, three, or four weeks down the road. It can also store deadline reminders a few days before the deadline looms (or however much time you would need to complete the project), as well as reminders of the next day's appointments.

Reading/research file

Use this as a comprehensive encyclopedia of information important just to you. It can be a life-long place to accumulate paper you want to retain as reference. Keeping a log will insure instant retrieval no matter how many items you store. (Figure 3.1, page 37)

This file is for all the articles, summaries, graphs, and similar information pertinent to your present and future information demands. You organize it by subjects of interest to you, for example: time management, law, computers, employee benefits. You create the subject categories you want and need. And don't be afraid to add, subtract, and reshuffle the categories as often as you need to.

To create the folders you'll need for an effective reading/research file, type up labels with the following headings:

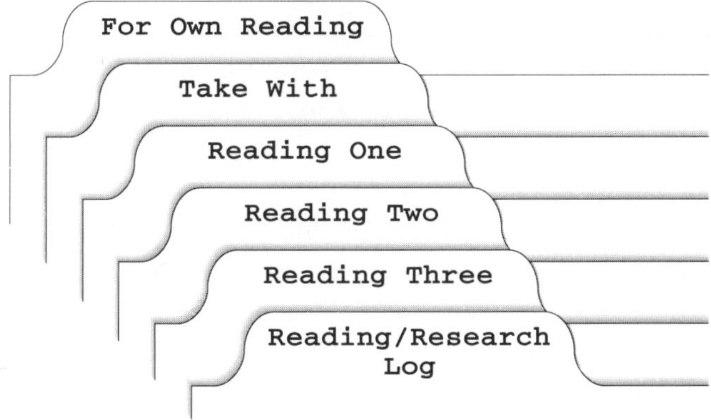

Then, keep a reading/research log by entering all new items at a single sitting every day, every week, or at the best frequency for you and your reading habits. To catch up on this reading, you can read by subject or by allotment. Either select all the items checked under a subject of interest and read them at a single sitting or set a definitive time for reading and skim in consecutive order all your recent acquisitions. When you find an item of interest, clip and save it. Don't read it, merely scan, mark, log, and file it. You'll read it when the appropriate time comes, later.

When you have enough clippings together, enter them in your log.

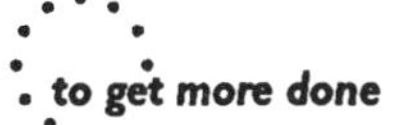

Number each item consecutively, and staple all sheets from one article together. Note on the log the title of the item, its consecutive number, and all subject categories to which it seems relevant. Then file the items in numerical order in magazine storage boxes or some safe place.

Some items are interesting but not worth saving. Clip and store these in your folders marked Reading One, Two, and Three. Carry the folders with you when you think you might have a spare minute to read. Skim the items and either mark them for filing or throw them away if not important.

Every Monday morning, throw out the contents of the third folder, and demote the other two piles of contents to make room for your latest "lightweight" clippings. Read One first, and heartlessly dump what you haven't read in the past three weeks. Store light reading of personal interest in the folder marked "For Own Reading." Take this home, on trips, or anywhere you might find a minute of free time.

Ideas and plans

This is your "creative reference" file. In it you can store good and bad ideas as they occur to you, as well as ideas that can be moved along from initial conception to implementation. The ideas and plans file is really a futures file that is perfect for keeping track of your concrete plans for future achievement, and of rough ideas and dreams which you hope to make concrete in the months and years ahead.

These folders can be labeled with such headings as: Ideas, Refined Ideas, Rough Projects, and Plans. Store under Ideas all the wild and woolly concepts that come to you in the middle of the night, in boring meetings, while working on other projects, etc. Don't worry about the details. Review the file periodically, and as some of the raw ideas grow more refined, move them along until you finally consider them "rough" projects.

At a certain point, a rough project becomes a real project with an appropriate place of its own in your working papers section. Plans for performance objectives, specific achievements, and any other future happenings stay in the "plans" folder for regular review, updating, and de-activation once completed.

Trip files

Store interesting information about places you go regularly, may go to soon, or would like to go to eventually. This is a simple geographic filing system with place names in alphabetic order, in which you can store items of interest regarding both regular, occasional, and hoped for business and pleasure travel.

Before each trip, pull out the appropriate folder and you're armed with information you can use on your journey. Use the "take with" folder to carry with you next time you leave your office. Whether you are going down the hall, across town, or around the world, you will most likely have a planned itinerary. And you'll also have accumulated items — plane tickets, hotel confirmations, phone numbers, contracts, and working papers — that must go with you.

Get in the habit of putting these items in your "take with" folder (and putting the whole folder in your briefcase or luggage) as they come to hand. Put them here and take this folder with you, and you'll never again leave something vital behind.

A-Z storage or correspondence files

Just as you use your alphabetic phone book to record names and numbers, here you can keep information — from copier instructions to correspondence — that you may need again.

These files contain general storage for people's names, maps, charts, and other general information that doesn't have a specific "tag" or work application. If you can't find a place for it in one of your special purpose files, you can store it here and be certain to find it later.

We adapted a new method of keeping our A-Z storage files — on January 1st of each year we begin new file drawers. Every file folder is labeled with a year on it. If data is pulled out of the previous year file it is refiled with a new year sticker on it in the current year's files. At the end of the second year the file is transferred to a storage box and moved to a storage area. About five years later somebody will make a fast "walk through" the box before discarding the entire box. That way, a file that had been marked "permanent file" will not be pitched.

Active and inactive files

One of the keys to swift information retrieval is carefully segregating documents according to how frequently you turn to them. Use your file log and your head to divide your files into the following categories:

1. Super-active – the files you turn to several times per day. Your time file and your project files certainly are super-active. Keep them within arm's reach: in a desk drawer, credenza, or a convenient rollaway cabinet.

2. Active – the files you normally use, but perhaps only several times per week. For example, current readings, A-Z files, some of the recently closed or soon-to-begin projects that don't require daily work. Store these within 10-20 steps.

3. Semi-active – the files you turn to infrequently but occasionally to clear up discrepancies or check on what someone did some time ago. Past correspondence, reading/research, and trip files are semi-active. Put these where you can get at them, but not in primary work areas.

4. Inactive – the long-term storage records you keep for legal, tax, or basic business purposes. By the time these files become inactive, they are carefully labeled, thoroughly purged of unneeded paper, and relatively disconnected from day-to-day and planning requirements. You can store these far from your workspace with no problem; even off-site, because you turn to them once a year or less.

General filing instructions

Appointments: note on calendar. File relevant papers, and/or appointment reminders in the time file. If paperwork has a regular place in your file system, store it there. If not, store it in the time file.

Articles: number and file consecutively, cross-referencing to reading/research log, relevant project folders, and anywhere else the item may be important. Scan it during your regular reading time, and read it only when it becomes "hot."

Books: same as articles, except books belong on book shelves in numerical order or by subject.

Letters: general correspondences goes in Correspondence 1 (routine, unimportant) or Correspondence 2 (important, expect to see it

using time management

again) in the A-Z section. Letters regarding specific projects can go in the "project" folder. Letters requiring response in the future can go in the time file. Letters giving important information can be indexed in reading/research log, or filed independently in A-Z by subject.

Memos: file in time file for the day before or the day action is due. Once action is complete, either discard or file under relevant "project," "trip," or subject in the A-Z section.

Notes: same as memos.

Projects: start a new folder as soon as a project begins to take shape, or when the assignment to project is official. One general project folder is enough to begin. Divide materials among more detailed folders for more complex projects. Keep all folders for a single project together.

Publications: scan the table of contents and the general short item sections for articles and items of interest. Skim the few that appeal. Clip those with relevance and valuable content. Log and file. Throw out what's left of the publication. Discontinue those from which you clip very little or nothing at all.

Reminders: file under the appropriate date in the time file. Also note the item on the calendar, where appropriate.

Reports: routine reports go into Reading One, and if unread after three weeks can go into "subject" or "project" folders, or can go into the trash.

Special reports of definite importance can be scanned, then indexed in reading/research log, to be read more thoroughly when needed or during regular readings. Reports linked to specific projects can go into the "project" folder, with a cross-reference to the reading/research log, if there is any general application.

Cross referencing

The basic rule of filing is, "if it's worth putting into your files, it's worth doing it correctly so you can find it again when you need it." Cross referencing is the most important means of finding items that might otherwise get lost, misfiled, or just plain whisked away.

Here are some guidelines:

- *Cross reference only when an item belongs in more than one place in your filing system, because it is directly relevant and should not be overlooked in two or more folders.*

- *Underline in red, or handwrite in red, all the key words that identify the subjects, topics, projects, ideas, or categories to which the item belongs.*

- *In one-page cases, it's easier, faster, and better to simply make the required number of copies and file each under a separate key word. For multi-page items, however, it's simpler, cheaper, less space-consuming, and faster to fill in a "cross reference" form and file that. Use pre-printed multi-part forms, pads of forms with carbons, or copy the filled-in form, whichever seems best for you.*

- *File the item itself under the first key word (except consecutive numbered files). Then deposit one cross reference form in the folders of every other key word you can think of. This way, no matter where you look, you'll get to the item fast.*

It has been estimated that fully cross referencing an executive filing system adds less than 10 percent to the number of items on file, but reduces 50 percent of the amount of time spent looking for specific pieces of paper.

- *Computers have changed the way we alphabetize in offices — before computers were invented we learned to ignore initials in filing — if a company was named, A. F. Price Company we would file it as "Price, A. F., Co" — today, computers would sort the name into the A category so we suggest that you pattern your correspondence files into a true alphabetic system as would a computer file.*

It has been estimated that fully cross referencing an executive filing system adds less than 10 percent to the number of items on file, but reduces 50 percent the amount of time spent looking for specific pieces of paper.

We would be negligent if we did not mention the opportunities of computer filing many documents through some of the more popular database programs. See Chapter 21 for more details on this subject.

Purging

Any good office supply house can provide you with a "records retention schedule" that covers your legal obligations on paperwork. In addition, work out your own rules for keeping what you need, but only so long as you need it. Throw out paperwork as soon — and as often — as you can. Record below how you and your boss want to handle purging your new information system.

	How often?	**Discard all older than:**
Time File	_________	_________
Project File	_________	_________
Reading File	_________	_________
Ideas/Plans	_________	_________
Trip Files	_________	_________
A-Z Storage	_________	_________

Another way to maintain a current filing system and stick with it is to start a new set of files for the new year. Keep as many of the old files as necessary, but mark the year they apply to in the tab. Then start a new file for this year.

For example, suppose you have all of one particular client's orders and notes in one file. Mark that file with the client's name and the year, such as "XYZ Manufacturing – 1990." Then create a new file for 1991. When a piece of information from the previous year's file is needed this year as well, retrieve it and file it into *this* year's file. After a couple of years, store the old files to free up space for current information.

These are the rules for a comprehensive and successful filing system. But the rules won't work unless you put them into practice. So start right now: you'll start working more effectively right away. ◐

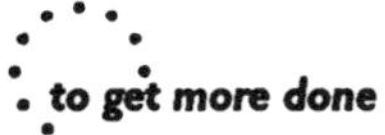

Chapter 14: Summary

■ **Keep hanging files within arm's reach for ongoing projects.**

■ **For quick tasks that don't warrant a whole file folder, keep three folders labeled Priority One, Priority Two, and Priority Three.**

■ **Keep an alphabetical filing system for research and reference materials.**

■ **Prioritize material to read by filing it into folders labeled Reading One, Reading Two, and Reading Three. Two additional folders can be labeled "For Own Reading" and "Take With," for reading to do outside of the office.**

chapter fifteen
Time Management For Personnel

"I'm working so hard on my time management that I don't get anything done." Obviously, if you hear these words from a colleague or staff member, it's a sign that something is wrong.

As you continue to foster enthusiasm for time management, it's easy to try to share your new-found knowledge with colleagues and subordinates. Whether you are president of the company or department supervisor, you have everything to gain by spreading the word about basic time management principles, and helping your fellow workers implement the time savers you've found so helpful. But unless these people can also realize the benefits and the "whys" of time management, they won't have the incentive to learn how it's really done.

Helping your people learn time management is similar to helping children learn the basics. You can't just tell them what you want done — you have to explain how and why it's done. Otherwise, you run the risk of having mechanical behavior that may please you on the surface, but does your people no good. Time management expert Merrill Douglass tells a story about a manager who expected his staff to clear their desks every night before leaving work. They did so to please the boss, but were really just aimlessly stuffing papers into their desks. The next day they had difficulty locating even important documents.

The solution is to take the time to teach employees about organization and filing — or expose them to time management publications. Or, if this is not possible, allow them to leave their desks as they wish, assuming that their own systems will work well enough for them, even if they are not "by the book."

The best place to start improving the time effectiveness of your firm or staff is yourself. Fortunately, that's usually the easiest place to start, too.

Perhaps the most important thing you can do is to show by example how time management principles, if used properly and all the time, can improve productivity and make work a lot easier. If you do this well enough, some of your co-workers should become interested on their own. Share with them what you have learned and little techniques you have picked up. It's easier to share your successful habits with people who work *for* you. But if you're tactful, you can pass along a set of To Do sheets to a peer or even to your boss, route a copy of this book to a friend, or take charge in meetings and steer the discussion back to the agenda.

Talk with your staff about ideas you have found helpful. Discuss it informally, on a memo or even in a lecture or two. Share books, publications, cassettes, etc. Route books you've found helpful, and, if you are in a position to do so, plan to rent a time management film for a staff meeting. Make your people aware that you support the idea of their attending a good time management workshop, and share brochures and flyers on such seminars. Encourage them to come up with good ideas as well. Time management should be a group activity and group goal.

Try to be a good example of a time management model. Do everything you would want your staff to do: keeping up with To Do lists, prioritizing, working to reduce paperwork, and emphasizing short- and long-term planning. You will have to spearhead the effort in this particular case.

Encourage people to tell you how you may be wasting their time. Try to learn how your habits slow others down. Show that you respect others' time as much as your own. Eventually, a give and take discussion may develop that lets you share your views about time wasting procedures in the office.

Help your assistant and/or secretary utilize time management principles. Perhaps you have a quiet hour each day from 9 to 10 a.m. Who is shielding you during that time? If it's your assistant or secretary, let him or her know you appreciate the help. Perhaps you can answer the phones or find a replacement to shield your helper at another time during the day so he or she can have a quiet hour too.

Have a time-saving suggestion box. If you have a suggestion box program, make people aware that time saving ideas are eligible for suggestion box awards. Or, set up a special time management suggestion program on a limited time or ongoing basis. Perhaps the best ideas could be shared on a regular basis in ten-minute staff meeting segments, or passed along in short memo form with a special binder for keeping the ideas handy.

Reward and recognize time saving improvements. If your people are improving, let them know it, if only verbally. If a pay increase or other reward can be arranged, so much the better. Tangible rewards may be incentive pay, bonuses, stock-purchasing plans and competitive salaries. Or, consider intangible rewards such as improving communications, answering questions, and involving workers in goal-setting. A kind word, thank you note, pat on the back, or notice in the company newsletter about a job well done are also important.

Finally, make sure employees feel a part of deadline decisions and priorities, as much as possible. Sometimes, foot dragging may be caused by resentment at having deadlines "shoved down people's throats" by managers who don't take the time to assess the performance required from the employee's point of view. Discuss projects and their deadlines with employees to get their views and make realistic priorities. This give and take will result in a consensus that allows teamwork toward a mutual goal.

Improving employee productivity

Traditional time management principles can sometimes hurt productivity. Some people work best with informal structure, lots of clut-

ter, and constant diversions. Those with artistic tendencies often have trouble doing detailed long range plans and adhering to routine and limiting ideas. Others are more methodical than creative — they prefer structure, lists, rankings, etc. Unfortunately, most business settings are methodical-oriented.

Here are some ideas to make creative people more organized and organized people more creative. First, focus on individual energy cycles. Try to allow people to work according to their mental and physical peaks. (We'll talk more on this idea later in this chapter.)

Recognize the benefits of taking breaks. It's important to put as great a priority on what you like to do as what you have to do. Breaks can be a reward for finishing tasks. They can also "decontaminate" work time of distractions. "If you keep contaminating your work time, that's a good indication you need more time to play," comments Ann McGee-Cooper in *Savvy*.

Michael Gelb of the High Performance Center agrees. He recommends not going for breaks for longer than an hour. Free-thinking time such as time spent walking or exercising often produces new insights and answers. Our minds are capable of high concentration only for so long. If we try to overwork them, the result may be a feeling of burnout later in the afternoon.

Breaks every hour? Sound too radical? Think of how strange our current business environments would have looked 50 years ago. Even over the last five or ten years, business operations have changed dramatically. Computers, interest rates, labor laws, recession, tax laws, and employees' approaches to their jobs have all changed with the times. According to William Maynard, executive director of the Effectiveness Institute, it's difficult for poorly managed firms to survive such changes. Managers must learn how to face newer and tougher management problems, how to manage productivity, and how not to manage productivity.

How to stimulate productivity

Managers will have to learn to blend technical and human skills as a way to improve productivity, according to William Maynard, executive director of the Effectiveness Institute. But this is simply a change in the managers' focus, not a change in their role. Here are a few suggestions to develop a good balance between these skills:

- *Improve productivity in all ways. There are seven pathways to reaching goals: technical skills, goal setting, interaction styles, problem solving, dealing with conflict, communications, and decision making. But most businesses use only two effectively: technical skill development and goal setting. In order to increase job satisfaction, the other five pathways must be developed and actively used.*

- *Have a productive climate. The corporate climate, or corporate culture, directly affects employee effectiveness. This is the perception of the people in the corporation — employees and executives — and how they behave according to those perceptions. Measuring the climate will enable a company to set the priorities to improve productivity.*

- *Recognize and manage stress. Great change can result in stress, which leads to illness or accidents.*

- *Have a balance between work and home. There needs to be a balance between life at work and life at home, even though it's not possible to separate the two. Managers need to develop the skill to balance work and personal life.*

- *Have skills to manage change. Most people don't want to change, even if there is a need for it. Managers must try not to force change onto employees to the point where they get hostile. At the same time, they cannot ignore the need to change, either.*

- *Balance productivity and satisfaction needs. Either area should not be emphasized too much — employees can feel great and get nothing done, or they can overwork and not get appreciation. Maximum productivity comes with a balance of these two elements.*

■ *Have knowledge of human behavior. Develop new skills in motivating and working with employees. No one should do things the
same way simply because that's how they had success before — that's
a good course toward trouble.*

■ *Develop versatile people skills. Wickham Skinner and W. Earl
Sasser pinpointed the patterns of managerial success in the Harvard
Business Review. The "new" manager deals well with relationships;
carefully analyzes decisions and their impacts; has an operating
strategy; handles no-win situations effectively and recognizes di-
lemmas; uses a variety of management skills; is flexible and adapt-
able according to the situation; motivates subordinates and satisfies
superiors; and manages his or her own work.*

In addition, Skinner and Sasser identified several patterns of managerial failure in dealing with subordinates. These include: avoiding
people-related problems; working haphazardly without an overall plan
or strategy; paying too much attention to detail; not working according
to priorities; moving slowly; tolerating ineffective subordinates for too
long; not seeking help or advice.

How not to improve productivity

Some common mistakes made when dealing with subordinates
include overusing power, overplaying technical skills, and not developing people skills. Here is a list of top mistakes managers need to avoid
when dealing with staff members:

■ *Managing workers poorly. The employees determine success — managers are not the ones who achieve the firm's goals. Instead, a manager
must properly manage his workers — they achieve the goals when
properly motivated and directed by the manager.*

■ *Not using human resources. Managers who look at the bottom line
results tend to disregard the development and use of human resources.
Productivity then suffers, along with those coveted bottom line results.*

using time management

- *Underplaying job satisfaction. An employee's job satisfaction and productivity have a direct bearing on each other. For example, if morale decreases, satisfaction decreases. As satisfaction decreases, productivity decreases.*

- *Overusing power. "Executives who control by the use of power and directive will eventually become extinct," says Maynard. There's a new work ethic developing — highly skilled people will work in a climate that suits their personal needs and gives an opportunity for achievement and satisfaction. The old-fashioned executive style doesn't foster that climate.*

- *Using "Band-Aid" solutions. Managers tend to use easy and fast solutions when under pressure — often refereed to as "Band-Aid solutions." But such a solution often affects only the symptom, not the problem, which is usually people-related. These are not easily or quickly fixed by structural solutions, and the approach often yields confusion, hostility, and a host of other problems.*

- *Overplaying technical skills and not developing people skills. Two elements affect an organization's productivity: technical skills and people skills. While most of the money and time are used to improve technical skills, improving and developing people skills is just as important, if not more so in some cases. The skills needed to effectively deal with people must be improved to increase productivity. Successful managers can effectively manage technical and human resources. They should also continue to improve the manner in which they work with employees.*

Productivity checklist

A productivity program is something many firms strive for, but what makes a good productivity program? The following checklist, reprinted from the *Management of Change* newsletter, details what's necessary to establish a productivity program in your firm.

1. Task force — to plan, organize, and steer the program.

2. Goals — specific areas where productivity needs to be increased, spelled out specifically.

3. Relationships to improve — this is a definition of what input-output functions specifically need to be improved.

4. Resource allocation — this can include money, time, and training.

5. Benchmarks — objectives and specifications of progress measurement — all in quantitative, measurable, and verifiable terms.

6. Training and education — for employees and management to learn productivity improvement and productivity management.

7. Specific tools — such as valuable engineering, work simplification, process-flow analysis, diagramming, creativity techniques, etc., should be made available for workers.

8. Programming of the productivity effort within a specific time frame.

9. Productivity teams, selected and constructed unit by unit and function by function, level by level.

10. Compensation program to assure all involved that in both monetary and non-monetary ways, they will be compensated for their increased productivity.

11. Feed-back system as well as measurement to evaluate and report results.

Knowing what workers want and improving morale

What do workers really want? Knowing the answer to this question is the first step in improving company morale. According to a survey by Kenneth Kovac, a professor at George Mason University, what employees want from work and what supervisors think they want are very different.

In order of popularity, most workers want:

1. Interesting work.

2. Full appreciation of work done.

3. Feeling of being in on things.

4. Job security.

5. Good pay.

6. Promotion and growth.

7. Good work conditions.

8. Loyalty to employees.

9. Help with personal problems.

10. Tactful discipline.

Managers think workers want:

1. Good pay.

2. Job security.

3. Promotion and growth.

4. Good work conditions.

5. Interesting work.

6. Tactful discipline.

7. Loyalty to employees.

8. Full appreciation of work done.

9. Help with personal problems.

10. Feeling of being in on things.

It is a wise manager who listens to complaints about employee morale. Good morale can help increase productivity, performance, and profits. Some managers describe morale as a means of developing the people in an organization into a working team. Marilyn Morgan, professor at the University of Virginia, describes morale as "the employee's reaction to the work situation."

According to Morgan, signs of low morale indicate that something needs to be done if the problem becomes widespread. These signs include: high levels of employee turnover, absenteeism, and lateness; complaints about the workplace, especially about pressure and the feeling that the company is not concerned about workers; complaints from

clients or other departments about service from the department with low morale; employees who don't seem to work hard or put much into the job.

This is where time management can help. A manager's leadership style is one of the top influences on morale. Getting workers to participate gets them actively involved and concerned — and gives them better self respect. Morgan suggests developing a participative leadership style by:

1. Delegating responsibility with the appropriate rewards or penalties.
2. Looking for ways to get the subordinates involved in the decision making process.
3. Providing employees with the needed information so they feel they know what is going on and how they are contributing toward those goals.
4. Having the manager and subordinate work together to establish collaborative goals.

Note that most of these suggestions are also discussed in similar forms in previous chapters on delegating, goal setting, and other time management topics. Chalk up another benefit for time management principles!

Another time management principle which offers the dual benefit of improving employee morale is installing a Flextime Plan. This allows employees to select their own working hours — within limits, of course. For example, during certain hours each day, such as from 10 to 3 excluding the lunch hour, most employees are expected to be present. But within those limits, workers can arrive as early or as late as they desire, and leave as soon as the full day's hours have been put in.

From a time management perspective, a Flextime program offers several advantages. These include letting employees choose their own peak working hours, making commuting easier, and improving morale. A morning person who hops out of bed at 5 a.m. can use that early-morning "peak" to work from 6:30 to 3:30. The night owl who would rather stagger into work by 10 a.m. can stay on the job until he "peaks"

using time management

— from 3 to 6 p.m., for example. And, when everyone does not arrive in the office at the same time, the urge to chat around the coffee machine or donut cart is cut substantially. Each employee arrives individually and gets to work without undue socializing.

A Flextime program also provides for built-in quiet hours. By setting up definite hours when everyone is in, such as from 10 to 3, you create built-in quiet hours at the beginning and end of each day. A logical extension of this schedule is to leave 10 to 3 as permissible hours for meetings and visitors, and keep the hours before and after this period free for individual work.

In addition, employees can skip rush hour train and auto trips if they choose to, thereby avoiding arriving at the office late, annoyed, or drained by delays, crowding, and traffic jams. Finally, employees are given control over their work hours, and can plan their doctor's appointments, children's school conferences, etc., without having to go into long explanations or calling in sick.

Management teams

The concept of the management team is growing in popularity these days, partly because a well-run management team can "synergize" human effectiveness and give you much more than the team's members could individually.

Your management team can be much more than a collection of subordinates who do what you could if you only had the time. With the emphasis on "team" as well as "management," you can mold the team into whatever the organization needs most: a strong guiding force to direct current activities, a forecasting unit to plan for and implement future programs, a research group to explore new ideas or ventures, even an efficiency center to make the best possible use of every resource.

Just as an entire football team can move the ball toward the goal much more effectively than any one or two players working alone, a well-chosen and well-developed management team can accomplish things that the team's manager could never do working as an individual. A four-step process — recruiting, training, development, and utiliza-

tion — helps you develop such a team for whatever purpose you determine. Results take time, but in most cases they are well worth nurturing.

Recruiting

Most of the team members you need may already be on your staff, but do not assume so. Evaluate your people on the basis of managerial strengths and weaknesses. To do this, you might use charts with columns showing their education, training, financial background, marketing background, or engineering background.

If you are too heavy in marketing and too light in finance, for example, keep this in mind when it comes time to add staff. Recruit new managers with the thought of building a more well-rounded team. In other words, do not start firing or laying off good people just because their specialties are too much alike, but when vacancies occur, hire new managers with strengths that your department could use. Transfers or promotions from other departments of the firm could help as well, especially since these employees would already have some experience with your firm and its quirks.

Training

Make sure that your people have an overall view of your business. Do not keep them cloistered in their own area of specialty; give them assignments that will make them interact with other departments to learn and teach. Let your own team members work together so that marketing pros start catching on to what data processing is all about, and so forth. This you-teach-me, I'll-teach-you concept does not have to be rigidly enforced. The smart managers on your team will automatically take advantage of the opportunity to learn from others, and they are the ones who will become your team leaders of the future.

Development

Foster team spirit and team interaction. Put the team members' offices in close proximity. Assign them to a variety of projects in different combinations. Have regular team meetings to discuss progress on these projects. Team members should share responsibility for each project. No one designated leader should shoulder the burden for everything. Rewards should come from decisions arrived at through a consensus; individual actions and approaches should be saved for a more appropriate setting.

Group trips to conferences and conventions may help to build good feelings among team members. Group-think sessions can be helpful as well, as can social occasions to celebrate successes and changes brought about by the team.

Do not do all this without revealing your motivations; it is helpful to explain to your subordinates that you are trying to build a team with their help.

Utilization

Once your management team is shaping up, identify a major project or two for the team to tackle. Explain the project, then get their input, advice, and support. Make sure the team has as much responsibility and authority as possible to deal with its particular problem area.

A valuable project — in addition to more immediate ones you may assign — is to have the team do a three- to six-year plan for the firm or the department. Several alternate paths can be explored, along with contingency plans and utilization outlines for manpower, equipment, and capital. ◑

Chapter 15: Summary

■ Time management students need to know
the "why's" of time management so they have
the incentive to learn the "how's."

■ Discuss helpful time management ideas
with your staff. Share books, newsletters, and
cassettes on the subject.

■ Strive to be a good example of a successful
time manager.

■ Stimulate employee productivity with high
morale, a productive atmosphere, flexible
hours, and effective management techniques.

chapter sixteen
Effective Delegating

*"Wanting to work is so rare a want
that it should be encouraged."*
Abraham Lincoln

What can you delegate? Think about this for a moment, even if you work without a secretary or other staff member to delegate to. Stop and list all the activities you do in a typical week or month. Are there research or word processing activities that could save you time if handled by someone else? Consider a part-time worker or word processing service.

Are there routine tasks that don't really need your personal attention but you do them anyway out of habit? We both have worked for executives who relished opening the mail. With hundreds of press releases, articles, invoices, checks and other information arriving weekly, this took up more than an hour of time on most days. Other stories of managers who can't delegate describe people who actually re-do all their subordinates' work. If this sounds familiar, ask yourself if it's worth your time to continue doing such tasks for the sake of routine. Passing off such responsibilities can help subordinates learn more about the business. It can also help to groom them for advancement and enhance your own chances for promotion.

Pitfalls of not delegating

Perhaps you tend not to delegate because you were always taught, "If you want something done right, do it yourself." It may be true that doing things yourself is one way to get things done correctly, but it is also the most time-consuming way. Do you truly believe that you must do everything your own way to have it done right?

This do-it-yourself philosophy is one you will have to rid yourself of if you hope to control your time. Think of it this way: if you insist on doing everything yourself, your career and your life will be forever stuck at the level where you can do everything yourself. Furthermore, your subordinates will become bored, since you refuse to give them anything new or challenging to do. Before long you may get a reputation as a poor trainer, or worse, as an easy boss who takes on all the subordinates' work for them.

Managers who don't delegate run the risk of having too much to do and no time to handle more important or more interesting projects that come in. Think of yourself as a lever, while those under you are the fulcrums. The more you use your fulcrums, the greater time advantage you will have. You can leverage time through fellow workers, outside specialists, and friends.

A common complaint in the business world is that managers are never really taught how to manage. Even the finest graduate business schools do not teach time management to potential executives. It's a shame, because people come out with MBA's who have no idea how to manage their daily lives. As a result, they continue to do the work they did as staff members, rather than overseeing others to do those tasks. There are probably a few instances where Chicago Bears coach Mike Ditka wanted to run onto the field and really participate in the game, but that's not his job. He's needed on the sidelines, giving direction to quarterbacks and other players. If you become a player rather than a coach, who's going to direct the game? Your job as an executive is to motivate the team and keep them on the right track — not to get down on the field and make the field goals yourself.

One of the best managers we have ever met was David A. Brown, who, at the time, was vice president of the Financial Systems Division at Rand McNally and Company, Chicago. He supervised about 30 people and spent very little time in his own office. He spent most of his time in his subordinate's offices talking to them about projects they were working on. He eventually moved on to become president of one of the major business forms manufacturing companies.

Finding delegates

Getting close to the people who work with you improves the time advantage because it takes you less time to influence friends than strangers. And the closer you get, the better you're able to judge who is right for each of your projects. Note that leveraging is not "manipulation." Leveraging refers to your sincere efforts to get people on the team and working toward coordinated goals.

You can leverage through subordinates, of course. But you can also leverage time through colleagues, friends, professionals, and resource specialists. Delegating household tasks such as cleaning, grocery shopping, preparing tax returns, or planning a party can also save valuable time. At work, look for other workers who may want to participate in projects but lack the initiative. If your firm is understaffed, part-time or temporary help may be another option.

When you concentrate your efforts on the people involved instead of the work, you can easily generate very favorable "time advantages." The result will be bigger projects and greater accomplishments at no extra time cost to you. In addition, your delegates will understand that you want them to succeed and do well, rather than simply get the job done by any means.

Working with delegates

Many managers admit that they do not know how to delegate effectively, or they fear delegating important jobs because they are afraid of competition from those who work for them. It's important to learn how to delegate, what to delegate, and specific skills that will help you get started with this crucial task. Learning these skills can bring so many rewards — primarily, time — that your fears will seem insignificant once you get started. In addition, you'll learn how to eliminate, pass on,

to get more done

or at least minimize time-consuming routine jobs that keep you from the primary tasks at hand.

Delegation can also help you upgrade your subordinates. You do not need to hold formal classroom sessions to teach those who work for you what the department is all about. Rather, give them assignments that will help them develop new skills and abilities. Do this step by step so that you can keep your subordinates challenged but not overwhelmed. Delegation gets training off the theoretical level and into the world of reality by making one cope with a specific assignment. A careful delegation program will mold confident, capable subordinates who will be highly promotable. It will also show who lacks the necessary skills to rise to management.

Delegation multiplies results. If you do it yourself, you can only get so much done. But if you and your entire staff work on a project or problem, the results multiply and expand. Again, that extra experience will also benefit your subordinates.

In today's business climate, it is essential to develop sharp delegation skills. Put the tips in this chapter to work for you now. Here are some reasons why: It is simply not possible for one manager to keep on top of the market in which he or she must function without help to keep the work flowing. Formerly, most parts of a business could be understood and handled by one person, but now, with computers, complex tax laws, and government regulations, a smart manager allows specialists to handle their areas of expertise, thereby freeing him or her to manage. It is no longer possible in most instances for a boss to expect military style responses to his or her commands. Delegation with thorough communication helps employees to understand why they are doing what they are asked to do. It also lets managers free themselves from trying to do everything and from not doing anything as well as it should be done. Through delegation, subordinates can get involved in their managers' jobs, expand their horizons, and try more complex tasks with guidance.

Delegation ways and means

The first thing you must do is to determine what needs to be delegated. Routine tasks, for example, even if you could do them quickly yourself, should be delegated so that you need not even think about them anymore.

Ask yourself the following questions when a project comes across your desk: Who else can do this? What would be a better use of my time? When can I start delegating this? How can I do it faster? Why am I the one to do this? The answers will help you determine if you should do the job yourself or delegate it.

Strive to delegate everything that someone else can do. Keep only the tasks you must do yourself. Things that you believe you do better than others should be delegated as well, especially if they are time-consuming. Teach your subordinates to do them and free yourself for the highest level work and thinking.

Certain things, of course, cannot be delegated. Do not delegate disciplinary action when this discipline should come from you as a department manager. In the same vein, do not delegate other work that you simply do not want to deal with yourself. If a subject is confidential, it is imperative that you handle it yourself. Otherwise, you risk losing your status as someone who can be confided in by upper management.

If you have several subordinates, it makes sense to set up an assignment chart so that you allocate the work fairly. Such a chart might have spaces to list each person's current assignments, special skills, areas of special education or knowledge, and current time commitments. A chart like this can help you determine the most likely candidate for a project in just a few minutes.

Do not always give the tough jobs to the few most qualified people. When you can, take the time to give your people training jobs in areas they are not familiar with. Encourage subordinates with special knowledge in these areas to help their peers develop. Show them how such teamwork is rewarded in higher departmental output, and respond positively to those who tutor others when review time comes around.

Get your subordinates involved

Here are a few areas to cover when you give your subordinates a new assignment:

- *The task – what it is you want done, in specific terms;*

- *Considerations – what you think is important to know as background information for task completion;*

- *The larger view – how this task fits into the big picture for the department and the firm;*

- *Accomplishments – specifically, what needs to be done to complete this task;*

- *Responsibility – both the scope and the limits so that the subordinates know how far they may go within the corporate structure;*

- *Authority – necessary so that subordinates will not be too timid or step on toes.*

Many people are frustrated when they are given the responsibility for a job without the authority to get it done properly. Make sure you set things up for your subordinates with other departments, and that they are recognized as your deputies and not as your menials.

Delegate to help others succeed. Do not tell them exactly how to do the job — let them tell you. Exercising their minds will help train them to do their own work in the future. Share information, background material, and considerations with them, but let them shape the form the project will take — but be available to answer questions, of course.

If the task you are delegating is new, you do not have to assign the whole job at once. Try outlining the entire project and asking your delegate to report when the first step has been completed. Then you can evaluate the actions to date and proceed with the next step.

It is up to you to make sure that the reports you ask for are delivered on time if your delegate does not volunteer them. Realize that delegation is the beginning, not the end, of the supervisory process. Make sure that your people know that you do keep track of what they have been assigned and that the jobs are not just busy work. Get briefed on progress, evaluate reports carefully, offer advice and suggestions — tactfully.

Also, make sure you and your delegate take time to evaluate the work on a job once it has been completed. This should be a private affair, especially if you must criticize the subordinate's work. If praise is in order, that can be given in public as well as on a one-to-one basis.

The nuts and bolts of delegation

Practice, practice, practice. You need to get comfortable with the art of delegation. Until then, it may seem easier to do the work yourself than to delegate it. Begin to practice by refusing to get directly involved with a project. Keep pushing your delegate to do it. If he or she tries to pass it off to you, stay aloof and merely give advice and pointers. Do not let that file folder or notebook land on your desk until the project is through. Be firm.

According to Bill Oncken, a management consultant, effective management means leaving problems in others' laps. Instead of taking them on yourself, you simply offer yourself as a coach, consultant, or advisor to people at specific times only. Each meeting about a problem should end with a clear assignment as to what the person must do next and by when.

Use a delegation file. In addition to the chart of subordinates that lists their current projects and areas of expertise, make sure you keep an up-to-date delegation file detailing the assignments you give to each person. Put the scheduled reporting dates in this file and on your calendar. If you do not postpone the reports, subordinates will get the idea that you mean business.

Take time to teach a task. How many times have you put off delegating a duty because it has to be taught to your assistant? Take the time once to teach that skill, and you'll be free of the task for good.

Listen well. After you have given the assignment clearly and explained reporting methods and times, listen carefully to what your subordinate says. It is up to you to act as an early warning device to head off problems. Watch for uncertainty about schedules, discomfort in discussions, fuzzy data, delays without basis. Investigate while the problem is still of manageable size.

Make sure that you are understood. Here is what a machinery company vice president says about delegation communications: "I find miscommunication is the biggest time-waster of all. If I give an assignment, for example, and there is miscommunication, all the time spent doing it is wasted, plus the time to correct it or recommunicate the assignment and have it done again. Also, subtle misunderstandings rob time from every day. Now I take the time to be sure I'm understood correctly the first time, even if I have to go over and over it again until we get it right. In the long run, that's the shortest route to speedy communications."

Do not solve delegates' problems for them. Too often, your delegate will come to you with a question, and you will end up working out the whole project. You have lost the time-saving advantage of delegation, and they have lost the opportunity to discover a personal solution. Insist that when your delegates have problems to discuss with you, they come armed with some possible solutions of their own. Then you can help them choose the best one and send them off to implement it themselves.

Test your delegates' readiness. If you doubt whether a certain subordinate is ready to take on a certain job, play a "what if" game and see. Identify two or three central areas of knowledge crucial to seeing the project through. Ask your delegate, "What would you do if one

using time management

of these areas started causing problems?" The answer will tell you how knowledgeable your delegate is in this area and how well he or she can handle the inevitable close calls.

The best test comes while you are away. The next time you go out of town, test your subordinates' new-found skills. Delegate some assignments you might have handled if you were in town, and see how your delegates do in your absence. How well are routine activities carried on without you, and which seem to need you around for guidance or watchdog duty?

Use meetings to serve two delegation purposes. Send a delegate to some of the meetings you usually attend yourself. This will, first, save you the time of attending. Second, it will expose your subordinate to some new activities and decision-making processes. Ask your delegate to write a concise report on the meeting (ten minutes maximum reading or hearing time). It will be challenging for the delegate to distill the important parts of the meeting for you, and you will get an edited report that will serve you almost as well as personal attendance in a fraction of the time. 

to get more done

■ The adage, "If you want something done right, do it yourself," can quickly squash time management efforts.

■ List all the tasks you do in a typical week or month and determine what could be handled by an assistant or outside service.

■ Remember that delegation multiplies results and grooms both the delegator and the delegatee for promotions.

■ Think of household tasks that could be delegated to outside services or other family members.

using time management

chapter seventeen
Two Big But Necessary Time Wasters — Meetings & Travel

"A leader is a man who has the ability to get other people to do what they don't want to do, and like it."
Harry S. Truman

Of all the activities that occupy a manager's schedule, meetings and travel may well be the biggest time drainers. At many companies, meetings occupy three to four hours a day and more. And, for middle managers working an average work week of 70-80 hours, business travel is the number one time waster, according to one survey.

Controlling your meetings

Meetings become great time wasters when they are held without adequate reason or when they are poorly planned and run, according to Charles Hamman, a California-based management consultant. Whether you spend one hour or 20 hours per week in meetings, it's a good bet that most of that time is wasted. And, although they are useful to inform, explore alternatives, and reach a consensus, meetings are expensive. In fact, their costs can reach hundreds of dollars if you total up the time investment of all those participating.

While there is little you can do about meetings held by your boss or peers, you can do something about your own. First, ask if a meeting is really the best way to accomplish your purpose. Would a memo or conference call suffice? If the meeting is only to be between a handful of people, consider having it in one of their offices so you can briefly state what you need to discuss, then leave when the meeting is over, eliminating the small talk.

Distributing an agenda in advance will help others to stick to the topics at hand. Have the needed data at hand. And limit the time to no more than 90 minutes. If you plan and run a good and effective meeting, perhaps others in the office will observe how you operate and follow your lead, says Hamman.

Most meetings have six basic "points of control." These include purpose, people, discussion, time and place, timing, and conclusion.

Purpose. This is the backbone of any good meeting. If you have a strong, clear purpose in mind, you can make your meeting extremely effective and exciting. If you can't state the purpose of your own meeting in one sentence, don't expect very gratifying results.

Meetings are generally for problem solving, planning, training, or news. Sometimes the purpose is two-stage. For example: a first stage to explore the possibilities for solving a problem, then a second stage for final decision making, or a first-stage discussion of a new pension plan, then a second stage to announce how the plan works. First and second stages can be one or two meetings, depending on the specifics.

Your purpose is generally your central control factor, and you should use it to help define the other control points.

People. The most basic rule is, the more people you bring in to the meeting, the more energy you must put in to make a good meeting. In general, you should limit attendance to the smallest number possible. Problem-solving and planning meetings work best with half a dozen or so people; training meetings can hold up to 20 or 30; and news meetings are limited only by the number of people that can comfortably hear your voice. But if you want feedback, keep news meetings under 50 people.

Controlling the attendance list helps to control the meeting. Limited attendance immediately creates an "in group" who feel more privileged and gain more influence than the group that wasn't invited. The desire to stay "in" or get "in" often provides a strong motivational

using time management

incentive that leads to greater effectiveness. In addition, including or excluding specific people allows you to influence the course, mood, and tone of the meeting. The people you invite are a big factor in determining the success and outcome of the meeting.

Discussion. This is the meat of the meeting. You can exert tremendous control over the content, direction, format, and outcome of the discussion through a variety of control techniques. Here are some examples:

Positive or negative feedback. Facial expressions, head movements, body and verbal language all carry feedback on what you think of the discussion. Use your feedback power to guide the talk along fruitful lines.

Degree of focus. Your questions — either more general or more specific — will unfocus or focus the discussion. Focus the meeting on valuable points, and open up the focus when the talk strays down the intended path. Tighten the focus to bring things to a pinpoint conclusion.

Recognition. A powerful tool to reward some people and punish others. For example, a slight nod is a pat on the back, raised eyebrows are a strong salute. Jot a note on your pad and others hear you clapping appreciatively. It works in reverse, too. Look bored and people hear your objection. Interrupt the speaker and you have objected even more. Simply direct a new question at someone else and you virtually shut off debate on the old point.

Summaries. A convenient means of meeting control. Move the meeting along with timely summaries and statements of "the consensus." Simply exclude points or options you don't like, opinions you cannot credit, and discussion you feel is way off the mark. Your summary is often the basis for the next phase of the discussion, and frequent summarizing in one direction can guide your meeting in the direction you want it to go.

Conclusions. Here is a way to "fix" the discussion in a pattern you appreciate. As you press for a definite conclusion, options fall away and people accept the current concept and assumptions. If you ward off a

conclusion by "unfocusing" and asking for "more study," you leave the field open for later conclusions that are more appealing.

Time and place. This is often an overlooked control point for your meeting. For effective problem solving and planning, as well as creativity, pick a morning time in a quiet, comfortable location. For news meetings and training, hold short meetings in-house, four- to eight-hour meetings somewhere else.

Timing. Here's another control point too often overlooked. A timed agenda not only controls a meeting, it controls the preparation by signalling how much you think each item is worth. Intelligent timing also helps you cut off the long-winded, and pace you to an upbeat ending.

Last five minutes. This can be the most important control point of your meeting, since these are the minutes people will remember the most. Your last five minutes can set a pattern and create respect for your meeting skill.

Provide an upbeat ending, particularly when your meeting has been too long, acrimonious, or fuzzy. Play it safe and prepare a short, snappy, satisfying item to end the meeting on a positive note. Do what you can to gain agreement on something positive, so people leave the meeting without a lot of hard feelings or pent-up frustration.

Then take two minutes to restate all assignments and their deadlines resulting from the meeting. Create a strong final note with definite instructions on what has been done, what must be done, and what still remains to be done at the next meeting.

Attending meetings

When it's you that has to attend the meeting — rather than plan it — you can also make the most use of that time by making an effort to learn as much as possible from the meeting. Insist that the planner of the meeting prepare and distribute in advance of the meeting an agenda of the meeting and then make sure that he/she sticks to the agenda.

One *Execu*Time®* reader, a health care manager in California, gave us this advice:

using time management

"I devised a useful and timesaving worksheet which accompanies me to meetings, and can be used for conferences, telephone or otherwise, and telephone conversations. At a meeting, each section can be allocated to an agenda item, and is especially useful when I wish to take either notes or minutes. Each section has an area for basic points discussed, summary of action to be taken, and a 'punch' list of action to be taken which denotes: self, other name, date due, delegated to, date completed, and comments."

Here is the basic format of the form:

Conference Worksheet (Meetings/Telephone)

Basic points discussed:

____

Summary of action to be taken:

____

Action to be taken:

____

Self: Other name:

____

Date due:

____

Delegated to:

____

Date completed:

____

Comments:

Some people prefer to write down or record on tape all important points of a meeting. This can be particularly useful for seminars and training meetings. One engineering executive believes in writing down everything you are taught. "Don't trust to memory. Jot down all that

is said and all that you observe (i.e., names of people involved) and refer to these notes constantly when you are working on your own," he suggests. "This will cut down on mistakes and time spent asking repeat questions about processes already taught. The result is saved money and more efficient work."

Another idea is to bring a microcassette recorder to training sessions and record the entire meeting. Then play the tapes over a couple times as you are driving to work, taking a walk, or doing mindless tasks in your office. Most likely you will get more out of the meeting then those who only heard the information once.

Travel

Business travel is not only time-consuming, it is also the most mentally and physically draining task that an executive can do. Running from the cab to the baggage check to the terminal — only to find that your flight is delayed one hour — can be frustrating. Not to mention the jet lag, time-zone changes, airline food, and other pleasures that travel brings.

What's the most effective time-saver in business travel? Don't do it at all! Find another way of accomplishing the trip — use the phone, send a subordinate, get the other person to come to you or totally avoid the trip altogether. Unfortunately, many business trips are unavoidable and the job is to figure out how to do it most effectively to eliminate the waste of time.

Conventions and trade shows

Even if you only travel a few times a year — say to an occasional convention or trade show, these can be hectic and confusing times. Peter Turla and Kathleen Hawkins outlined a few ideas to help people be organized and prepared for conventions. Their suggestions, taken in part from *Success* magazine, appear below.

Think ahead before the convention. Give your office the phone numbers of your hotel and convention message center. Let staffers know that you expect everything to run smoothly in your absence — unless they call.

Outline the staff's responsibilities. Encourage staffers to do as much of your work as possible so you aren't swamped upon return.

Let a travel agent make the travel arrangements, unless the company is handling them. Get information on the city and area you're visiting, especially if the family is coming along. Check the weather forecasts and pack accordingly.

Read the convention materials and agendas ahead of time. Plan out some of your time in advance so that you will get the most out of the activities and sessions.

Set goals for the trip. What exactly do you want to get out of it? Write down the goals and refer to them every day so that you'll focus on what you wanted to learn, not just on what's happening.

During the convention. Never arrive at the exhibits at peak hours. Go either when the booths first open or the last hour before they close, although going early will probably be more productive, as some people close up their exhibits early. If there are many exhibits, go to the most important ones first. Visit the remaining exhibits in the order of their value to you. If there are good sessions scheduled at the same time, ask whether tapes or transcripts are available. If not, share notes with someone who was at the other session. Tape meetings or take notes. Dictate the important ideas afterward while they are still fresh.

Be organized. Put all receipts in the same place, such as a folder or pocket. On the back of business cards from people you meet, note what was discussed for later reference.

After the convention. Share what you learned in a short presentation or report. Work with the others to put any new ideas into action. Stay in touch with the people you met at the convention. Send them follow-up notes or cards on occasion.

According to *Boardroom Reports,* another convention time-saver is to stay in a hotel near the convention site — preferably in the same hotel

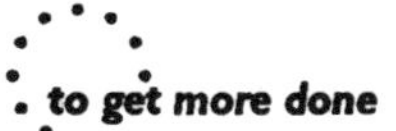

as the show or within walking distance. You'll avoid traffic tie-ups, time spent searching for buses and taxis, and time-consuming commuting.

On wings or on wheels

Whether you're traveling by car or plane, careful planning and organization is also important. It's a real time waster to jump on a plane to a faraway destination, have one "rush" meeting, and fly all the way back home again. By planning your travel schedule in advance, you'll be able to coordinate several stops in one city — or interim stops on the way or coming back — so that you can complete all your needed travel for a month in one trip. This is much less of a strain on you, your employees, and your family than one fast trip per week. One four or five day trip is no more straining than two two-day trips! Make your trips longer and make fewer trips.

When flying, there are several steps you can take to make your trip more effective.

First, have a travel agent book your flight and arrange seat reservations ahead of time, preferably in first class or to an upgraded seat so you can be either the first or the last to board. Book any connections you'll need to make far enough apart so that you're not panicked when your first flight is invariably behind schedule.

If possible, take a limousine to the airport to save on parking time and other frustrations. Make sure you have your ticket in hand before arriving at the airport so you don't need to stand in line. Arrive at the airport at least 30 minutes before flight time. Check in at the airline's frequent flyer desk or club room to avoid waiting in line with masses of humanity. You may think you're saving time by running like Carl Lewis through the airport, two minutes before take-off, but the possibility of missing the flight, forgetting something, or getting so keyed up that you can't work or relax during the flight easily cancels out the few minutes of time saved.

Join one or two airline clubs so you can get some work done while waiting for a delayed flight. These are also good places to meet clients if you are flying in to see one specific person.

There are two schools of thought regarding the "check or carry your luggage" debate. The first says that carrying your own luggage saves time waiting in the baggage claim areas, as well as the frustration of finding out the important notes you needed for that meeting in Toronto are now on their way to Tokyo. With extensive trips, however, that luggage can be a burdensome load to carry everywhere. Checking it with the skycap before entering the airport puts it out of your mind and lets you enjoy your trip that much more. Other than a single one night trip where you have light baggage we strongly recommend that you always check your baggage — the few minutes you save carrying your luggage on is not worth the aggravation. Here's a case where convenience rather than time saved makes good sense. Usually we'd recommend you carry your attache case on board though so that the important papers for the meeting are not misdirected and, in case the flight is delayed, you have material to work on in the airport waiting area.

When traveling by car, there are a number of easy preparations that will save you time, worry, and inconvenience. The first is to make sure your car is equipped. This includes a car phone, so you can keep in touch with the office, call clients, confirm directions, and summon help in an emergency. Other important equipment include a comfortable driver's seat, cruise control option, a holder for toll change, and a highway emergency kit.

In addition to a car phone, other items can be brought to help turn your car or hotel room into a portable office. While some people even have facsimile machines and answering machines hooked up in their cars, most would be satisfied with an "office on the road" kit in their briefcase. This is a convenient, compact set that includes stapler, staple remover, ruler, scissors, paper clips, pens, and other compact items. The kits can be found at office supply stores or other supply houses and are handy to have in a hotel room when you're trying to do some paperwork.

Take the time to plan your route before you leave. Try to make some extra, productive stops without going out of your way. Call a few prospects or clients that are in the area where you'll be going and try to set up appointments that will use your time away to the fullest advantage.

Keep a supply of local maps for the areas you cover, as well as a road atlas. Make sure you know all the details of how to get to your client's office — just knowing how to get to Podunk without street directions can waste a lot of time. Ask about one-way streets and other traffic patterns, too.

Finally, take along educational or motivational cassettes to use your driving time effectively — and bring a microcassette recorder for notes and memos.

Accommodations

Naturally, your travel standards will depend on your expense account limits. Staying at a Marriott or Hyatt is great for the morale but too many companies insist on using the Super 8s, Red Roofs or Budgetels.

But if you want to be able to get some work done from your hotel room, ask if the motel or hotel has an executive room available. Red Roof, one of our favorites amongst the budget hotels, has what they call an "Executive King" room. For $3-4 extra dollars per night, these include king-sized beds, full office-sized desks and credenzas, a telephone on the desk — not by the bed — and a modem jack. Lauren's biggest complaint about hotels rooms is that they don't contain a nice La-Z-Boy® Chair so that he can sit and relax in front of the tube.

A health club, or at least an indoor pool and jacuzzi, helps travelers relax and ease stress. Many hotels are also offering in-house massage services for the same purpose. And don't forget to pack two bathing suits so you've always got a dry one to get into, unless you like jumping into a cold wet swim suit. Two other options to look for in a hotel/motel are a decent restaurant that offers room service, so you don't have to leave the building at the end of the workday, and a parking space near your room.

We recommend ordering breakfast from room service to arrive at a specified time in the morning, thus saving the line in the coffee shop. Evenings can be either in the restaurant or room service as you prefer.

Working on the go

Bring along two types of work to do: heavy and light. Do the heavy work during your prime time; save the light reading for the end of the day, the long flight home, or while sitting in distracting waiting rooms. On long flights, plan time for both working and relaxing. Travel is a good time to catch up on the newsletter file that you've got in your desk drawer and have been placing light "catch up" reading. It's easy to read a four-page newspaper while spending 10 minutes waiting for a plane and it is quite productive and helps the hours in the air pass quicker. Also be sure to pack a novel for "bedtime" reading or when you don't feel like doing anything serious.

A laptop computer can also help improve productivity while on the road. On longer trips, disks can be mailed back to the office so subordinates can act on a task immediately. Portable computers and electronic organizers are also useful for listing phone numbers and addresses of clients, car rental agencies, hotels, restaurants, and other things to do in the various towns you visit. The one drawback of carrying a laptop computer is that you can't check them and they must be hand inspected at the airport. Warning: do not let the laptop go through the radar machine or you can expect to be missing much of your data! If you're at gate G-93 you'll wish you had left the laptop at home because the average laptop weighs from about six to 16 pounds and the mile walk to the gate can make the laptop feel like 93 pounds. But for convenience in the hotel room they can't be beat! Use your judgement as to whether you want to tote one along or not.

Additional time-savers

As former editor and publisher of *Execu*Time*® and an independent marketing and time management consultant/public speaker, at one time Lauren spent about 80 percent of his time traveling. Here are a few of his own tips:

- *Avoid sudden one-day trips. Schedule trips far enough in advance so you can stop and give a speech in Chicago, have dinner with a customer in Denver, visit regional offices in Seattle and Los Angeles, and then linger over a weekend of golf in San Diego to help bring you back to life before making the trip home.*

- *Take a limousine or cab to the airport — you avoid the congestion and save another 30 minutes. For distance, limousines are actually more reasonable than taxis.*

- *Avoid (at all costs) traveling near the holidays, Monday mornings and Friday evenings, as these are peak times. If possible, avoid the busy airports like Chicago O'Hare, Atlanta, and New York LaGuardia, and opt for the smaller airports where you can walk to the terminal without having to pack a lunch. I try to avoid getting up at 5 a.m. to catch a 7 a.m. flight. Better I get a dinner flight the night before, check into a comfortable hotel and wake up refreshed for my meeting.*

- *Stay at a hotel where you can get a complimentary shuttle van to and from the airport. Consider renting a car at the counter in the hotel instead of at the busy counter at the airport. I always rent a luxury car (Lincoln Town Car, Cadillac) instead of a mid-size (usually about $4-5 a day more than the mid-size), or at least a car that is no smaller than the one I normally drive. I've found Budget Rent A Car to have the best deals on luxury car rentals — but check with some of the other companies too.*

- *Use the exercise facilities at the hotel for your normal daily workout, or make sure your daily run is as long as it would be at home. A quick swim in the hotel pool and hot tub before you go to bed will relax you and make you sleep better, as well as help you work off a heavy dinner.*

- *Reduce your liquor intake for the trip and you'll feel less tired. In the four years since I've been a total abstainer from alcohol I've found much less stress in my life so you may want to discontinue alcohol consumption altogether. Alcohol is a stress producer and 10 percent of us in the American population are allergic to the stuff anyway. If alcohol is a daily habit or is giving you problems then it's time to quit.*

■   *Finally, if it fits into your schedule, extend your trip for the week-end and take your golf clubs or tennis racquet along. A couple of personal days tacked onto the end of a business trip is much like a mini-vacation and will make business travel more enjoyable. The added weekend that consists of "time for myself" is a great stress reducer and one that too many executives forget to do frequently. A few years ago while doing some consulting in Florida I spent six consecutive weeks there. I brought my golf clubs along and checked into the PGA Sheraton in West Palm Beach instead of flying home every weekend. It was like being on a six week long vacation and the resort atmosphere of the PGA Sheraton made me feel refreshed. I played a quick nine holes every night after work, played 36 on Saturday and Sunday, loafed around the pool and generally acted like I was rich for the week. It was great, particularly since I was traveling on the client's expense account for the trip.*

Look for ways to make your travel more enjoyable. A simple "Saturday" tacked onto the end of a Thursday-Friday trip in which you become a "tourista" in a strange town and return on a Sunday morning flight can make an otherwise grueling two-day trip into an enjoyable four-day holiday. ◐

Chapter 17: Summary

■ To keep meetings on track and within time limits, distribute an agenda to those attending the meeting.

■ Know the purpose of your meeting. Can you express it in one clear sentence?

■ The best way to reduce time wasted traveling is to find another method of accomplishing the job at hand.

■ Be as organized and prepared as possible before a business trip. Outline what needs to be done at the office while you're away.

chapter eighteen

Dressing For Better Managerial Effectiveness

"Style is effectiveness of assertion."
George Bernard Shaw

in the movie remake of "The Fly," Geena Davis asks Jeff Goldblum why it is he always wears the same outfit. Shocked that she would think him such a slob, he proudly opens his closet. It holds five identical outfits. "Albert Einstein did this," he explains. "It saves time and energy for more creative pursuits."

It would certainly be nice if we could don this type of uniform in the corporate world. Gone would be the time wasted each morning deciding what suit, what shirt, what tie, what earrings. Suddenly, we'd have ten more minutes to spend talking to the children, reading the paper, or riding the exercise bike.

But alas, this solution may not be accepted too well by our bosses and colleagues. Nor would it be ideal for creative types who see their clothing as a personal expression. What busy people can do to save time in this area is to spend a little time planning. We've already talked about how managers can quadruple their effectiveness with a few minutes of planning their workdays. Why not plan your wardrobe?

In our society, appearances are important. Thus, they are worth a little planning. As one commercial puts it, "You never get a second chance to make a first impression."

Planning pays off in saved time, saved dollars, and an improved corporate image. It may take a little homework, but the benefits are well worth the effort.

How to plan your wardrobe

Let's face facts. Many people hate to shop. Others may enjoy it but rarely have the time. And some would probably enjoy it a whole lot more if money were not involved. (Too bad we couldn't reverse the process and receive money as an incentive. "Good choice, Sam! You've earned $50!")

Planning a wardrobe, on the other hand, eases the pain and frustration of shopping because the buyer knows what he or she needs. With a well-planned wardrobe intact, most people need only to shop once or twice a year to freshen up or expand their wardrobes. Even adding one simple accessory can create several new outfits.

Or, consider getting your wardrobe in shape without spending your own time on the project. Call in a wardrobe consultant! These services are available for about $100 to $400, and are even offered as a benefit by firms who want to make sure their representatives are impressively attired.

The first step in planning a wardrobe is to develop a "color capsule," suggests M. J. Cross, a consultant to many major corporations and nationally-known speaker and seminar leader on corporate image and executive dressing. (One Brighton, Oak Brook, IL, 60521, 708/574-8323, FAX 708/574-7373) This involves not only knowing what colors are best for you personally, but what colors are appropriate for your particular job, and what colors and image will affect the response you desire. Centering a wardrobe around a few basic colors can make dressing for everyday office, as well as packing for travel, a breeze.

For men, there are three basic colors appropriate for business suits. According to Lois Fenton, author of *Dress for Excellence,* these are blue, gray and tan, ranging from medium to dark, and light to medium tan. Of course, this may vary slightly through seasons or warmer climates, but generally there are no browns, no greens, no bright or powder blues in the board room.

President Ronald Reagan probably lessened this "rule" as he was well known for wearing brown suits during his White House years. Generally you need be more cautious with the color of brown for a business suit than you do the other colors.

Although women have more choice in the matter of style and color, just a few suit colors are safe in any business situation, writes Emily Cho in *Looking, Working, Living Terrific 24 Hours a Day*. These include brown, beige, gray, black, navy, burgundy, camel, and rust. Other colors can be added to the look with blouses, scarves, or other accessories.

Once you decide what colors your wardrobe will center around, take stock of the items already in your closet. Remove anything that's worn, that clashes with your color scheme, or that hasn't been worn in at least a year. It may sound extreme, but once a wardrobe is more focused it will make getting dressed a lot easier. And look at all that free room for new items! Think of a closet as you would a filing cabinet. Would you rather hold onto unnecessary and outdated files "just in case," only to double or triple the time you spend looking for the files you really need? Or do you purge those unnecessary files periodically to simplify the process?

Mistakes to avoid

Common mistakes are made by both men and women. And ignorance is no excuse. If the following pitfalls sound familiar, they could be tarnishing your professional image or sending out mixed signals about who you really are. A sales representative who's trying to convince a client that his product line is state-of-the-art and up to date, for instance, may not go too far if it's obvious that his polyester shirt was a high school graduation gift.

According to Cross, fashion mistakes made by men often result from being too frugal. "Polyester does wear pretty well but if it pills or becomes outdated, it still needs to be replaced." Nothing replaces the wool blend suit for best appearance and long life. Yet some people feel they need to hold onto these items until the elbows are worn through.

Some men have difficulty realizing what items go together to create a coherent style, she adds. They may combine a conservative suit with casual shoes or a sporty watch. Or, they wear excessive jewelry when they need to look conservative. Wing-tip loafers are not casual shoes though are just as comfortable as a pair of penny loafers.

When is it acceptable for a male executive to spend the day working without a tie? A survey by search firm Robert Half International Inc. asked respondents this very question. The results: only two percent answered that spending the working day without a tie is always acceptable, while an overwhelming 69 percent said the practice is never acceptable. Twenty-six reported that it was generally not acceptable; two percent said it was generally acceptable; and one percent said working without a tie was generally acceptable, except when meeting with visitors.

We feel that there are exceptions to this rule — mainly in very small (under $10 million in sales or 200 employees) companies where an informal atmosphere prevails and the standard "dress" among the entire management staff becomes slacks and golf shirts or open collared shirts without ties and sport coats for going out of the building. But even in a situation like that it is desirable for the executive to keep a good suit, white shirt and tie hanging in the office to make a quick change when a client meeting is necessary. Of course, most entrepreneurs working from home-based offices abandon the shirt, suit and tie regimen when working in their own office.

The same survey also asked how acceptable it is for a company's executives to work without a jacket. This met with a little more approval. The majority of respondents — 36 percent — said this is generally acceptable, except when meeting visitors, while another 35 percent simply said it was generally acceptable. Twenty percent of respondents said the practice was always acceptable; 8 percent said it was generally not acceptable; and only 1 percent said it was never acceptable.

Because women's fashions offer more variety, it can make choosing what's best a difficult decision. Often the various choices offered lead us to become fashion victims. "Flamboyant styles don't translate well to a professional image," says Cross. Some women mix the wrong accessories — extravagant earrings, for example — with conservative suits.

It's important to know what items are meant for work and what's "after five." If a look is too flamboyant, it can distract people from the business at hand, adds Cross.

Another problem that both sexes make is taking the fit for granted. Too often, people tend to pull items off the rack and "make do," says Cross. They don't allow for their body's idiosyncracies. To avoid calling attention to a wide derriere, or looking like you're wearing clothes a size too big, know what type of tailoring is necessary to show you at your best. If you can afford it, custom-tailored is always the way to go.

For men, Mortimer Levitt, author of *The Executive Look: How to Get it — How to Keep it,* offers the following suggestions:

Wear two plains, but only one fancy. If you wear a suit that is patterned, striped or checked, your shirt and tie should be plain. If you choose a fancy shirt, try it with a plain suit and plain tie. There are a few exceptions to this rule, but for quick dressing, keep it in mind and you'll avoid mistakes.

The base color (suit) may be accented by a brighter color (tie and/or shirt). In business environments, the suit should always serve as the base color, such as gray, navy, or tan. Say you've chosen a plain gray suit and a blue accent color. Try a blue shirt and a blue and gray striped tie. Or, with a gray plaid suit that has burgundy accents, wear a plain maroon tie for accent, with a light gray or white shirt.

Wear light with dark and dark with light— but not all light or all dark. Dark suits look best when you wear a light shirt and tie. And light suits are set off by darker shirts and ties. But if you have dark skin or a suntan, a light suit can be quite attractive with a white or cream-colored shirt.

Don't choose your shirt collar on size and style alone. You should also look at the height of the collar at the back and at the front from the base of the neck upward. Ill-fitting collars are a common flaw in many people's dress — too tight, or poorly-suited to the length of

their necks. Men regularly make the mistake of buying too small a shirt collar size just because they have always taken that size — but collar size is affected by weight gain.

Other hints from Levitt, as reported in *Money* magazine, include:

■ *avoid gaudy cuff links and tie clips;*

■ *cuffs improve the hang of trousers, though not popular today;*

■ *a white handkerchief improves the appearance of suits while perched in the top jacket pocket but very few people wear them anymore;*

■ *Hong Kong suits are more often than not disappointing and not the bargain that is often advertised;*

■ *made-to-measure London suits are always a good investment, but you must be in London two weeks for fittings, etc. The famed Regent street tailors are very expensive but worth every penny you pay. Mr. Januz has bought several custom-made suits and sport coats in the shopping area just off Picadilly Circus with great success and a 4-5 day turnaround. Shops in that area tend to look more like fabric stores but most have custom tailors on premises and are half the cost of the Regent Street tailors. Use caution in shopping in London for executive suits and you won't go wrong;*

■ *your overcoat should be at least two to three inches below the knee — or up to six to eight inches if you like a long coat;*

■ *polyester shirts don't wrinkle, but their appearance is seldom as good as cotton. There is seldom a substitute for a good broadcloth cotton blend shirt. Button-down Oxford cloth usually presents a good appearance unless you're quite heavy, in which case they should be avoided.*

Organizing your wardrobe

Once you have the suits, the shoes, and the accessories to project the image you want to convey, these items need to be organized so your investment doesn't go to waste. Kim has several items that she wears about once a year because they wrinkle so easily while being smashed against other clothing in my closet. Don't do this! There are too many nifty gadgets and organization systems on the market to justify a messy closet.

Before you spend any money on these gadgets — and it's easy to do — organize what you have by hanging like items together. For example, put all long sleeve shirts or blouses in a row, then short sleeve shirts, then dress pants, followed by skirts and suits. Within each category, it's also helpful to group things according to color, such as hanging blouses from white to dark.

Specialty "organization stores," discount stores, and department stores are finally realizing that we don't have the time to stand in front of our closets for twenty minutes looking for that gray suit. They've come out with a host of space-saving ideas, some of which are better than others. The products Kim has found to be successful include:

- *Special hangers designed to hold five pairs of pants or skirts by layering several hangers vertically;*

- *Clear plastic storage boxes for shoes and small items. Look for the kind with a pull-out drawer so you don't have to unstack them to get to the bottom box;*

- *Canvas or nylon shoe bags that fit over the closet rod or back of the door. These are good for everyday shoes that you turn to often;*

- *A grid system, which features pegs to hang scarves, belts, and similar accessories. Try to fit as much in your closet as possible. Things in a closet are easier to find and easier to put away than items in a dresser drawer;*

- *"Elfa" or similar closet systems. These are entire systems, available by*

component and designed to make clutter a thing of the past. You pick the components you need: stacked drawers, double closet rods, shelving, even a drawer for ties or jewelry. A double closet rod system - one above, one below — is probably one of the best investments an executive can make , believes Lauren.

With the variety of interesting products available, it's easy to waste a few dollars on things that aren't really necessary. Know what you need before you start looking for it, or you'll be buying strange new gadgets and saying, "I'll find some use for this."

Other products sound good in theory, but don't translate well into practice. For example, the vertical clips that hold five hangers in the space of one (see illustration) are all right for pants and sweaters, but not for shirts that could wrinkle. These items need a little breathing room. Hanging nylon sweater bags, which feature six or so fabric "shelves," present another problem: they're not sturdy enough to hold the weight of more than three sweaters. Look for plastic instead. Finally, throw out your cardboard shoe boxes. They usually end up collecting nothing but dust, space, and a pair of shoes that can never be seen, and are rarely worn as a result.

Once you've established a place for everything, it will take far less time to find the outfits you need — and find them in good shape. At the risk of sounding *too* obsessed, another time saver is to take a few minutes over the weekend and line up your outfits for the workweek. Even going so far as to hang ties, jewelry, and other accessories with your suit will really save some time. Let that morning energy go toward an activity more important than deciding if you should wear black two days in a row.

Along with dress go a few other comments about the executive appearance and image.

The attache case — while the "*Land's End*®" canvas bag has become very, very popular for some managers, it probably doesn't belong in the hand of a person who is a vice president or above. There is little short of the Hartmann attache bag or a deluxe Canadian belting

using time management

leather for the best image. In our opinion, the Hartmann bag is not only overpriced but also too heavy for practical trips, although Lauren has had exceptional luck with a good 3" Canadian belting leather bag.

Unless you're in sales try to avoid the 5" attache case and avoid any molded plastic bag — they look too "repairman" oriented. Try and stick with a good 3" attache and expect to pay $300-400 for a good bag that will take travel well and still be looking good in two years or so.

The car driven by an executive should be reflective of the position. While the red or yellow sporty vehicle is fine for the younger middle manager a dark-colored (grey, black, blue, maroon) full-sized four-door sedan is the only appropriate vehicle for a senior executive. If you opt for imports consider a luxury import over the cheap Oriental imports for the right image. A CEO who drives up in a Toyota or Toshiba just doesn't create the proper image. Volvos, Saabs and other less popular cars create a "liberal college professor" image and usually not a good image for a senior executive. With the possible exception of the new Lexus avoid the Oriental imports. Nothing will replace the black or gray Lincoln Town Car, Cadillac, Chrysler or the big Mercedes for proper executive image. Avoid bright colors at all costs — conservative colors contribute toward executive images. Bright colors spell youth and immaturity. Needless to say, a twice-weekly trip through a full-service car wash is worth every penny it costs to help the image.

A senior executive who pulls up in a two-seater sportscar or a convertible presents an image of a playboy (or playgirl) and probably should be avoided.

Your pen set — an investment in a gold-filled *Cross®*, *Shaeffer®* or *Garland®* pen is probably the best investment an executive can make to enhance the right image. The new "dull black" finishes and "wood finishes" are fine but avoid any pen that has somebody's advertising imprint on it unless it is a simple corporate crest on the pen clip and then only if the crest is a Fortune 500 company or your bank.

Your watch — a *Rolex®* watch spells success automatically, but any deluxe dress watch with a conservative band can do the same.

Gimmick watches such as "diver's watches" or a watch with nautical flags do not contribute to the personal executive image. Avoid the *Timex®* or other "over the counter brand" that looks cheap. Digital watches are now passe and can be bought in any drug store for $25. The historic Hamilton type watch with arms is part of success. Expect to pay $300-1000 for a good executive watch. Lauren has a fake "Rolex" watch that he bought in Tijuana that looks identical to the real thing. If you go to the Orient or Mexico you may be able to find one for as little as $25.

How executives dress and the pens or briefcases they carry has an effect on how others respond to them. Choose them carefully. ◐

Chapter 18: Summary

■ **To save time in the mornings, plan your wardrobe just as you plan your week.**

■ **Know your "color capsule": the colors that best suit your personality and your job.**

■ **Avoid overdressing with too many accessories, a mistake more commonly made by women than by men.**

■ **Examine the many closet organizers on the market to save time searching for certain items.**

using time management

chapter nineteen

Using Time Management In The Home

"The difference between life and the movies is that a script has to make sense, and life doesn't."
Joseph L. Mankiewicz — All About Eve

Should To Do lists and other time management techniques be used at home? Many dual career couples think so. So do many parents who are also full time professionals. In this era of striving for the "superparent" or perfectionist model, managing stress and crises is an ongoing challenge. Intelligent use of time has become just as important in our personal lives as it is at the office.

When a job takes 40-50 hours of our time every week, how can we cope effectively with demands from children, spouses, household tasks, health problems, or other personal problems? A licensed daycare mother in Indiana offered a valuable solution, which she gleaned by reading her husband's issues of the *Execu*Time®* newsletter.

"As I have four children, run a licensed daycare home, am enrolled in an English Composition class, and am public relations coordinator for our area Girl Scouts, I find it necessary to be as organized as possible," she begins. "I use a loose-leaf folder as a calendar with one page for each day of the week. For example, I type one daily schedule to use every Monday of the year, then I photocopy 52 copies for my folder. On this schedule I include whose library books or gym clothes should be put out for the following day, any regularly scheduled piano or dancing lessons for the kids, and household tasks which are done every Monday, such as watering plants, laundry, and planning meals for the week. As a result, I no longer have to waste time writing the same To Do list every Monday. I simply write in any extra activities I want to accomplish." In addition, she simplifies meal planning tasks with a master menu designed to include two weeks of breakfasts, lunches, and snacks. Only the dinner menu needs updating. She also has a master list of grocery needs specifically created for her family.

Have you ever been out of town on business, only to remember your mother was celebrating her birthday as you were making that connecting flight? Try writing birthdays and anniversaries in your calendar, as well as a tickler reminder a few days before so you have enough time to send a card or gift.

Every executive juggles three parts of himself or herself: personal needs, professional needs, and family needs. At times, any one of these balls may "drop," but the challenge is to keep them all successfully in the air, at least for most of the time. Doctors Barrie S. Greiff and Preston K. Munter have studied this balancing act and come up with some important guidelines for the executive and the dual career family. They include:

- Constantly think in three dimensions: self, family, and organization.
- Don't become too rigid.
- Keep your eyes open for problems in the making.
- Constantly reassess what you're doing and how you feel about it.
- Allow time for yourself and your needs.
- Find satisfying hobbies and interests outside of work.

A compensation consultant for a Chicago financial firm handles the personal/family/work balance in a similar manner. "To keep everything balanced, you need to maintain good relationships and to do things for yourself physically, spiritually, and intellectually." At 45 hours per week, her work is her intellectual outlet. In addition, she works out three nights a week in aerobics classes, attends a weekly bible study group and church on Sundays. This type of activity helps her to put her all into her family and professional life.

"You need to manage your priorities according to the stages of your life," she adds. Realize that you can't do everything at the same time. Greiff and Munter agree. Concepts like "success," "goals," and "objectives," they say, should not be written in stone. They vary depending on the circumstances. Be flexible and be prepared to change emphasis if one area of your life needs attention.

Thirdly, they add, it's important to face facts promptly regarding career advancement, problems in your marriage, kids' shortcomings, etc. Putting your head in the sand will only complicate matters when they come to a head and you're forced to deal with them.

When negative feelings surface, get away from the hustle and bustle for a bit to sit down and think things out clearly. Don't forsake spontaneity for organization. Spend some time with family and friends to get away from routine responsibilities once in a while. Finally, spend time getting to know yourself and developing interests outside of work. This will help keep your self image from being totally dependent upon success in your career.

To add time to their crowded schedules, many people's first reactions are to forgo the exercise class or other personal interests. Yet taking care of yourself — both mentally and physically — will also help you cope better with household and family demands. A good analogy cited in a magazine article about this subject reminds us that, on plane flights, parents are instructed to don their own oxygen masks before helping children in the event of an emergency. If it were done the other way around, the parents just wouldn't be as effective.

Dual career guidelines

When both spouses work, it's necessary to look at the "balancing act" from another perspective, say Greiff and Munter. First, articulate your goals and make sure that both spouses are aware of individual, mutual, and family goals. Be able to delegate and use outside sources to further your goals, for everything from report writing to cleaning the

to get more done

house. The "superman" or "superwoman" syndrome often results in guilt or disappointment.

If you feel guilty having fun while laundry, errands, and other household tasks go begging, consider delegating the tedious work to others. If your children are old enough to take on more family responsibility, perhaps they could help. Or, look at the costs of outside services. Many people tend to write off household help as too expensive and are surprised to find out how little some types of help cost. Why spend an entire weekend washing windows or wallpapering if an outside service can do it for a reasonable price? Still, many well-paid managers, not realizing the value of their own time, hesitate to spend a few dollars an hour for hired help. The trade-off comes down to this: examine what is available in terms of money and time. Learn to budget personal time just as you do money.

Dual career couples need to make sure their energy levels can accommodate their hectic schedules. If you don't have the necessary high energy level, something or someone will suffer — and it may well be you or your children. They also need to make decisions promptly, using whatever information is available. Be resourceful, suggest Greiff and Munter, have back-up babysitters, meals, and transportation lined up and ready for emergencies.

The debate between mothers who work outside of the home and those who make their households a full-time commitment has been going on for decades. Dual career pairs are sometimes subject to comment by family members and more "traditional" couples who may resent their success. Don't let guilt get to you! It can lead to biting off more than you can chew. Assess your own lifestyle and priorities and accept the fact that you cannot coach every team or run every bazaar in town. Community work can be done, however, as can help with children's activities.

Many successful time managers are well-rounded individuals with deep feelings about community involvement and career development. But a busy executive — especially one with a travel schedule to contend with — may have real difficulty making a regular commitment to weekly community activities. Here are a few alternatives.

using time management

- *Sign up for concentrated activities. Perhaps you can't commit every Tuesday to a boys' club meeting, but you could arrange an annual camp-out or fund-raiser. The same goes for working mothers who can't commit as room mothers for their children's classes because of work schedules. Perhaps they could volunteer for a Saturday bake sale or help arrange an evening open house.*

- *Do community work that can be completed on your own time. Keeping books for an organization, making phone calls, and other vital work can be done at a time that suits you.*

- *Arrange for a monthly commitment. Perhaps you can't be around every week for an activity, but many community boards meet only once a month. Planning around just one date is much easier than around four or five each month.*

Another problem working couples with an endless lists of commitments complain of is not having quality time together. Try to schedule time to do things as a couple and remember what it is that draws to you to this person. Make an appointment for dinner with your spouse Saturday night and keep it as scrupulously as you would a business date.

Finally, realize that if you have children, their lives will necessarily be different than the lives of kids with a parent who stays home. Accept this fact, and work out your own way of quality child rearing.

Additional time-saving tips

To Do lists and quiet hours can be just as effective at home as they are in the office. Try making up a To Do list for the weekend, making sure to include plenty of time for rest and relaxation. Schedule time for a ball game to balance those two hours spent working on your taxes. Write down a reminder to call relatives or friends out of town. If you do a bit of advance planning, you'll find Mondays will not always lead to that lost "where did the time go" feeling.

Everyone needs some time to themselves, but busy managers — especially those in two-career families — must do some real planning

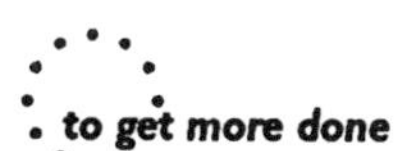

to carve out that special time. Perhaps you can plan to get up an hour before anyone else in the family and have a quiet hour to sort out your feelings, plan your day, read for pleasure, or take a restful walk or brisk jog. These quiet moments can help relieve tension, which is just as harmful at home as it is in your business life. Some busy parents enjoy spending a few hours alone on Saturday mornings to visit the library and catch up on personal reading.

Below are a few other time-saving ideas for organizing your home and family life.

Use the mail. Why bank or pay bills in person? You can shop by mail or phone, too. Even postage stamps can be bought by phone or mail. If you must go to a store in person, at least call ahead to find out if the store has what you are looking for.

Save time grocery shopping. Avoid long lines — do your grocery shopping early in the week instead of over the weekend. Around 6 p.m. on weekdays and 8-9 a.m. on weekends are the least-crowded times. Consider shopping every two weeks or once a month for staple and frozen items. Then make short weekly trips to a local produce store for fresh fruits and vegetables. Keep a list in the kitchen of things you need, and have your family write down items as they run low. Or, consider making up a master list of everything you ever buy in the grocery store, preferably conforming to the layout of the store you shop in. That way, instead of writing out a list each week, you can simply check off the items you need.

Organize your finances. Have a financial corner in your home, and keep all money-related items there. Stack bills in a "due" folder or file, and set definite times to pay them in a batch — perhaps once or twice a month. Some people prefer to take this folder with them while waiting for doctors' appointments, etc.

Choose your service people well. Make sure they are truly time-saving and do not just do what seems expedient. For instance, should your dry cleaner, auto repair shop, and shoe repair shop really be in your home neighborhood, or would you be better off dealing with someone near work? Try to find services on your commuting route to save time. Use the same services repeatedly to become a known and valued customer, and you may then be able to get special fast service when you need it.

Don't be glued to the tube. Schedule your television viewing. Limit yourself to a few favorite shows each week, rather than flopping down and watching whatever comes on. Or, tape the shows you must see but watch them only when it's convenient. Spend more time reading, exercising, or catching up on rest than you do watching television.

Keep sets of spare keys. Keep duplicate keys for your home, car, and office in a safe, handy place, such as your briefcase, wallet, or purse. If you misplace your main keys, you will be covered. This is a real time-saver for the absent-minded.

Get the family together in the morning. With parents at work, children at school all day, and activities and relaxation scheduled for the evening, it may be difficult for the family to get together to talk or share things. Try doing this at breakfast. Get up a bit earlier and assign each person a job: the little ones can set the table, older children help cook, and everyone clean up. Newspapers, television, and radio should be left firmly in the "off" position to encourage conversation. Make sure you start early enough so that everyone can linger a bit, enjoying an oasis of leisure before the hectic day begins.

If mornings are too difficult, another idea for family togetherness is a regular night out at an inexpensive restaurant. The distractions of TV, homework, or drop-in visitors are avoided, and everyone will have more energy for communication without having to worry about cooking and clean-up chores.

Forget perfection. Especially where two-career families are concerned, perfection in household management is an outmoded goal.

to get more done

Strive simply to make everything adequately clean, comfortable, and complete. Clean only what's at eye level on a regular basis, leaving the other areas for times when they really need it.

Keep in touch with the family. Make sure you have a "communications center" in your home so that people going in and out know where to look for the latest family bulletins. The kitchen is the best place or right by the door where everyone comes in. This is where children can leave notes stating their whereabouts and where the day's chores or appointments can be posted.

Bunch your appointments. If you have to sit in the doctor's or dentist's office and wait, make sure you do it only once. Get check-up appointments for yourself and all the children at the same time, and do the same for other types of appointments whenever possible.

Teach your family systems and make them practice them. Don't simply tell children to clean the bathroom or do a load of laundry without telling them how to do it — unless you don't mind turning those wool slacks into Bermuda shorts. In addition, make sure children understand how often various household chores need to be done. Make sure they know that cleaning rooms, dusting and vacuuming can be done weekly, but making beds is a daily task, for instance. If your son feels he should vacuum his room only every two weeks instead of weekly, accept it as long as he sticks to that schedule. Having him do this job every two weeks is still better than having you do it every week.

Sort laundry as it collects. Get a laundry cart with three compartments — one for whites, colors, and delicate items. Train your family to put their clothes in the proper areas to cut down on sorting. This also makes it easier to do a load of laundry when you really need a particular sweater washed, for instance.

Keep paperwork under control. At the very least, sort through your mail and other papers once a week before you create a monster.

Make sure bills are put in the "Bills Due" folder. Read school reports, sign, and return. Mark invitation days and times on your calendar. File useless items in the circular file to avoid shuffling them over and over.

Shop only twice a year for clothes. With planning, you can do your major shopping in spring and fall trips to your favorite stores, all at once. Do the same for your children. And use the phone or mail order catalogs to order standard items your family needs.

Keep repairs under control. When you remove a garment, check it for needed cleaning and repairs and set it aside if such help is needed. Get the item to the cleaner or tailor, do not hang it up and put off repairs or an important part of your wardrobe will be out for the season.

Do your social calendar every month. Have a social calendar on which you list parties, birthdays, weddings, and activities. At the beginning of the month, list all the presents you will need and buy them, along with wrapping paper and cards, all at once. Or, order gifts by mail or phone and have them wrapped and sent to the recipient. Some department stores offer a gift-buying service, in which personal shoppers select, wrap, and deliver gifts.

Entertain simply and stay calm. Guests enjoy a relaxed barbecue or buffet much more than a tense seven-course dinner. If you scale down the formality of your entertaining, your guests will probably be relieved and do the same when they return the favor.

Accept invitations selectively. Learn to say no to social engagements that do not interest you. You do not owe it to anyone to spend an evening just being social if you do not find it pleasant. Refuse politely and with thanks; this is much more sincere than a reluctant acceptance.

Schedule idleness on your vacations. Busy executives cannot hope to take whirlwind vacations and return refreshed. The purpose of an executive's vacation is to wind down and get a new perspective on things, so opt for the Caribbean beach vacation rather than the ten-day, eight-country European fling.

Have a Blondie's "Job Jar". The comic strip "Blondie" used a "job jar" for Dagwood Bumstead to have projects around the house that had to be attacked. This really was a great time management idea — a jar of "projects" that the kids or parents can attack. Every Saturday morning a number of jobs are drawn for projects for the weekend from the job jar. An estimated time should be put on the slip in the job jar so that you don't select too many projects to attack on a Saturday/Sunday.

Look for other household time-management tips. Service magazines and other publications often feature articles and columns on time management and household shortcuts, so read them and use them wisely for a richer, more rewarding home and family life. ◑

Chapter 19: Summary

■ **Use To Do lists for household chores, just as you use them at the office.**

■ **Keep duplicate copies of master lists to simplify such tasks as grocery shopping or meal planning.**

■ **Realize that you can't do everything at once. And delegate chores that could be handled by another family member or outside service.**

PART IV
Tools For
Effective Time
Management

chapter twenty

Office Automation

In this chapter, we use the term office automation to describe the tools and machines available to make an office more productive. We'll touch on time-saving equipment such as computers, facsimile machines, and copiers. Dictating machines and telephone systems are described in detail later in this book.

Some people shy away from learning about these products. They may reason: "It's not my responsibility to learn about computers — I'm a salesperson," or "Things are changing so fast, what's the point of trying to learn about them today if they'll be obsolete tomorrow?"

But according to an Accountemps survey, familiarity with bytes, modems, disk drives, and cursors is an absolutely necessary weapon for that trek up the corporate ladder. The survey showed that 70 percent of top personnel executives believe that some computer proficiency is either important, very important, or essential, while the rest are almost unanimous in their opinion that such knowledge is, at the very least, helpful.

If you want to control your own destiny, or even your own *day* for that matter, your input in these equipment purchase decisions can only help you. Otherwise, you'll have no one to blame but yourself when you're standing over the facsimile machine without an automatic feed, thinking about the more important things you could be doing in those fifteen minutes.

To the other extreme, some managers are so obsessed with new, automated products that they begin to focus on technology and information generation for its own sake. This is the finding of office technical specialist John J. Connell. He says executives need to remember that their focus should be on the function of the office — that combination of people, machines, support services, and facilities that makes for productivity.

Too many data processing managers get hung up on having the latest toys, points out Connell, instead of recommending a more modest computer set-up that might serve the office more effectively at a lower cost.

Amazement at the reams of reports that a new computer system can spin out may lead managers to create such reports unnecessarily, leaving hundreds of managers with computer print-outs flipped over their desks like Slinky toys. Because the reports are so cumbersome, they're seldom read.

Connell's suggestion: rather than "hooking in" to new technologies, today's manager should come up with goals and a business plan to achieve them before looking for a technological solution. "One cannot manage the office, and the people, machines, and facilities used in the office, without also being concerned about what the office is all about: the acquisition, processing, storage, retrieval, and dissemination of information — information that is the lifeblood of the enterprise. Some philosophy of information management has to emerge or we will have information chaos. But too little is known today about information and its characteristics to make it the basis for addressing the future office."

Personal computers

Without a doubt, the computer has made the most important contributions to time management. If used correctly, it can save managers from repeating steps, typing the same material twice; it can even dial their phones for them. Just about every profession can benefit from these features.

One Chicago attorney often complained of a time management problem that found him spending too much time managing his practice and not enough time at the practice of law. The time he had to spend working with changes in laws, procedures, regulations, and other details cut down on the challenging and lucrative time he could actually spend working with clients. He purchased two word processors, one which serves mainly to maintain a diary of client phone conversations, and the other for giving instructions to his staff. The result has been a 50 percent improvement of productivity among his three secretaries.

While an entire book can easily be devoted to the subject of what to look for in a computer (and, in fact, many such books are available), we'll try to cover the basics.

First, decide what you need to computerize. What information could be better managed by a computer system? The idea is to find a computer system that fits your business, not to change your business to suit the computer. A vital part of this decision is to take a good look at software programs available for your industry. What exactly <u>can</u> be computerized? According to computer experts, novices often make the mistake of choosing the hardware system without proper regard for what type of software will best benefit management. Many of the best business software programs are available for IBM PC and compatible systems. And while the Apple systems are terrific for graphics, desktop publishing, and educational needs, not too many of them are found in the executive suite. Apple is popular for desk-top publishing applications and strong in education but it hasn't made a strong bite (no pun intended) in the quest for the office market. DOS (IBM's operating system) is far and away the leader in that marketplace.

Service and flexibility are also important areas to consider. If the computer has to be shipped back to the manufacturer to be serviced, can you afford the time to do that? Often companies become so dependent on their computer systems, the answer is no. While looking for a personal computer for her business, Kim had to rule out what looked like a great deal for a similar reason. When she asked the sales representative at the newly-opened (and cheap) "Dan's Computer Outlet" where she could have the computer serviced, he replied "You bring it back here."

Wonderful, she thought, and where do I bring it *next* year after Dan disappears in the bankruptcy court?

The Association of Computer Users, Boulder, Colorado, (P.O. Box 9003, Boulder, CO 80301) offers a service called "Benchmark Reports," which publishes a regular report on "How to Select a Small Computer." The association also offers "Ten Pitfalls to Avoid in Buying a Small Computer." They are:

1. **Don't "buy backwards."** Determine first what you need the computer for and what you expect it to do. Many people make the mistake of choosing a machine for its flashy image and then finding that it is not suited for the work at hand.

2. **Don't buy without a contract.** Make sure the agreement to purchase includes all terms of importance, such as warranty, service, timing, etc. Otherwise, you can be "left in the lurch" with a purchase of thousands of dollars that is "out of commission" for a long period of time.

3. **Be sure you test out the equipment.** Would you purchase a new car without taking at least one test drive? Surely not. But many computer buyers bring the equipment into the office without even trying a software program to see how it performs. Use some "live" software — not a demo program which may be set up to hide the performance limitations of the equipment.

4. **Determine your specifications.** Unfortunately, many computer purchasers "buy blind" without a list of exactly what the machine's capabilities should be. Have someone study specific requirements so that you can set them forth for your salesperson.

5. **Don't pass the buck on decision making.** It is tempting to delegate the entire computer selection and purchase to a lower-level employee, but such a purchase usually requires a much more broad view of the company's needs and goals. Otherwise, you may end up

with a machine which suits the needs of only one department, or
will be hopelessly inadequate after a planned spurt of growth.

6. **Don't expect the computer to be an overall panacea.**
    Computers are wonderful machines, but they will not save a failing
    business, make decisions for you, or explain things that you don't
    understand. Nor will they allow you to make immediate staff
    reductions in most cases.

7. **Understand the full cost of what you buy.** In budgeting,
    don't think of the computer alone, but also consider the software
    costs, hardware extras, installation, extra personnel, etc.

8. **Make sure you get a good supplier.** Computer salespeople
    may come on as technical types, but they are salespeople — make no
    mistake about it. Do not consider them to be totally "on your side."
    Look for recommendations for a good computer vendor.

9. **Strive for a long horizon.** A computer is a large capital invest-
    ment, and you should do all you can to make sure it serves your
    needs far into the future. Don't buy a "dead end" machine — look
    forward to the extra capacity and functions you will need "down the
    road" and purchase the computer that can grow with you.

10. **Do you really need a computer?** The fact that competitors
    have them, or that it feeds your ego to have a computer does not
    mean that you need one. Think this through carefully — the reason
    to get a computer is to help you make more money or reduce costs.
    Can a computer do that for you?

Other items to consider before you buy hardware include the keyboard,
monitor, and storage capabilities. How does the keyboard feel? Are the keys
positioned in a comfortable and familiar location? You should feel comfortable typing on it for any length of time. Also, consider whether you'd prefer
the keyboard attached to the computer or not.

Many software programs work well with color monitors. WordPerfect, for example, can run on either a color or monochrome monitor but color helps to differentiate various features, such as large type. If you choose a monochrome monitor, be sure to get one that puts less strain on the eyes. An amber monitor, for instance, is better than a black and white version.

How much memory, or K (kilobytes), can the computer hold? Although more memory is more expensive, it also makes the system easier and faster to run. If you're going to be running graphics or desktop publishing programs, additional memory is usually necessary. Can you expand it later if necessary, or add another drive? Try to buy as much memory as your budget allows, and certainly as much as the software you've selected requires. About 640K to 2MB (megabtyes) is a common range, although most MS-DOS compatibles can be expanded to as much as 8 MB or bigger. Pocket computers today frequently come with as much as 64K and portables frequently come in 2 MB or more. If you have any intention of running a program such as Microsoft Windows (more on this later) make sure to put an *absolute minimum* of 2 MB in the computer, preferably 4MB.

Modems

Modems allow your computer to communicate over the phone lines. A modem can automatically dial a phone number, work in combination with a computer fax-board, transmit documents to the computer of a client or co-worker, and access on-line information services. In this respect, they are a real time saver. Various data banks offer news reports, encyclopedias, stock information, and news of interest to your specific industry.

The speed at which a modem operates is called the baud rate. This refers to the number of electronic bits transmitted per second. Typical baud rates are 1200, 2400, and up to 9600. Speeds of 2400 baud are usually necessary to load large-scale text or graphics. Although modems do not have to be of the same speed to communicate, the unit with the slower speed will set the pace. Look for a "Hayes" or "Hayes-compatible" standard. We have a "Zoom" brand modem that we're delighted with. An internal modem today costs as little as $150-300 — hardly something you can pass by anymore!

Laptop computers

Laptop computers can be a real time-saver for executives. At six to eight pounds, the battery-operated units can easily fit in a briefcase and be toted along on business trips, on the daily train commute, to the library, or to meetings. Many of the units offer full-sized keyboards with a smaller sized screen than is available on a regular PC. They can be used for word processing, appointment scheduling, and telephone and address logs. Or, you can install the same programs used at the office. A word of caution about laptops: be sure to back up everything you do on a laptop daily and make sure the vendor has a service facility in the U.S.A. — Lauren had one Canadian built laptop blow its hard disc seven times over a nine month period. Each time he lost all the data on the hard disc and each time it had to go to the factory it had to go through Canadian customs — a round trip of about six weeks time. Fortunately, he was backed up!

Copying machines

Yes, even a copying machine can be a time-saver — if you look for the right features. Automatic sheet feed, collating, and stapling save people from doing these tasks manually. To save time and avoid subjective decision making, here are some points to keep in mind when comparing office copiers:

- *What will the copier be used for? Do you need one or two copies of many different items or large quantities of fewer items?*

- *How reliable are the brands you are comparing? What kinds of warranties do they have?*

- *Compare costs, but also compare financing arrangements. In these days of skyrocketing interest rates, the difference can be substantial.*

- *When you call for service, how long will you have to wait? Ask for references who can vouch for the salesperson's answers.*

- *Compare copy quality for the price — do you need perfect copies, or suitable reproductions?*

- *What is the anticipated monthly or annual volume of copies you'll make? Have you chosen the most economical machine for this volume?*

- *Compare reputations of the copier firms you're considering. Get input from reliable sources as to which copiers have performed best for them.*

Other areas to look at include ease of use, speed, paper capacity, and enlargement and reduction capabilities.

Facsimile machines

It's been called "the Superman of document transporters." With it your business can make leaps in productivity, decrease postage costs from 25 cents to two cents per page, and save hundreds of dollars on phone bills.

It is, of course, the fax machine. As competition in this field has increased, prices have gone down. Fax machines are now available for anywhere from $500 to about $4,000. That price buys the ability to transfer a one-page document for the same price as a one-minute phone call; unattended, automatic reception; and a simple-to-use machine that will no doubt boost productivity.

Just look at previous methods used for a quick telephone inquiry. A phone call is made and after a transfer or two and a minute on hold, the intended party comes on the line. If the person is a familiar contact, there will probably be a minute or two of "Hi, how are you, how was that vacation, etc." before getting to the point of the phone call, perhaps followed by another minute on hold or worse, "I'll get back to you." With a facsimile machine, the inquiry is sent in about a minute, allowing you to get on with other work while someone else follows up on the request. Another boon: because of the immediate delivery of information, in written form, it often conveys a sense of urgency.

Features to look for in a fax machine include:

- *Group Three compatibility — the most popular and economic models.*

- *Speeds of 9,600 bits per second — the longer it takes to send a page, the higher the phone bill.*

- *Automatic document cutter — saves time trimming each page from one long roll. It also makes documents neater in appearance.*

- *Automatic document feeder — so you don't need to "babysit" the machine by feeding one page at a time. Capacities range from five to thirty pages.*

- *Autodialing capability — this allows you to use speed dialing for regular clients and to redial busy numbers automatically.*

The latest entry in the facsimile market is computer fax modems, which can send images to ordinary fax machines or to other fax modems. This saves time printing documents produced on the computer in order to transmit them via fax. Instead, they're simply transmitted directly from the computer. It also conserves on expensive thermal paper — so often wasted on "junk fax" —because the receiver can view the document on the screen before deciding whether or not to print it. The disadvantage is that you're limited to transmitting or receiving documents from one computer to another.

These are just a few tools that will help improve time management methods in the office. In the next chapter, we'll look at a range of software that will make those tools more efficient. ❿

Chapter 20: Summary

■ **Before buying a computer system, decide what office functions need to be computerized. Then look at software, service, and expandability.**

■ **Laptop computers are a big help for people who work in several places: at home and at the office, at the office and on the road.**

■ **Facsimile machines are tremendous time-savers. Look for automatic feed, high speeds, and autodialing features.**

chapter twenty one

More Tools For
Time Management — Software

imagine this scenario:

Jack Grimes, an important criminal lawyer, has a horrendously full week ahead of him. He has status calls in court rooms, motions to prepare, appointments with clients and three brief full trials, one for assault, one for driving under the influence and a third, a jury selection for a murder trial that will go into the following week. In the past, he carried a Daytimer appointment book with him to record items in the court room, but was forever getting notes misplaced. He kept a manual To Do Today pad on his desk but his secretary often complained of things being lost on it. She also maintained a schedule in her word processing program and kept the office version of a Daytimer as a master record.

Today, instead of using a manual To Do Today pad, he simply enters the many tasks to accomplish in his computer and punches in his appointments for the week. As his To Do list grows smaller and smaller, tasks left to accomplish are automatically carried over to the next day. An important client needs to meet with Jack over dinner. His secretary accesses his schedule through a computer network. She pulls up his schedule and sees: Dinner with Mom and Dad — 35th anniversary. "How about lunch?" she asks the client. Voila! A disaster has been avoided. At the end of the business day the secretary prints out an updated To Do Today list for tomorrow — and a complete list of all future appointments and court dates for the next 60 days. She makes one copy for herself and one for him. He carries the copy in his coat pocket or briefcase as he makes his rounds of court rooms, having, instantly at a glance, his entire schedule for the next 60 days or longer.

Is there a program that can keep you that well organized? You bet. It's called OnTime, and although there are similar time management programs on the market, this is the best we've seen yet. The program is a combination appointment book, To Do Today program, pocket secretary, desktop planner, tickler reminder system, and alarm clock.

OnTime is available for all IBM PC-compatibles, Macintoshes, and for the most common networks (Novell, Lantastic, 3-Com, 10-Net, etc.) It presents your calendar in a way that immediately communicates time availability and conflicts, and it graphically illustrates the time plotted out for various events (See Figure 21.1 on page 259).

The week at a glance screen provides an overview of your week and prints out your itinerary for a day, a week, a month, or even years in advance. The Day Planner screen displays your day in one hour, 30 minute, or 15 minute increments. You can enter dates through the year 2079. It will automatically schedule repetitive meetings, such as the staff meeting every Monday at 9 a.m. The program is easy to learn and includes a 60-page manual. In addition, users can toggle back and forth between the To Do list and the appointment list. OnTime can be installed RAM-memory-resident — it takes up less than 5K of RAM — for a single user or network system. The program comes with a user manual but we learned to use the program without ever reading the manual — we could not be without OnTime today. (You can order OnTime through us for $89.95 for the single user version plus $6.50, shipping and handling. Desktop Graphics Inc., 26940 N. Longwood Rd., Lake Forest, IL 60045-1071.) Please send check with order.

In addition, several programs are available to enhance the efficiency of a manager's computer system. These include hard disk menu programs, environmental software, and database programs. And, of course, numerous spreadsheet, word processing and miscellaneous software programs also make life easier.

Thanks to vast improvements in these programs, the computer has now become the right-hand assistant of many managers. They turn it on first thing in the morning to check their schedules, read electronic mail messages, or jot down ideas that may have occurred to them since the day before.

Without a doubt, the computer is one of the easiest ways to make professionals more productive in the time they have available. For some businesses, many tasks once handled by a clerical person are now performed easily on the computer. Managers who can type reasonably well, for instance, often find it faster to input their own letters rather than go through a tedious dictation process. For other companies, the fact that many tasks can now be delegated to the computer means that secretaries and other clerical personnel can assist with other, more valuable projects.

To explain just how efficient a computer system can be, we'll describe the programs that have made our lives easier. Because we felt more comfortable discussing the programs with which we have some personal experience, there are obviously many others that we don't have the space, or the knowledge, to touch on. A software store, consultant, or computer magazine could surely be of help there.

Hard disk menu

A hard disk menu program organizes various software programs — such as WordPerfect, Lotus 1-2-3, OnTime, or TeleMagic — into easily accessible easy-to-use menus. This lets you organize programs on your computer by categories (word processing, spreadsheets, desk-top publishing, accounting, database management, etc.) HDM-IV is extremely user friendly and anybody with just the basic knowledge of DOS can set it up. We've been using this program now for three years and could not survive without it.

This also lets you avoid having to remember complicated DOS-commands to get into your programs but also saves the user consider-

able time jumping back and forth between the different, but essential, programs. The version HDM IV that we use can be easily installed, and is available for $50 with a user manual from Jim Haas, P.O. Box 447, Richfield, OH 44286-0447. This is another very low-cost program that really speeds up access into and out of your computer. We suggest that the program is so good that you send him the $50 up front for it — and be sure to tell him that you're a friend of ours!

Environmental software

Eventually, these programs may take the place of the hard disk menu, as they too simplify the transition to and from other software. But for the moment, they offer users a "glorified hard disk menu," along with memo pad and FAX functions.

Microsoft Windows is one such program. Its intent is to simplify everyday computing needs and give users more time to spend on more important tasks. The program includes an on-line help system, paintbrush program, macro recorder, personal calendar, dual-mode calculator, and communications software, all of which are designed to improve productivity. It also enhances the abilities of function-specific programs like Microsoft Word, for word processing; Microsoft Excel, for spreadsheets; Microsoft Power Point, for graphics; and Microsoft Project, for project management. It'll cost you about $100 for Microsoft Windows from your favorite software store but that simply is the umbrella software. To that figure add about $300 for each additional program to make it usable. Super efficient but mighty expensive — you'll end up spending $1000 or more for just a few simple programs.

Between the time we delivered the manuscript to the publisher and the time we received the proofs of the book to check we had a good chance to learn how to use the Microsoft Windows 3.1 environmental software. It requires 2 MB of memory and a 386 machine. We would be remiss if we did not insert a couple paragraphs at the last minute into the manuscript about our experiences.

Windows is a complex and somewhat difficult to learn program but is well worth the time, trouble and expense. We acquired the Microsoft Windows "Office" package which includes Word for Windows (word processing), Excell (spread sheet) and Power Point (graphics). We also bought Aldus Pagemaker which requires Windows and is probably the best known DOS-based desktop publishing software. We have WordPerfect for Windows version of word processing on order.

In order to learn these programs we have taken a one day seminar in the basics of using Windows. We are in the middle of an 8-week class to learn Pagemaker. And we're signed up for a seminar on WordPerfect for Windows (we have that package on order now) and a 4-week class on Word for Windows.

We've gotten far enough along in using Windows and PageMaker to tell you that we are, indeed, impressed. We're not about to give up our faithful and lovable WordPerfect 5.1 but we're going to begin moving in the direction of the Windows environment. There are problems in using some of our non-Windows software through the Windows menu system (for example, we can't print from within WordPerfect if we boot it through Windows, so we still use WordPerfect from DOS). We doubt that WordPerfect for Windows is going to change our love affair with WordPerfect, particularly since we're signed up for a desktop publishing class using WordPerfect. But it behooves you to learn Microsoft Word and PageMaker today and possibly a graphics program such as Microsoft PowerPoint for Windows, Harvard Graphics or Express Presenter.

We strongly urge you to go to your local community college and sign up for a basic course in Windows and evaluate the environment yourself. While you're there check out some of the other PC courses available. Most community colleges are relatively low cost for their computer training and have both seminar type one-day programs and full 8-16 week courses.

We've been taking computer courses off and on now for ten years and, because of it, we're relatively proficient in the use of a PC. We just don't have the patience to sit down and try to learn page-by-page a program from the manual. The few dollars we pay are a real bargain. We've been taking college courses now for 35 years and probably have the equivalent of about six years of undergraduate courses. We now take them largely to keep abreast of the computer technology and have a lot

of fun — and meet some interesting people along the way — doing it.

Central Point Software's PC Tools Deluxe is a combination desktop manager, data recovery, hard disk back-up, and DOS shell program. Management functions include: modem and fax board support, notepads, data base, telecommunications, appointment scheduler, calculators, macro editor, and outliner. It costs about $100 and well worth every penny for the person who doesn't want to learn all the DOS commands to move files around and to help you back up your programs.

So how do you know these features are really helpful, and not just bells and whistles? To be truthful, there are a few bells — such as an alarm that sounds to remind users of appointments, or the ring that will sound in a client's office when the system automatically dials their number. Sound helpful yet? PC Tools' Desktop Manager also allows users to create appointment schedules and To Do lists; access CompuServe, Easy Link, MCI, or other on-line services via modem; send and receive program files; send and receive fax transmissions; organize a multitude of information through the database; and use the notepad application for word processing.

Word processing

With good reason, WordPerfect 5.1 is the most popular word processing program. WordPerfect is probably the most comprehensive word processing program available. They have a simpler version called WP Office for those who don't need all the bells and whistles and still want compatibility to WP.

In the full blown WordPerfect program macros allow users to type in often-used phrases such as company names, addresses, and memo headers only once. A merge feature reduces the time needed to send out a form letter to mere minutes. Users simply key the addresses, salutations, and other specific information in one file, type the basic form letter in a second file, and merge the two. Other time-saving functions include outlining, spell check, thesaurus, search and replace, footnotes and headers.

The latest version of WordPerfect makes it easier to create tables, print mailing labels, import spreadsheets, and add graphics to text.

Your authors are both dedicated users of WordPerfect version 5.1. As a freelance writer, Kim has used WordPerfect for everything from drafting articles and columns, writing memos, producing camera-ready copy for newsletters, and creating invoices for completed jobs. And it can produce just about everything else, from resumes to graphics to annual reports. Lauren uses it to write advertising copy, newsletters, do major marketing plans for consulting clients, and daily correspondence. This book was written by swapping WordPerfect discs back and forth between Kim and Lauren with each adding input into each chapter.

Other good word processing programs include Microsoft Word, PFS Write, Word Star, Scripsit and several others. WordPerfect is a little more complex than some of the others but is becoming so universally accepted in the business world that we suggest you consider Word Perfect over any of the others. Our second choice would be Microsoft Word because it'll fit into the Windows environment. On our new computer we'll have about three different programs — WordPerfect, Word and PFS Write because various clients prefer different programs. We don't have it now because we're out of disc space — but that new 200MB hard disc will give us all the room we need.

Database programs — sales call followup systems

For executives who need to track client prospects and related information on a database, these programs can enhance time management, organizational, and marketing efforts.

In the old days, sales people carried 3 x 5" cards to record the dates they called on a prospect, what transpired during the call, and what the customer bought. In its simplest form, that was database marketing. Theoretically, the sales person had a card on every prospect in his or her territory, and regularly logged the activity with the prospect. Simply put, this was a salesman's marketing database and he used it daily.

Although the concept is the same, today database marketing is more sophisticated. Simply put, it means building a prospect and customer mailing list, and computerizing the list in such a way that the list can be used effectively by telemarketing personnel, sales service personnel,

field sales personnel, customer service, credit, other departments, and management to have a combined marketing effort that will maximize sales activity and results.

There are numerous programs that enable a marketer to do a good job of building, updating, and maintaining a data base. The program we use and strongly recommend is Telemagic Software (Remote Control Inc., 5928 Pascal Court, Carlsbad, CA 92008; 619/431-4000, about $500.) Even a customer list consisting of a few hundred names can be maintained practically and effectively on a database management program. Needed selling information can be kept up to date from an easy-to-use screen on a PC, and marketing information about the customer can be continually input so that when a salesperson makes a telemarketing or personal visit, he or she will have the information needed to do an effective selling job. Word processed letters through mail merge techniques can easily be sent from the data base by making various selections to mail only those parts of the list you want to mail. At *Execu*time®* we maintained our subscription file as a Telemagic Database and had nothing but the highest praise for it. The computer can be trained to dial your phone, print your invoices and run mailing labels as well as word processed letters.

After all, isn't becoming more effective what time management is all about? Without a computer on your desk you're severely limited — with the computer you need the right software. We suggest that a combination of a Hard Disc Menu, OnTime to schedule your appointments and maintain your To Do Today pad, a good word processing program, a data base manager, such as Telemagic, and a utility program such as PC Tools are the nucleus for any good desktop computer system. To this you can add spreadsheets (Lotus, Multiplan, Quatro Pro, etc.), desk top publishing, purchasing or invoicing systems. And don't overlook some good cheap programs in the public domain — available through many catalogs for $3-5 each. If you buy public domain software, be sure to get a copy of Central Point anti-virus software to make sure you don't have problems with virus laden software.

The programs mentioned here are some that we've found helpful to us. You may want to look at them as well as some of their competitors. ◑

Figure 21.1 Sample OnTime screen displays

Day Planner with Appointments

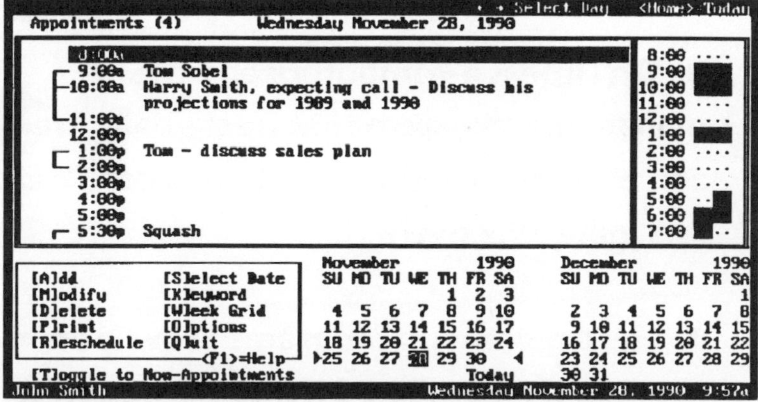

Day Planner with Appointments and other To-Do's

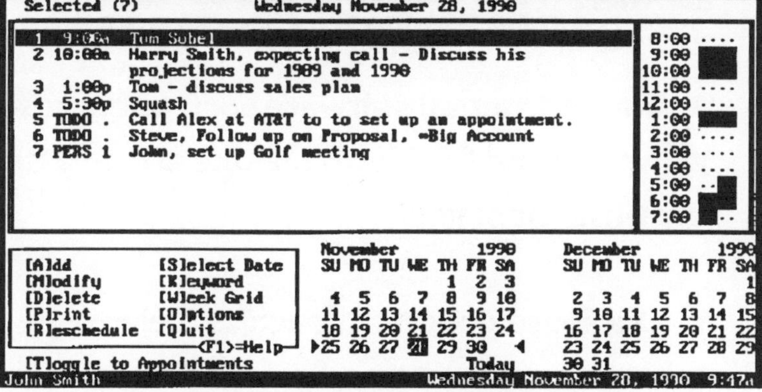

Week Grid with Appointments Time Grid

Chapter 21: Summary

■ **OnTime is a computerized time management system that tracks daily, weekly, and monthly schedules, and manages To Do lists quite effectively.**

■ **Hard disk menu programs allow users to move easily from one software program to another.**

■ **Environmental software such as Microsoft Windows and PC Tools Deluxe are an asset to any time manager.**

■ **Database programs such as Telemagic can enhance marketing and sales efforts, as well as time management and organization.**

chapter twentytwo

Time Management In The Office At Home

*"We cannot do everything at once but
we can do something at once."*
Calvin Coolidge

One of the cornerstones of time management is to
avoid performing the same tasks twice. We've talked about how group-
ing like tasks together, such as phone calls, saves the time involved in
starting and completing each individual call. We've also explained how
to use macros and other functions on your computer to avoid typing
repetitive information.

So how can people maintain this efficiency in a home office? For many
executives, having a den or work area at home, in addition to the outside
office they report to all week, is a necessity. More and more people are
earning their living in their own businesses working out of a spare bedroom,
basement, or attic, for an office. Certain projects are often easier to tackle
at home where interruptions from telephones, meetings, colleagues, and
visitors are eliminated or at least minimized. But it's often difficult to keep
these two areas organized, and to avoid repeating tasks. How can a supple-
mentary home office be a help and not a hindrance?

First, let's look at what can — and should — be duplicated. Many
of the same organizational tools used at work can also be used in the

home office to increase efficiency there. Try to design your workspace in the same manner as well, arranging frequently-used tools such as the telephone, computer, or typewriter at arm's reach.

Lauren's office at home from where he does consulting, writes advertising copy for clients, this book and a wide variety of other material, is a virtual duplicate of his former office "at the office." Both rooms are about the same size — 22x22 and both are just as full of his useful "toys". His desk is the same size (40x80+), and the credenza contains full-sized file cabinets. A computer, typewriter, and facsimile machine are also nearby, just like they are set up at his full-time office where he runs sales/marketing activities of a $10 million company. He has identical chairs in both offices — all of the same programs on the computer, but he uses them for different businesses. He can easily transfer data between office and home on a floppy. He also carries a laptop computer for note-taking when he travels, and he has both laser and dot-matrix printers.

When a project is large or complicated, and even a quiet hour or two in the office won't suffice to complete it, he remains home for a day and works in that office for peace and quiet. The key here, of course, is to shut off the phone, put on an answering machine, or tell the secretary or assistant at the office to take messages for call-backs later. Sometimes he takes a "mental health day" and works from home rather than going to the office.

About 35 million people preferred working at home so much, they've made their home office their primary work locale. Many of these people operate part-time or full-time businesses from their homes. But for now, we'll concentrate on those managers who use their home offices as a supplement to their regular business offices.

Where to set up shop

Where should you locate your home office? A separate room, such as a den, extra bedroom, attic, room, or basement, is the preferred choice for several reasons. Kim's office, for example, is a spare bedroom in her home from which she writes articles for dozens of business magazines.

A detached garage can also be remodeled, heated and improved into

using time management

a delightful office. If you're seriously considering an office at home we strongly recommend that you get hold of the magazine, *Home Office Computing*, available on most newstands. It gives dozens of good ideas on setting up your home office.

Using an entire room for your home office helps to keep your family and business lives separate. One of the advantages of working from home is to minimize interruptions and increase concentration time. This is hard to do when "Ninja turtles" are duking it out on your desk. Second, deducting a portion of rent and utilities on your taxes is possible if the space is used exclusively for work. If you don't have the luxury of an extra room, try using screens, room dividers, or bookcases to block off a work area into a "created" room.

Improving productivity

If you're going to be working in your home office for at least a couple days per week, you'll want those days to be as productive as possible. Lighting, color, and wall coverings can all affect productivity. For example, there are certain colors that affect moods and productivity in the office, writes Bobbi Digerness in *Administrative Management*.

Red overstimulates and increases blood pressure, although it can also create feelings of warmth in areas where people are there for short periods of time. (Red also makes us hungry, according to many restaurant owners. If you want to eliminate trips to the kitchen for a snack, keep this in mind.) Black and brown create feelings of fatigue and decrease the perception of light. This is why dark paneled or painted walls often lead to fatigue.

Blue is very relaxing, and reduces blood pressure and stress. But over-using blue can cause sluggish behavior or even a sense of depression. White, on the other hand, is neutral, giving no strong feelings in any way for productivity. Yellow can strain the eyes if too bright or overused. But it can also be cheerful and raise the spirits. Finally, green is thought of as the most normal color, but overuse can be monotonous. It can be light and sensitive or cool and cold. It's often a favorite room color.

When choosing a room color, Digerness suggests looking at the room's function, where it is located, and what effect it should have on

the occupant. Do you want to relax and unwind or do you need to roll up your sleeves and get to work?

Lighting options range from natural lighting to incandescent to fluorescent lighting. Of these, the most desirable choice is natural daylight. If you'll be working at a personal computer, you'll want to reduce glare and eyestrain, which is often caused by fluorescent light. Consider neodymium-based bulbs, which simulate daylight.

Ergonomics — another productivity booster

Drop a load of laundry in a washing machine and an alarm will sound if the load becomes unbalanced. In effect, the machine is letting the operator know that it needs proper balance to do its job efficiently.

That's just one difference between machines and humans. While the washing machine will signal when something doesn't feel right, a human worker will simply adjust to the new position and continue. It is, after all, what we're used to doing. Ergonomics is out to change this practice. Also referred to as "human factors engineering," ergonomics is the study of human characteristics for the appropriate design of the living and working environment. Its goal is to create safer and more efficient work practices.

In the office, ergonomists look primarily at computer terminals and work stations. For workers who sit in front of a computer all day, greater comfort and ease increases productivity. One government report found that productivity increased 25 percent when workers were placed in ergonomically correct work stations.

In your home office, you have the advantage of being the decision maker. You can learn how the position of your computer or the height of your chair can affect comfort and productivity. Let's look at four problems that are fairly easy to correct.

Eye strain

More than half of all visual display terminal (VDT) operators suffer eye irritation, fatigue, or focusing difficulties, reported *Fortune* magazine. When reading, the average distance between the eye and printed material is 14 to 16 inches, while a VDT screen is about 25 inches away. People who wear bifocals often have a hard time working at a VDT, and almost all eyes tire when working at the VDT.

The worst eye problem is glare. Too much illumination from the overhead lights or windows can dim the contrasts on the screen. Filters, which are available from office or computer supply stores, are a partial solution. Locating the monitor away from a light source, or lowering the intensity of the light source, can also help. In addition, consider resting the eyes for at least 15 minutes every two hours, or 15 minutes each hour if work is particularly demanding.

Aches and pains

VDTs often exacerbate lower-back problems. Posture at a VDT is rigid, forcing the operator to stare longer and harder. Reflections make the viewer twist around or tilt the neck to look over glasses, which also causes aches.

Seating is also a factor. Ergonomists have changed the way the average chair works. Many chairs now adjust easily to the operator's weight and size. Ergonomists are also designing more comfortable work stations. Keyboards, for instance, are no longer always attached to the computer, allowing the operator to sit more comfortably.

Excessive fatigue

A tired, depressed feeling is the most common symptom found in VDT operators. It may be due to eye strain and poor posture, but there is often more to it. One expert says the computer pushes people harder to keep working because it never tires. Fatigue also results from the designs of the furniture. Not everyone, obviously, is of the standard size and weight for which the seats and tables are designed. Again, try to stretch frequently and take periodic breaks.

Stress

This is the ultimate complaint of most VDT users. Part of it comes from just trying to keep up with the quick and tireless pace set by the computers — which can get frustrating. Although ergonomists have

identified this as a problem, it's up to you to come up with a solution.

Furniture

A good chair can add as many as 40 productive minutes a day, says professor E.R. Tichauer in a United Press Syndicate column by Porter Shimer. Sitting, according to Tichauer, can put as much strain on the back as bending over to lift something. He offers these suggestions to help you get a more comfortable chair:

- *It should have a rounded front. A sharp front edge can restrict the blood flow, causing numbness and poor circulation in the legs and feet.*

- *It should be adjustable in height. Set your chair at a height that allows the feet to come into firm contact (but not too firm) with the floor. Seats that are too high bring pressure on your thighs and low seats strain the lower back.*

- *It should be firm enough to allow you to squirm. Squirming is a way of giving your rear end the movement it needs to ensure good blood flow. Seats that are too soft restrict the movement.*

- *It should have adjustable back height. The chair's backrest should extend at least a third of the way up your back. It should also have an open space or indentation just above the seat, which encourages better posture.*

Most experts favor a backrest that tilts to support several working positions: edge-of-seat intense, relaxed for reflection, or leaning back for a stretch. If your chair doesn't resemble this model, try placing a small pillow above the small of your back so you sit with a forward arch, raise your seat with a firm cushion, or "lower" it by using a footrest.

Computer or working tables and stations should also be adjustable in height and angle. Detachable keyboards, keyboard drawers, and a mouse can all make the computer easier to use. About 26 inches from the floor is a good height for a keyboard. A CPU stand, which can position your CPU vertically next to the computer desk, frees desk space for the monitor. Your eyes should be looking 10 to 30 degrees downward at the monitor, rather than upward or straight ahead.

Mail order catalogs offer a good idea of the products you'll need for your home office. You'll probably want a desk to accommodate your computer. Buy this after you buy the computer itself, so you can find furniture to accommodate the computer system, rather than vice versa. Furniture manufacturers offer many options for computer work stations. The Sears catalog has an excellent selection of computer furniture for the office-at-home. First there are the traditional wood computer desks, which are slightly smaller than a normal desk and feature a hutch over the top for shelving, monitors, etc. The modular designs are good because they can be expanded later should you need to add more components. There are also portable computer desks, which hold the monitor, CPU, printer, and keyboard on shelves, one over the other. These are a good idea if space is at a premium.

Time management tools

A calendar, appointment book, and an efficient filing system are important time management tools for the home office. Ideally, try to use the same appointment book at home as you do at the office to avoid duplicating your work. Some people prefer to keep personal appointments in a separate organizer that they keep at home.

Add a couple of desktop trays to hold reading material and perhaps mail that needs to be sorted. Another tray or file stand could hold projects that you've brought home from the office. Remember the "out of sight, out of mind" theory. Leaving these on top of a desk or credenza, rather than inside it, is probably the best way to avoid having to tell your boss "I forgot my homework."

Many electronic products and telephone services allow people to link their home offices to their employer's or client's office. Electronic mail, or E-mail, is one example of these services. This allows you to send data from your computer to other E-mail users. Modems and facsimile machines also allow people to transmit information from one location to antoher. (These are discussed in more detail in Chapter 20.)

Some companies offer a communication device that combines phone, fax, and modem, or phone, fax, and answering machine. The FAX Line Manager from Inmac, for instance, automatically routes calls to the appropriate source — phone, fax, or modem. With the latter product, callers hear something along the lines of, "Hi, this is Jane Smith. If you'd like to leave a message, press *. To fax, press #. Or, stay on the line and I'll be right with you."

Modems enable people to send and receive information 24 hours a day. Libraries and reference services offer on-line data banks, so users can access valuable reference material without ever leaving their desks.

Voice mail, which is available from the phone company, can act as a receptionist for your home office. The service is similar to an answering machine, but without the equipment. If you're on the phone or away from your home office, callers will hear your pre-recorded message and can then leave their own messages. The messages can be replayed by punching a couple buttons on the phone. The service also offers other benefits not available with an answering machine.

The phone company also offers a few other services that can save time and help the home office project a more business-like image. For instance, services from Illinois Bell Telephone Company include:

Call forwarding – calls to your office can be automatically forwarded to your home office or car. (Clients never even know you're working three feet from your bedroom!)

Call waiting – allows people to receive important calls by putting one call on hold while they answer another.

Distinctive ringing and multi-ring – enables users to tell if a call is business or personal. With the multi-ring option, a single phone line can accommodate up to three different numbers, each of which sounds a separate tone. With distinctive ringing, a unique ring sounds for incoming calls of up to ten different people.

Repeat dialing – automatically redials busy numbers.

Speed calling – frequently-dialed numbers can be dialed with one or two digits, which increases both speed and accuracy.

Three-way calling – works just like the conference call feature on the office phones. Allows people to have quick meetings over the phone by talking to two people at once. No time wasted with the old "let me call them and get back to you."

Make sure your office has a good door that can be closed — and locked from the inside — so when the Ninja turtles want to invade your office you can bar the door so that the invasion is prevented. Working from an office at home requires discipline and the discipline dictates that other than office helpers are relegated to another room during your working hours. ◗

Chapter 22: Summary

■ **For people who use a home office or work area as a supplement to their normal offices, the objective is to make the area as efficient as possible without duplicating efforts.**

■ **Ideally, base the home office in a private portion of your house, such as an extra bedroom, attic, or basement.**

■ **When setting up your office, be sure to include ergonomically-designed furniture and layouts to improve productivity and overall health.**

chapter twenty-three

Effective Telephone Use

it's amazing how often the tools we invent to simplify our lives turn into "Frankensteins." In other words, the very tools we created end up controlling us instead. The telephone is one of those monsters. Its original intention was admirable. We'd save the time and energy walking or hopping the nearest horse to deliver important information to a neighbor, a relative, or a business. But did Alexander Graham Bell ever imagine that one day his invention would have people skipping lunches and staying out of showers for fear they'd miss a call?

People are equally guilty of this behavior at the office. They run across a room to answer their ringing phone, interrupt an appointment or a conversation with a colleague to take an unexpected call. Often, they prefer to pick up the phone as a way of procrastinating on more important matters at hand.

The situation can be frustrating, as this *Execu*Time*® reader tells us:

"Why is it that people will answer the telephone under most any circumstances — convenient or not? People jump out of the bathtub, interrupt conversations with scheduled visitors, stop on their way out to important meetings, just to answer that insistent jangle. I've stopped doing it — but I don't miss anything important. I have a telephone answering machine at home, and at the office my secretary is trained to screen all calls and save all but the most vital for my intensive 'phone period' each day. Then, when I sit down at the phone with my stack of messages, I can get them all out of the way at once instead of breaking my concentration many times."

Another reader offers a similar solution to dealing with phone demands. "I am convinced that one reason why people drop current activities to answer the phone is because it is so darn loud — a ringing phone is terrible to try to talk or work over," the person writes. "If you own the phone, take out the metal parts from the bells. Or take the phone to a repair shop to have a repairman quiet down the phone. All that is needed is a dull tinkle — the loud/soft dial on most phones is not adjustable enough."

These people have offered good, simple solutions on how we can control the phone, rather than letting it control us. If used properly, the telephone can be one of your best time savers. There are many ways to control phone use in the office. One is to let a secretary or receptionist make and take all your calls. Pick up the phone only when you know there's someone you want to talk to already there. Or, give the secretary three lists of people: those you don't want put through at all (ignore them or call them back when it's more convenient); those you will talk to during normal hours but not when you're concentrating or in conference; and those few you'll talk to anytime. Make sure the lists are kept current. Or consider putting in a "private line" on which only certain people can call. That phone would not be answered if you're out of your office which will save them time as well as you.

Second, think before you dial. Get out of the habit of reaching for the phone every time it occurs to you. Ask yourself whether calling is the most time-effective step at this moment. Try not to make calls that would have to be followed up with confirming paperwork anyway, to people who will not be able to give you an answer until they've been able to think about the answer or consult another source for it, or to people who would have to have the item you are calling about approved by several other people first. Instead, dictate a note and get the ball rolling at your convenience instead of interrupting your train of thought — and that of the person you would be calling — for a phone call that may get diverted to unrelated topics.

Working the late shift at a 24-hour convenience store in college was probably when Kim first learned the world will not come to an end if she lets the phone ring. "If you have a customer in the store, let the phones ring," the owner told him. "We're open all night — they can call back."

While most offices are probably not open 24 hours — nor should they let their phones ring endlessly — this concept can work just as well if you screen incoming calls, then limit return calls to a certain hour of the day. This way, the priorities you set are your own, not those of an outside source who doesn't have the insight to see that you're working on something more important.

When you have carved out time to concentrate on a report, to see a long-awaited supplier with a fine new product, or even to take your well-deserved fifteen-minute break, why should you answer the phone just because it is ringing? If a secretary or assistant cannot field the calls, try taking turns with an associate, to allow each other quiet hours. Or, install an answering machine or voice mail system. Answering machines range in price from about $50 to $250, while the latter are available from the phone company for a few dollars a month.

Schedule an hour or so each day to make the calls you need to initiate or return. Have all the relevant material handy so you don't need to get up and search through files as you are talking. Also, keep some paperwork or reading material at your side to fill in time waiting to be connected, or to initial or skim during routine calls.

You may prefer to make all your outgoing calls and return any messages left earlier at the same sitting. Or, you may want to divide the phone time so that all your important outgoing calls, say those made to clients or vendors, are made first thing in the morning. That way, you'll be at the top of their To Do lists for the day. When you need to return calls where other people have requested information from you, group those together as well.

You'll probably find that making those phone calls all at once helps get the momentum going and helps you to keep a time limit on each call, because you know there are a number of calls still left to make.

Herschel Shosteck, a survey researcher and consultant from Washington, DC, solved the problem of keeping a tickler system up to date when the people he needed to call were not available. He puts his tickle calls on 3M Post-It-Notes™, listing the party's name, reason for the call, telephone number, and date. Then he places the note in his calendar book on the appropriate date. If he calls on that date and needs to follow up, he changes the date on the note and forwards it to the new date in his calendar.

Taking notes before making a call is also a good idea, because they outline exactly what you need to discuss. Then take notes during the call on what was actually said. This may seem tedious, but it actually saves many hours of wrangling about who said what, as well as hours saved doing things wrong and having to do them over, or trying to remember what you talked about during your last phone conversation with a particular client.

If you want to save time on the phone, don't mix business calls with pleasure. Many people have the habit of conducting business on the phone for a minute or two and then saying, "So, how's everything?" or "How have you been?" You can almost feel the climate of the call changing from business to socializing. And you don't have time for too much chitchat if you are going to finish your To Do Today list.

If a business associate starts to steer the conversation to a social level, just reply, "I'd love to tell you all that's been happening, but I'm swamped at the moment. How about lunch next Wednesday?" (Or substitute a tennis date or whatever else that may be appropriate.) Set the social date, then get off the phone and back to business, or you may be in for thirty-minute bull session that can put your whole schedule out of whack.

If a supplier or other person you do not have outside social contact with starts in with chitchat, simply answer the open-ended "How's everything" question in this way: "Everything's fine, but really busy. I'd love to chat, but I must run. Thanks for calling." Take the initiative, and politely but firmly end the call.

If you consider the phone a "message system" rather than something closer to a personal visit, you'll cut out a lot of the conversational fat. Get right to your point, and when you're done, conclude with "I have to go now." When someone calls you, immediately find out why. Discuss what's relevant for as long as necessary; then quickly get off.

Features to simplify your lifestyle

For people who use the telephone frequently, phone companies and office stores offer several conveniences to make life easier and improve time management skills. Most of them are inexpensive when you consider the amount of time and aggravation they can help you save. Talk to your telephone service representative about conveniences available through your phone company. Others are available commercially, most often from office-supply firms.

Probably the easiest way to waste a few minutes on a phone call is to hold indefinitely. Make your own policy about how to handle being put on hold. You can refuse to be put on hold and call back later in your phoning period. Or, if the person is especially hard to reach, keep some paperwork or reading handy so that you don't waste the time spent holding.

One *Execu*Time®* reader wrote in to say that a telephone amplifier, or speaker phone, is priceless in this respect. It frees you to walk around the room and handle other work while you are waiting. But if you get one get a good one — the older and cheaper ones make it sound like you're talking from within a deep tunnel because of the echo they cause.

Other time-saving phone features include:

Let your secretary dial your calls. If your secretary dials your phone calls you don't have to wait — or work your way through somebody else's switchboard or secretary.

Telephone headset. For people who use the phone a great deal, this has the added advantage of privacy that amplifiers lack. Be sure to get one with a long, elastic cord.

Message center. Keep this next to your phone to take and place all messages for easy access during your "call-back" hour.

Telephone charge card. You can make calls from pay phones without having to scramble for change, or even from a client's office. Anyone with a phone can have one, and you get an automatic record of the calls you place using it.

Call waiting. This allows you to talk as long as you need without worrying about missing other calls. If another call comes through — signalled by a click or a discreet "beep" — you simply put the first call on hold and answer the second. Then it's up to you to decide which call you'd like to continue. If you prefer not to be interrupted during an important conversation, most phone systems allow you to temporarily deactivate the call waiting feature for that particular call.

Conference calling. This feature can be used both at home and at work to add a third party to the conversation, thus saving time calling back and forth.

Cordless phones. A portable receiver definitely makes life a lot a easier because you can move around while you talk and do two things at once, such as straightening up files or opening up the mail.

Voice mail. Similar to an answering machine, it allows callers to leave a message when you can't take the calls personally. Those trying to reach you will simply hear, "Hi, you've reached the office of Jane Doe. I'm either on the phone or away from my desk at the moment. Please leave a private message at the beep and I'll get back to you as soon as possible." To retrieve messages, just dial a private code and they'll be played back over the phone. The only equipment necessary is a touch-tone phone.

Pager/beeper. Executives who are often away from the office, or who frequently visit the plant and other areas where it's difficult to take

using time management

calls, may find a pager/beeper to be the solution to their problems. To page you, the caller simply dials the phone number assigned to your pager. A beep or vibration tells you have a message, and displays the number to call. Wristwatch pagers, for business and personal use, will also soon be on the market.

Cellular phones. While the price of cellular phones has gone down substantially, the reception quality has gone up. The phones are available in a portable version, which can be toted in a briefcase, or they can be installed in your car. Cellular phones also offer last number redial and multi-number memory. A hands-free operation lets you keep both hands on the wheel while you talk, although you run the small risk of looking a little silly as you talk to your sun visor.

Automatic dialer. A speed dialer or auto-dialer stores and selects more than thirty phone numbers for you, and dials them faster and more accurately. These can be found at supply stores that carry office, telephone, or electronic merchandise. Particularly with long distance calls, this can save considerable time looking up and dialing numbers.

Call forwarding. This is another service that phone companies offer in many areas. If you are working at home or at a client's office for the day and do not want to miss important calls, you can use this feature to have your calls sent wherever you are. By punching a simple code into your phone and then dialing the number where you'll be, you don't have to miss a single call.

Phone etiquette

In this fast-paced society where people must learn to talk to machines, send impersonal fax transmissions, or use electronic mail, a little phone etiquette can go a long way. If you insist on having a live voice answer your calls to add a personal touch, the last thing you want to hear a client mutter is "I'd rather talk to his machine" when a snide receptionist takes the call.

Here are some quick tips on phone protocol from *P.S. For Personal Secretaries:*

1. Always answer on the first or second ring.
2. Identify yourself and your department when you pick up the phone.
3. Don't transfer calls unless the caller agrees. It's annoying to be told "I'm going to transfer your call."
4. Don't forget calls that you put on hold. It's extremely rude to leave a caller on the line for extended periods without checking back.
5. Be polite — avoid curt comments. The best way to convey politeness is to use "please," "thank you," and "you're welcome" liberally.
6. Be discreet when screening calls. It is important to make sure the caller knows you're helping to try and place the call rather than being nosy.
7. Don't argue. If there is a disagreement, be firm but polite.

Additionally, having the switchboard operator or assistant include the correct name spelling and phonetic pronunciation on a message saves time and embarrassment, according to Merrill Douglass. Staff members who take calls and messages can also improve time management considerably by taking as detailed a message as possible. That way you can have all the needed information before picking up the phone or returning the call. The reverse is also true: if the party you are calling is out, leave a precise message that includes your name and phone number, the purpose of your call, and the type of response you need. In many cases, the message-taker can relay the message and get the answer for you.

Finally, let people know when you are not available to take phone calls. For the convenience of those who call you often, try to schedule and stick with your quiet hour and phone hour. Let frequent callers know the best time to reach you. Or, if they want to call and leave a message, let them know when you usually return your calls. 🕐

Chapter 23: Summary

■ **Control your phone use — don't let the
telephone control you.**

■ **Consider making all your outgoing calls
during a "phone hour."**

■ **Take notes before and during business calls
to remember important items to discuss.**

■ **Look into time-saving products and features
available from the phone company.**

using time management

chapter twentyfour

Dictation as a Time Management Tool

*"To say the right thing at the right time,
keep still most of the time."*
John Roper

as more professionals find their personal computers make wonderful right-hand assistants, dictation is probably declining in its use as a correspondence tool. Nevertheless, there are still a few instances where dictation can come in handy.

For people who travel, whether locally or across the globe, bringing along a microcassette recorder, or portable dictation unit, can simplify expense records, correspondence, and instructions to the staff at the office. Other managers can also benefit by using dictation for personal note taking or letter writing.

So many times we hear people wishing hopelessly, trying to add more time to their days. Yet many of them are afraid to try different techniques, such as new and simpler ways to handle the "busy work." Dictation is one example of a time management technique that many people shy away from, perhaps because they don't see the value in it, or because they're a little "mike-shy."

Many executives write out their letters and memos by hand before turning them over for typing. If you are one of these handwriters, try a little test to show yourself how much time you are wasting. How many words per minute can you write, or even type? Twenty? Thirty? Perhaps 60 if you are a pretty fair typist? Now consider the fact that the average number of words we can speak in a minute is about 150.

If you usually write your letters by hand, you can quadruple your speed by switching to dictation equipment. Even if you dictate directly to your secretary, there is room for improvement, as you are probably capable of speaking twice as fast as he or she is able to take down your words.

Dictation units are convenient, too. They can be used in the car, in the office, even on an exercise bike for note-taking, delegating, or dictating. If you need to write a report on something you've read, for example, think of how much easier that task could be as you make notes directly into the recorder while you are reading.

If your assistant or secretary rebels at the thought of using dictation equipment, propose a test for several weeks. Some firms will give you a "loaner" to try for a while before you purchase. Many stenographers find using the dictation machine a liberating experience for them as well — they can now transcribe and type to suit their own daily schedules.

Dictation machine uses

What can you dictate? Because the tapes are nearly one by two inches small, you can easily bring along different tapes for different subjects: one for expenses, another for ideas, a third for correspondence and notes to people you delegate to. With these tiny idea-capsule types of cassettes, you can carry a number of them in a very small space. They are so small that you can even mail them back to the office for transcribing if you are on the road.

At meetings, try keeping a record of what was discussed on tape. Sometimes you can even eliminate the need for minutes if you record the meeting. That way you have a true record of what went on, although you need not transcribe it unless a question comes up later. Make it known that you save these tapes for an agreed-upon length of time and then erase them to use again.

Have people report to you on tape. The chief operating officer of a supermarket chain told *Execu*Time®*, "I used to waste time requiring written reports from my subordinates, then reading them during valuable office or home hours. Now I ask them to dictate their reports, and I listen directly to their cassettes while I drive to work. This saves input and output time, and usually results in better understanding, too."

Delegating can also be simplified by recording instructions to staff members. For example, go through your mail and explain on tape what needs to be done with each item. Then give the cassette and the mail to your secretary. If you are working late and want to leave some instructions for staff members, leave the To Do list on a cassette and your secretary or assistant can listen to it first thing in the morning.

Doctors have also found a special use for dictation. As one physician explains, "I use a portable cassette recorder to dictate my findings and recommendations in the presence of each patient. The dictation saves me time and gives me three other advantages:

1. I get the work done while the facts are fresh in my mind;
2. I let my patients know exactly what I'm saying about them to myself and others; and,
3. in the case of instructions, I double the impact by letting the patients hear me dictate them, and later handing them the typewritten copy."

How to dictate effectively

If you are a novice at dictation, you may want some pointers on how to dictate effectively. Libraries and bookstores carry entire books devoted to this subject. But here are some of the basics, which will be enough to head you in the right direction.

Time management expert Merrill Douglass offers a few objectives and reminders to help keep you on track when you dictate. First, be prepared. Preparation requires you to be clear about your objectives and to outline them. Have all necessary references at hand when you begin. Allow enough time to dictate effectively without interruption. Execution should begin with instructions: is it a letter or memo, what kind of letterhead, and so on. Speak distinctly. Write for the recipient,

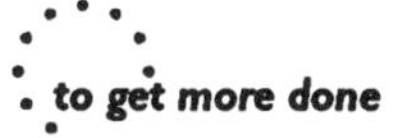

and be conversational, but concise. Spell difficult words and include unclear punctuation, such as a hyphen or a colon.

Try making a card or poster with the following points on it. Keep this on your bulletin board or in front of you as you dictate.

Preparation
- Objectives
- Outline
- References
- Take time

Execution
- Instructions
- Distinct
- Conversation
- Spelling

Preparing your material can also help save time on the part of the person transcribing the material. "In our office we use a Dictation Guideline, which is stapled to an envelope or file folder," explains a broadcasting executive in South Dakota. "We then file all of the letters and materials which need to be used in preparing the dictation, and enclosed in the letters or other mailings, right inside the envelope. The Dictation Guideline carries the date, name or subject matter, code number, and special instructions. The code number allows the secretary to locate the item and the special instructions let her pick out the items which need to be enclosed. Instructions may also include special letterhead, personal stationery, forms, news releases, or other keys for the typist. We have found this helps organize and speed up the dictation process."

Instructing your secretary to put the recipient's phone number on the letter may also be a time saver. Explains a Massachusetts architect, "Whenever I am dictating or writing letters to my clients, I always include their area code and telephone number directly under their address so that whenever I pull a copy of the correspondence out of the file for a follow-up call, the telephone number is already in front of me. This saves valuable and repetitive look-up time."

Overcoming mike fright

Some people never get started dictating because they have a phobia about microphones. A gradual approach may work best. Start with simple one-sentence memos and then dictate three- or four-paragraph directives. When a longer report is required, prepare and dictate it in sections that you have outlined in advance. You may fool yourself and become an ardent advocate of the very microphone you tried to stay away from. Many executives who have become accustomed to using microcassette recorders probably wouldn't know how to get along without them.

Seven steps to better dictation

Auren Uris is an expert in memo-writing and other management techniques. His seven steps will help even the beginner dictate successfully with a bit of planning:

- *Decide what to dictate. The longer the job, the greater your potential for time savings. Memos and other jobs with formats are ideal because your secretary can fill in the beginning and the end and you can just dictate the meat.*

- *Steno or machine? Machines are a bit harder to correct than a human being, but you can do it by playing back or just saying, "Scratch that completely." You must be clear with a machine; the transcriber cannot tell you how garbled the sound is until it is too late.*

- *Organization. Collect all your information and reference material, then make a rough outline. Open books to the pages you will refer to and get comfortable. Then you are ready to start.*

- *Getting started. Double check your preparations to enhance confidence. Plug in with something easy, just to get started talking.*

■ *Continuing the effort. Follow your outline exactly; do not let your-self ramble. If you get nervous, try alternate means. (Use a machine if a secretary bothers you, a human being if the machine seems too impersonal.) If you get stuck on a word or idea, just say, "Some-thing, something," and continue; fix it on the typed draft letter.*

■ *Improving your copy. Normally you should strive to have the first draft be the final one. But for important papers, get a transcript and perfect the draft. Cut repetition and overwriting. Remember your mistakes and try to avoid them when you dictate next time.*

■ *Improving your technique. Practice often until your portable cas-sette recorder is an indispensable aid. Spot your weak points by studying the typed copy. Improve your outlines and concentration to make the end product more effective.* ◑

Chapter 24: Summary

■ **Dictation can be a wonderful time-saving tool for people who travel. The recorders can be used in the car, or even on an exercise bike.**

■ **Make a permanent record of important discussions by bringing a dictation machine to meetings.**

■ **Executives on long trips may even drop the tapes in the mail to be transcribed back at the office.**

chapter twenty-five
What We Have Gained

"Success is simply a matter of luck. Ask any failure."
Earl Wilson

Congratulations!

You've almost finished reading what is probably the most comprehensive book on time management ever written. You've heard from the experts and you've read highlights from thirteen years of *Execu*Time®*, *the Newsletter on the Effective use of Executive Time*. We've talked about what time management is and isn't, how to get organized, how to set and work toward your goals, and how to deal with interruptions, crises, and personnel management. You've also read about the tools of time management: a calendar, a computer, the telephone, and other electronic aids. We've shown you that success at time management means having more time to do the things you want to do as a result of managing your time better.

So what happens when a colleague asks, "All right, now you're the time management expert. Tell me how to manage time." Of course, you can't compress 25 chapters into a ten-minute conversation over the water cooler. And it may be difficult to know where to begin. You have three choices: one, explain politely that you don't have the time for this conversation, then hand him this book and laugh as you retreat to your office; or two, explain only a little at a time. Or, three, suggest that he/she buy a copy of this book and consider attending a time management seminar.

Think about what you personally would like to accomplish this month in the area of time management. Then develop a plan to work toward that goal. Next month, you'll start to work on another area. The truth is, we can't change our habits overnight. Even quitting smoking cold turkey is followed by a month or two of mental coaching, gum chewing, and other tricks to replace the habit.

Improving time management methods needs to be taken one step at a time. Here's an overview of some of those first steps:

Remember the real goal. Why do you want to manage your time in the first place? Do you want to spend more time with your family, exercising, relaxing, or working on a hobby? Perhaps you've been given increased responsibilities at work and you want to manage them without working longer hours.

Learn to compress your time. If you use the right tools, time can be compressed much like air. These tools include following routines rather than re-inventing the wheel; using checklists and comparison ratios; using evaluation forms for employee reviews; and using form letters, memos, and dictating equipment.

For example, three hours studying a balance sheet can become one hour of concentrated analysis with a checklist of comparisons and ratios to look at. An hour evaluating a subordinate becomes 15 high-energy minutes with a form that asks for specific comments on specific aspects of performance and potential. Routines are another way to compress time. Instead of delegating little assignments one at a time, give all of one kind to one person.

Communication time is also highly compressible. Form replies, dictation machines, phone calls instead of letters or memos are all intelligent choices that allow you to communicate effectively and precisely at less time-cost.

Rather than starting each task from scratch, these tools allow you to jump right into the heart of the matter. By systemizing your work, you can compress your time and efforts.

Streamline your office. Aquariums, artwork, and other conversation pieces may be attractive, but they encourage visitors to talk about them, and not about the purpose of the visit. Time management expert Ron Davis suggests that you make sure all the signs and pictures in your office relate to company and personal goals. That way, when your eyes wander, you'll be encouraged back to work instead of into a daydream. What's more, visitors will have less to digress about — more incentive to be goal-oriented with you when they take in your surroundings.

Put a personal computer on your desk. Like it or not, this is the computer generation and the executive who doesn't use a computer as a daily tool is living in the dark ages. (If you can't type now's the time to go take a night school course at your local community college or high school adult evening program and learn to type so you can use a computer efficiently.) For starters we'd suggest the following programs — OnTime, WordPerfect 5.1 (or Microsoft Word), Telemagic, and a good spreadsheet program such as Quattro Pro (or a current version of Lotus 1-2-3). You very well may want to consider the Microsoft Windows environment but, unfortunately, it requires 2MB of RAM so many older PCs can't handle it — we upgraded to a bigger computer recently and put Microsoft Windows and the Microsoft office environment on our new computer.

Learn to use these few programs and you'll have 90 percent of everything you'll ever need. Don't bypass some of the simple little public domain programs that are available for miscellaneous tasks such as cutting purchase orders, invoices, etc. If you refuse to use a computer then a dictating machine is an absolute must.

Never write your address again. Get yourself a rubber stamp with your name and address — better yet, have several for different locations and your home and office addresses. If you write to the same person frequently, have a stamp made up with the address as well. Printed self-stick labels are another alternative. Or, print out a sheet of computerized labels. Your contacts will appreciate labels with your company's address, too, as it makes mailing things to you much easier.

Don't waste time waiting for appointments or meetings. Bring your reading files, review your To Do list, answer some correspondence. Try to do these tasks while holding on the phone, or making phone calls that don't require high concentration.

Listen to motivational or educational cassettes. Learn to improve your effectiveness or stay abreast of your field by listening to tapes as you commute, sit back for a plane ride, ride your exercise bike, or take a walk. Or, try to relax more by picking up a novel on tape. Consider owning some of the "new age" music tapes for a soft background music (with no commercial interruptions) in your office or for relaxing after a busy day at the office before you begin your evening schedule.

Learn to say no. When handed a request, don't just say yes automatically. Ask yourself if you really do have the time to do this project or if there is a good reason why only you can do it. Or, try a trade-off and delegate one of your tasks to the person making the request.

Plan your time. An hour of planning can result in three or four hours of productivity! Plan for at least one hour each week, if not more. At the end of each day, plan out what you'd like to accomplish the next day. Write it down on your To Do list. It's easier to work toward a goal once it's written on paper.

Focus on high-priority work. According to William Yeoman, author of *1,000 Things You Never Learned in Business School,* you need to be aware of the work that is most important to you. People who work on their top priorities are leaders, while those who work on low priorities are clerks. Yeoman advises getting a big calendar that displays one month at a time with spaces big enough to write in. At the start of the year, go through each month and mark off holidays, vacations, and trips. Pencil in standing meetings and lunches, and block out tentative times for regular events, such as budgeting and performance appraisals. Block out time for No. 1 priorities.

Each Monday, take a long view of the week. Adjust your calendar so that you can devote as much time as possible to high-priority work. At the start of each day, make a list of all the tasks you have to do. Tasks related to your No. 1 priority should be done first. Then take on the No. 2 priority items. Skip or delegate the No. 3 priority tasks.

Schedule the hardest tasks for the time when you're at your mental peak. Group like tasks, such as phone calls — it's easier than doing one here and one there — and budget time for them in the calendar.

Schedule a daily quiet hour. Use this time to work without phone calls or other interruptions, to really concentrate on priority items or to get organized. Insist on not being interrupted during this time by having a secretary or co-worker screen your calls and putting a "Quiet Hour" sign on your door or desk. You'll be amazed how much you can get done in one quality block of time.

Beat the "CULPRITS." Time management teacher and consultant Donna Goldfein says these are the culprits that will let you use your time better once you beat them:

C – clutter

U – unfinished work (you say "yes" too often)

L – lots of anything (clothes, magazine subscriptions)

P – procrastination

R – racing through each day (work smarter, not harder)

I – interruptions (minimize them)

T – telephone (when you allow digressions)

Try the buddy system

Another way to help implement your new lifestyle is to find a friend or co-worker who would also like to improve their time management skills. A partner can help sustain interest and enthusiasm in a time management program — and almost anything else, including dieting, exercise, and other support groups. "Going public" increases commitment and helps prevent regression to old, bad habits, says Alec Mackenzie in *New Time Management Methods.*

In the buddy system, two or more managers agree to meet regularly (once a week) for lunch to check on each other's progress in managing time, and make commitments on what they want to achieve in the next week. The "buddy system" is often effective in maintaining progress or changes developed in seminars and meetings. And it sure beats doing it alone.

Where do we go from here?

Time management skills need to be reinforced so you can constantly improve your efficiency and effectiveness. The more effective you are, the closer you'll come to reaching your goals, whether you want to be promoted to vice president, head up your own business, retire at age 50, or spend time with your family.

Some people believe that time management is something which can be learned and never forgotten, like riding a bicycle. But on the contrary, time management is more like a sports skill of higher refinement, such as tennis or golf. In order to keep yourself "playing well" and/or improving, regular practice is required.

Strive to learn more about time management by continuing to look for time management advice. Below are a few suggestions to get started. Chapter 26 lists various time management resources in detail.

While *Execu*time's*® first book, *Time Management for Executives* (published by Charles Scribners, 1981), co-authored with Susan K. Jones, has been out of print and not available in bookstores for several years, we still have an inventory of a few hundred copies. Should you want a copy of that book send a check for $17.95 plus $3.50 shipping and handling to Desktop Graphics Inc., 26940 N. Longwood Rd., Lake

using time management

Forest, Illinois 60045-1071 and, as long as quantities hold out, we'll ship you a copy directly. Allow about 3-4 weeks for delivery.

Take time to attend a seminar. In Chapter 26 we've provided you with a list of providers of time management consulting, seminars, etc. Some of these are seminars are put on as open seminars that you can simply sign up and enroll in. You may want to consider attending such a seminar. Should your company or professional association be interested in having a time management seminar put on for your group, Lauren, as well as the resources listed in the back of the book, is available to provide your company or organization with a one- or two-day time management seminar.

Keep up with time management basics. Don't neglect to use a To Do list, and if you feel you are losing control of such planning, try a time log to see where your "time drains" are. Before important meetings, review your meeting "musts," such as a good agenda, timing, etc. Practice delegation and consider how best to handle an increase in your staff from a time management perspective.

Be on the alert for time management advice. Remember, don't say you don't have time to read — simply allocate 15 minutes a day to read (or listen to) subjects of importance to you. In a year's time, you will have covered an impressive bank of knowledge.

· · ·

Please take a few minutes to drop us a note at Desktop Graphics, Inc., 26940 North Longwood Road, Lake Forest, Illinois 60045-1071, FAX 708/362-0496, and tell us about how you've gone about implementing a time-saving technique in your life.

May your fun time get better, because you've organized your work time more efficiently! Don't forget that having fun in life is what life is all about. If you organize your business time to make available to you more time to do the things you want to do then we have achieved our purposes! As for us, Kim is off to Hawaii for a two week vacation, while Lauren is off to New York for a few days on business and then later will spend two weeks fishing in the Caribbean! We can take time to have fun in life because we've organized our business lives to the point we have!

May God Grant You the Serenity to Accept the Things You Cannot Change, the Courage to Change the Things You Can and the Wisdom to Know the Difference. May God be with you and grant you a full life! One Day at a Time! ◗

Chapter 25: Summary

■ **Decide on your time management goals, then develop a plan to work toward those goals.**

■ **Remember why you wanted to better manage your time: would you like to get more work done, spend time with your family, or save time for working out?**

■ **Continually expand your time management knowledge by reinforcing what you've learned and turning to other material for new information.**

using time management

chapter twentysix

Other Time Management Resources

Cassette Tapes & Films

An extensive catalog of motivational tapes including several on time management are available from

> Nightingale Conant Corporation
> 7300 Lehigh Avenue, Niles, Illinois 60648
> Phone: 708/647-0300

Other instructional films and cassette tapes are available from your local library. In addition, many cassettes on time management can be found in various book stores.

Best-known Time Management Consultants/Writers/Speakers

All of the consultants on this list are personally known to us. A further list of lesser known speaker sources follows this list. This is neither an endorsement nor a criticism of the individual involved — it is simply that we've known these people personally for a decade or more and believe that they are competent time management professionals who provide competent advice.

William H. Blades, Republic Speakers Bureau
8890 S. Grandview, Tempe, AZ 85284
Phone: 602/470-0699

Blades' primary seminar is titled "Spending Major Time on Major Things," and is geared toward sales and management personnel. He is also the author of *Leadership Strategists*. A veteran of the time management business.

Edwin Bliss, El Rancho Loma Serena
2220 Carolyn Street, Kingsburg, CA 93631
Phone: 209/897-1569

Edwin Bliss is an old-timer in the time management profession and one of the top time management consultants and author of several books on time management. Bliss teaches both corporate seminars and seminars for the professional seminar companies. He is a solid time management teacher.

Dr. Merrill Douglass, Time Management Center
1401 Johnson Ferry Rd., #328D6 , Marietta, GA 30062
Phone: 404/973-3977

A full-time college professor and the author of numerous books on time management, Douglass leads many time management seminars sponsored by the American Management Association. He consults on time management, stress management, and change. If you have one or two people who need a time management seminar we suggest you consider sending them to one of his AMA seminars.

Lauren R. Januz, Januz Consultants/Desktop Graphics Inc.
26940 North Longwood Rd. Mettawa-, Lake Forest, IL 60045-1071
Phone: 708/362-0024, FAX: 708/362-0496

Januz conducts fully customized seminars and keynote speeches on time management, industrial direct marketing and catalog marketing. He was for 13 years the editor and publisher of *Execu*Time®, the newsletter on the effective use of executive time,* and the co-author of this book, *Using Time Management to Get More Done* and *Time Management for Executives,* (co-authored with Susan K. Jones). He also puts on alcoholism awareness/prevention seminars on college campuses and corporate environments and is available as a marketing consultant specializing in direct response marketing and marketing via catalogs.

John Lee, Hour Power Inc.
Lake Ellen Executive Center, Box 398 , Crawfordville, FL 32327
Phone: 904/926-7121

One of the long-time time management consultants. Has written several time management books and does extensive consulting and puts on seminars.

Dr. Sam Lilly, Learning Resources Institute
5202 Washington St., Suite 6, P.O. Box 271, Downers Grove, IL 60515
Phone: 708/963-0398

Lilly is a highly professional public speaker who speaks on a wide variety of subjects including time management. He is a generalist on time management but a very competent speaker who is entertaining and well worth his fee.

Dr. Alec Mackenzie, Alec Mackenzie and Associates
P.O. Box 130, Greenwich, NY 12834
Phone: 518/692-9626

A well known time management consultant, Mackenzie (a lawyer and college professor) has also authored more than 80 time management articles and several books on the subject, including *The Time Trap* and *Time for Success*. His material is excellent, however Mackenzie is best known for his books and for the fact that he takes a very theoretical or academic approach to the subject. He is well known as a corporate consultant.

Fred Pryor, Fred Pryor Seminars
P.O. Box 2951, Mission, KS 66202
Phone: 913/384-6400

Pryor's company offers a variety of speakers with varying expertise in time management. Pryor himself no longer teaches seminars but the company promotes seminars on a wide variety of topics. If you have just 2-3 people to attend a seminar on time management, rather than looking for an in-house corporate seminar his programs probably will fill your bill. Speakers on his staff are well trained in the subject.

Greg Risberg, MSW
295 Church St., Elmhurst, IL 60126
Phone: 708/833-5066.

Risberg is a practicing psychologist whose main subject is
interpersonal relations in business and the art of touching in the
business world. He is an excellent and very entertaining luncheon
or after dinner speaker at a time management or sales meeting.

Sally Scobey, Total Communications Services
412 Lindsay Lane, West Dundee, IL 60118
Phone: 708/425-5626

A former regional NBC NEWS anchorwoman, Scobey is a speaker
on both stress management and time management. She is a
dynamic, very experienced public speaker who puts loads of
enthusiasm into her presentation and keeps the audience sitting on
the edge of their chairs for her entire presentation! Sally is one of
our favorite time management speakers and we highly recommend
her for an entertaining and competent performance that will keep
her listeners on the edge of their seats. She speaks on several other
subjects as well and does corporate seminars.

Additional Speakers and Consultants

We can neither recommend nor endorse any of the speakers on the
following list only because we are not personally acquainted with them or
their credentials. We suggest that you review each speaker's credentials
individually and select the appropriate speaker for your needs.

Frank and Monica Adick, Dew Point International Ltd.,
522 Ocean Centre, Harbour City 5, Tsimshatsui, Kowloon, Hong Kong
Phone: 01/852-730-1151

Larry Baker, Time Management Center
1590 Woodlake Dr., Suite 111, Chesterfield, MO 63017
Phone: 314/230-0900

Darlene Bordeaux,
P.O. Box 2674, Rancho Palos Verdes, CA 90274
Phone: 213/370-4328

Gayle Carson, Gayle Carson Presents
2957 Flamingo Dr., Miami Beach, FL 33140
Phone: 305/534-8846

Stuart Crump, Personal Communication
P.O. Box 1519-CJ, Herdon, VA 22070
Phone: 703/787-4647

Dr. Stanley R. Frager, Frager Associates
3906 DuPont Square So., Louisville, KY 40207
Phone: 502/893-6654

Patricia Fripp, Take Charge
527 Hugo St., San Francisco, CA 94122
Phone: 415/753-6556

James Hennig
P.O. Box 18055, Green Bay, WI 54304
Phone: 414/499-5550

Donald L. Kirkpatrick, University of Wisconsin
1920 Hawthorne Dr., Elm Grove, WI 53122
Phone: 414/784-8348

Laura N. Miller
1640 Redwood Way, Upland, CA 91786
Phone: 714/949-7342

Alan J. Parisse, Alan J. Parisse & Associates
6114 LaSalle Ave., Suite 438, Oakland, CA 94611
Phone: 415/531-7585

Marshall E. Reddick, Management Development Seminars
5151 State University Dr., Los Angeles, CA 90032
Phone: 818/780-8103

to get more done

Michael Woolery
3205 NW 63rd St.,Oklahoma City, OK 73116
Phone: 405/840-1751

<hr>

Speaker's Bureaus that Represent Time Management Speakers

John Palmer, National Speakers Bureau
222 East Wisconsin Avenue, Lake Forest, Illinois 60045
Phone: 708/295-1122

A well known speaker's bureau that represents big name figures in
business, politics and sports. Personally known to us as one of the
top bureaus in the business!

Cheryl Miller, Speakers International Inc.
51-W Sherwood Terrace, Lake Bluff, IL 60044
Phone: 708/295-5866

In addition to time management speakers, Ms. Miller represents
many big name sports, business, political and public pesonalities.
Ms. Miller is personally known to us and is highly recommended
by us as an extremely competent and ethical speaker's agency/
bureau!

Dottie Walters, Walters International Speakers Bureau
18825 Hicrest Rd., P.O. Box 1120, Glendora, CA 91740
Phone: 818/335-8069

Ms. Walters represents a wide variety of speakers of many types.
Many of her speakers are lower in price and somewhat less well
known that those listed by the two bureaus above.

National Speakers Association (NSA)
3877 North Seventh St., Suite 350, Phoenix, AZ 85014
Phone: 602/265-1002

NSA is an association of speaker's bureaus, professional speakers and
those who would like to become speakers. Membership in the
organization is open to anybody who wants to speak professionally.
Their membership directory lists several hundred additional speakers
who claim to speak on the subject of time management.

Most of the speakers on the preceeding pages are members of NSA.

using time management

However, nothing in the NSA membership screening procedure does anything to check the time management competence or expertise of a speaker member. We strongly suggest that you review each speaker's credentials very carefully before contracting with the speaker you choose. Many time management speakers listed as NSA members are not only totally unknown to us but were not even listed by NSA in their previous year's membership directory. Accordingly, we suggest that you "proceed with caution" before hiring any time management speaker as only those listed on the previous pages are known well enough to us that we can recommend their credentials. We strongly urge the use of a good speaker's bureau if you deviate from the list of speakers preceding.

chapter twentyseven
Other Books on
Time Management

Adelman, Conrad, **How to Manage Your Sales Time.** IBMS Incorporated. ISBN 0-933738-090-5.

Allen, Jane E. **Beyond Time Management—Organizing the Organization.** Reading, MA: Addison-Wesley Publishing Company, Incorporated, 1986.

Allen, Nancy. **Expand Your Time Use Potential.** Mentor, OH: NETWIC, 1987.

Allen, Robert F. **A Program for Personal Change on Stress Resolution.** Human Res. Inst.

Alexander, Roy, **Commonsense Time Management.** AMA Worksmart Series. 120p, Paperback. Amacom Books, New York, 1992.

Anderson, Richard C. & Dobyns, L.R. **Time: The Irretrievable Asset.** Correlan Publications.

Applebaum, Steven & Rohra, Walter F. **Time Management for Health Care Professionals.** Aspen Publishers, Inc. 1981. ISBN 0-89443-378-4.

Armstrong, Richard. **The Time Of Your Life.** New York: Christophers, 1977.

Auger, B. Y. **How To Run Better Business Meetings.** New York: Amacom, 1972.

Baer, J. L. and Fensterheim H. **Don't Say Yes When You Want To Say No.** New York: McKay, 1975.

Barkas, J. L. **Creative Time Management — Become More Productive & Still Have Time For Fun.** Englewood Cliffs, NJ: Prentice Hall, 1984.

Barnes, Emilie, **The Fifteen Minute Organizer**, 258p, Harvest House, 1990,   ISBN,0-07-005584-X

Becker, Selwyn W. **The Efficient Organization.** New York: Elsevier, 1975.

Belken, Loren B. **The First Time Manager,** Amacom Books, 1986. ISBN 0-8144-   5950-2.

Benson, Herbert. **The Relaxation Response.** New York: Morrow, 1975.

Billingsley, Ann V. **Getting the Twenty-Fifth Hour.** Hearth Publications, 1988.

Bittel, Lester R., **Right on Time: The Complete Guide for Time-Pressured Managers,** 1990, ISBN 0-07-005584-X, McGraw Hill, New York

Black, Roger. **Getting Things Done: A Radical New Approach to Managing Time & Achieving More at Work.** Viking Penguin, 1990.

Bliss, Edwin. **Getting Things Done.** New York: Scribners, 1976, rev. 1983.

Bloch, Arthur. **Murphy's Law.** Los Angles: Price, Stern, Sloan, 1977.

Bond, William J. **One Thousand One Ways To Beat The Time Trap.** Hollywood, FL: Frederick Fell Publishers, Incorporated, 1982.

Brooks, William T. **High Impact Time Management.** Prentice-Hall, 1989.

Brown, Ronald. **From Selling to Managing: Guidlines for the First-time Sales Manager.** Amacom Books. 1990. ISBN 0-8144-7746-1.

Carrington, Patricia. **Stopping to Gain Perspective: A Skills Training Program for the Management of Stress.** Pace Education Systems.

Christie, Les. **Time Allocation–Getting A Grip On Time Management.** Wheaton, IL: Victor Books, 1984.

Cochran, J. Wesley. **Time Management Handbook for Librarians.** Greenwood Publishing Group, 1991. ISBN 0-313-27842-3.

Cochran, David W. **Getting Things Done –A Home Study Course.** Blawenburg, NJ: Fruition Publications, Incorporated, 1981.

Collins, Cathy. **Time Management for Teachers: Practical Techniques and Skills that Give you More to Teach.** Prentice Hall. 1987. ISBN 0-13- 921701-0.

Cook, L. P. **No Down Time: Six Steps of Industrial Problem-Solving.** Paperback. Addison-Wesley Publishing Co., Inc., 1991. ISBN 0-201-55065-2.

Cooper, Joseph. **How To Get More Done In Less Time.** Rev. ed. New York: Doubleday, 1971.

Cooper, Robert K., **The Performance Edge: New Strategies to Maximize Your Work Effectivess and Competitive Advantage,** ISBN 0-07-005586-6,McGraw Hill, New York, paperback

Crisp. **Practical Time Management: How to Make the Most of Your Most Perishable Resource.** Crisp Publications, Inc., Paper. 1-56052-018-3.

Criswell, John W. **Maintenance Time Management.** 1991. Fairmont Press, Inc. ISBN 0-88173-116-11.

Culp, Stephanie. **How To Get Organized When You Don't Have The Time.** Cincinnati: Writer's Digest Books, 1986.

Davenport, Rita. **Making Time, Making Money–A Step-By-Step Program To Se Your Goals & Achieve Success.** New York: Saint Martin's Press, Inc., 1982.

Davidson, James. **Effective Time Management.** New York: Human Sciences, 1978.

Dayton, Edward R. **Tools For Time Management.** Grand Rapids, MI: Zondervan, 1974, rev. 1983.

Dobyns, Richard C., and Dobyns R.L. **Time: The Irretrievable Asset.** Watsonville, CA: Correlan, 1973.

Dorff, Pat. **File...Don't Pile.** St Martin, 1986.

using time management

Douglas, Baker. **The New Time Management.** R. R. Bowker, 1987-1991.

Douglass, Merrill E. **Timely Time Tips.** Grandville, MI: Time Management Center, 1975.

Douglass, Merill and Douglass, Donna. **Manage Your Time, Manage Yourself.** New York: AMAcom, Div. of Amer. Mgt. Assn., 1985. ISBN 0-8144-7632-5.

Douglass, Merrill E. & Goodwin, Philip H. **Successful Time Management for Hospital Administrators.** Books on Demand, Inc., 1980. ISBN 0-317-26716-7.

Drawbaugh, Charles C. **Time & It's Use –A Self Management Guide For Teachers.** New York: Columbia University, Teachers College, Teachers College Press, 1984. ISBN 0-8077-2706-7.

Drucker, Peter. **People And Performance.** New York: Harper and Row, 1977.

Dunsing, Richard J. **You And I Have Got To Stop Meeting This Way.** New York: American Management Assn., 1978.

Eisenberg, Ronnie & Kelly, Kate. **Organize Yourself!** Macmillan, 1986.

Engstrom, Ted, and Mackenzie, R. Alec. **Managing Your Time.** Grand Rapids, MI: Zondervan, 1967, rev. 1988.

Erickson, Kenneth A. **Christian Time Management.** Concordia Publishing House, 1985. ISBN 0-570-03972-X.

Evatt, Crislynne. **How to Organize Your Closet...& Your Life!** Ballantine, 1981.

Fanning, Tony, and Fanning, Robbie. **Get It All Done And Still Be Human; A Personal Time Management Workshop.** Open Chain Publishing Co. 1990. ISBN 0-932086-22-5.

Feldman, Edwin B. **How To Use Your Time And Get Things Done.** New York: Fell, 1968.

Ferner, Jack D. **Successful Time Management.** John Wiley and Sons, Inc., 1980. Paperback. ISBN 0-471-03911-X.

Finn, Kennet R. **Time Management.** (Simulation Game Serv). Didactic Systems, Inc., 1975. ISBN 0-685-78118-6.

Flannery, Raymond B., Jr. **Becoming Stress-Resistant: Improved Well-Being Through the Project SMART System.** Continuum, 1990.

Frailey, Lester E. **Handbook Of Business Letters.** West Nyack, NY: Prentice-Hall, Inc., 1965.

Frame, J. Davidson. **Managing Projects in Organizations: How to Make the Best Use of Time, Techniques and People.** Jossey-Baas Inc., Publishers. 1987. ISBN 1-55542-031-1.

Fitzwater, Ivan. **Time Under Control: Efficient Self-Management In and Out of the Office.** Corona Publishing Company, 1988. ISBN 0-931722-63-2.

Goldfein, Donna. **Everywoman's Guide To Time Management.** Millbrae, CA: Les Femmes, 1977.

Goodloe, Alfred; Bensahel, Jane and Kelly, John. **Managing Yourself - How To Control Emotion, Stress, & Time.** New York: Franklin Watts Incorporated, 1984.

Grossman, Lee. **Fat Paper.** New York: McGraw-Hill, 1978.

Groves, D.L. & Groves, S.L. **Developing a Time Budget.** Appalachian Assocs., 1978.

Hashmi, Sajjad A. **Make Every Second Count.** National Underwriter, 1989.

using time management

Haynes, Marion E.; Crisp, Michael G. and Mapson, Ralph. **Personal Time Management.** Los Altos, CA: Crisp Publication, Incorporated, 1987.

Haynes, Marion E. **Practice Time Management.** Tulsa: PennWell Books, 1984. ISBN 0-897814-273-8.

Heimer, Ray G. **Time Management for Engineers and Constructors.** AmericanSociety of Civil Engineers, 1991. ISBN 0-087262-793-4.

Hemphill, Barbara. **Taming the Paper Tiger: Organizing the Paper in Your Life.** Hemphill & Associates, 1990.

Herzberg, F. **The Managerial Choice.** Homewood, IL: Irwin, 1976.

Hirsch, Grechen. **Womanhours: A Twenty-One Day Time Management Plan That Works.** St. Martin, 1983. ISBN 0-312-88710-8.

Hobbs, Chalres R. **Time Power: The Reveolutionary Time Management System that Can Change Your Professional and Personal Life.** HarperCollins Publishers, 1988. ISBN 0-06-091490-4.

Hockheiser, Robert. **Time Management (Business Success Series).** Barron's Educational Series, Incorporated. 1992. Paperback.

Holmes, Ivory H. **The Allocation of Time by Women Without Family Responsibilities,** U. Pr. of America, 1983.

Hoyt, John S. **Personal Time Management Manual.** St. Paul: Telstar, Incorporated, 1981. ISBN 0-931975-15-8.

Hoyt, John S. **Personal Time Management Study Guide.** St Paul: Telstar, Incorporated, 1981.

Hughes, Charles L. **Goal Setting: Key to Individual & Organizational Effectiveness.** Books on Demand, UMI.

Hunt, Diane. **Tao of Time.** 1991. ISBN 0-671-73411-3. Fireside, S & S Trade, 1991.

Hunt, Diane S. and Hait, Pam. **Studying Short: Time Management for College Students.** Harper Collins Publishers Inc., 1990. ISBN 0-06-463733-6.

Hutchins, Raymond G. **Time Tracker.** Prentice Hall, 1991. ISBN 0-13-9-21859-9.

Januz, Lauren R., and Jones, Susan K. **Time Management For Executives–A Handbook From The Editors Of Execu-Time.** New York: Scribners, 1982.

Januz, Lauren R. and Jones, Susan, K. **More Time Management for Executives.** Springfield, IL. Smith Collins, 1992.

Januz, Lauren R., and Magon, Kim M. **Using Time Management to Get More Done.** Smith Collins, Springfield, IL, 1992

Jefferies, Stephen C. **Time Management Study Guide: A Manual to Accompany The Coaches Guide to Time Management.** 3-ring notebook. Human Kinetics Publishers, ISBN 0-931250-98-5.

Joyner, Gail W. **Super Mom's Organized Scheduler.** Supermom, Inc., 1991. ISBN 0-962842-0-6

Jungiohann, Kathy & Schenck, Becky R. **How to Understand & Manage Your Time.** Science Research Assocs., 1986.

Karaffa, Melanie C. **The Time Saver.** 1991. Practice Management InformationCorporation, ISBN 1-8784870-15-9.

Kast, Verena. **The Creative Leap: Psychological Transformation Through Crisis.** Chiron Publications, 1991.

using time management

King, James P. The Trace System: **How to Get Organized, How to Stay Organized.** Brown House, 1986.

King, Pat. **Time, Making It Work For You.** Lynnwood, WA: Aglow Publications, rev. 1986.

Kozoll, Charles E. **Plan For Success–Time Management For The Pre-Med Student.** Champaign, IL: National Association Of Advisors For The Health Professions, Incorporated, 1984.

Kozoll, Charles E. **Coaches Guide to Time Management.** Human Kinetics Publishers, 1985. ISBN 0-931250-97-8.

Laird, Donald A., and Laird, Eleanor C. **The Techniques Of Delegating.** New York: McGraw-Hill, 1957.

Laiken, Alan. **How To Control The Time Of Your Life.** New York: Norton, 1978.

Laiken, Alan. **How To Get Control Of Your Time And Your Life.** New York: Wyden, 1973.

Leas, Speed B. **Time Management. Creative Leadership Series.** Abingdon Press 1978. ISBN 0-687-42120-9.

Lebhar, M. Godfrey. **Use Of Time.** New York: Lebhar-Friedman, 1958.

Le Boeuf, Michael. **Working Smart.** New York: McGraw-Hill, 1980.

Lebov, Myrna. **Practical Tools & Techniques for Managing Time.** Executive Enterprises Publishing Co., 1981. ISBN 0-917396-38-8.

Lehrer, Robert N. **Work Simplification.** Englewood Cliffs, NJ: Prentice-Hall, 1972.

Le Tourneau, Richard. **Management Plus.** Grand Rapids, MI: Zondervan, 1976.

Levinson, Jay . **The Ninety-Minute Hour: Combining Time-Saving Technology with New Age Psychology to Take You Beyond Time Management.** Dutton, 1990. ISBN 0-317-02816-2.

Levinson, Jay. **The Ninety Minute Hour: Technological and Psychological Breakthroughs Take you Beyond Time Management.** Dutton. 1990. ISBN 0-525-24851-X.

Lewis, James P. **Project Planning, Scheduling and Control: A Hands-On Guide To Bringing Projects in One Time and Budget.** Probus Publishing Company Inc., 1991. ISBN 1-55738-204-2.

Lieberman, H. and Rausch, Erwin. **Managing And Allocating Time: Industrial.** Cranford, NJ: Didactic Systems, 1976. ISBN 0-894012-060-3.

Lieberman, Harvey and Rausch, Erwin. **Managing and Allocated Time: Non-Industrial.** Didactic Systems, Inc., 1976. ISBN 0-685-73582-6.

Liebling, Henry E. **The First Personal Productivity Handbook.** Hoboken, NJ: Skill Builders, Incorporated, 1983.

Linder, Staffan B. **The Harried Leisure Class.** Columbia University Press, 1970.

Loen, Raymond. **Manage More By Doing Less.** New York: McGraw-Hill, 1971.

Longeward, Dorothy and James, Muriel. **Born To Win.** New York: NAL, 1978.

Love, Sydney. **Mastery And Management Of Time.** Englewood Cliffs, NJ: Prentice-Hall, 1978. ISBN 0-13-559971-7, Buen.

using time management

Lowe, Sydney. **Mastery & Management Of Time.** Englewood Cliffs, NJ: Prentice Hall, 1982.

McBee, Wanda B. **How To Enhance & Control Your Time, Life & Career.** Fort Collins, CO: Workshops Unlimited, 1986.

McClelland, David. **The Achievement Motive.** New York: Appleton, 1953.

McConkey, Dale. **No-Nonsense Delegation.** New York: American Management Assn., 1974.

McGill, Michael E. **The 40 To 60 Year Old Male.** New York: Simon and Schuster, 1980.

McKay, James T. **The Management Of Time.** Englewood Cliffs, NJ: Prentice-Hall, 1958.

Mackenzie, R. Alec. **New Time-Management Methods For You And Your Staff.** Chicago: Dartnell, 1990.

Mackenzie, Alec. **The Time Trap.** New York: Amacom, 1972.

Mackenzie, Alec. **The Time Trap: The New Version of the 20-Year Classic on Time Management,** AMACOM, 1990.

Mackenzie, R. Alec. **The Time Trap,** McGraw, 1975.

Mackenzie, R. Alec, **Teamwork Through Time Management: New Time Management Methods for Everyone in your Organization.** 1991. Dartnell. ISBN 0-85013-182-0

Mackenzie, Alec & Waldo, Kay C. **About Time! A Woman's Guide to Time Management.** McGraw, 1981. ISBN 0-07-044651-2.

Maltz, Maxwell. **Psycho-Cybernetics.** Englewood Cliffs, NJ: Prentice-Hall, 1960.

Management Update, Ltd. Staff. **Making Effective Use Of Executive Time.** New York: State Mutual Book & Periodical Service, Limited, 1986.

Marcus, Jay B. **The TM And Business.** New York: McGraw-Hill, 1977.

Materka, Pat R. **Time In, Time Out, Time Enough–A Time Management Guide For Women.** Englewood Cliffs, NJ: Prentice-Hall, 1982.

McRae, Bradley C. **Practical Time Management; How to Get More Things Done In Less Time.** International Self-Counsel Press. 1988. ISBN 0-0-88908- 673-7.

Meyers, Fred E. **Motion & Time Study: Improving Work Methods and Management,** Prentice Hall, 1992.

Merrill, A. Roger & Merrill, Rebecca R. **Connections: Quadrant II Time Management,** Institute for Principle-Centered Leadership, 1989.

Messina, James J. **The Time Management Handbook.** Tampa, FL: Advanced Development Systems, Incorporated, 1982. ISBN 0-931975-15-8.

Miller, Elizabeth L., and Burns Carol J. **I Just Need More Time.** Wichita Falls, TX: Woman Time Management, 1984. ISBN 0-9610530-0-3.

Mintzberg, Henry. **The Nature Of Managerial Work.** New York: Harper and Row, 1973.

Munoz, Tisziji. **Time Mastery–The Beginner's Book.** Schenectady, NY: Illumination Society Publications, 1987.

Murphy, Dennis J. **Supervisory Handbook, 3 volumes, including Successful Time Management for Supervisors: How to Get More Done, Improve Quality, Meet Deadlines & Control Your Time.** Professional Training Assocs. Inc., 1981.

Nauman, Ann & Dearman, Marvene. **Making Every Minute Count: Time Management for Librarians.** Library Learning Resources, Inc. 1991. ISBN 0-931315-06-9

Neal, Richard G., and Felts, Frances I. **Managing Time–An Administrator's Guide.** Manassas, VA, 1982.

Newman, William H. **Administrative Action.** Englewood Cliffs, NJ: Prentice-Hall, 1963.

Nichols, Ralph and Stevens, Leonard. **Are You Listening?** New York: McGraw-Hill, 1957.

Odiorne, George. **Management And The Activity Trap.** New York: Harper and Row, 1974.

O'Frank, Milo. Rubenstein, Julie, Editor. **How to Have a Successful Meeting in Half the Time.** Pocket Books. 1990. ISBN 0-671-72601-3.

O'Hara, Bruce. **Put Work In Its Place: How to Redesign Your Job to Fit Your Life.** New Ways Publishing.

Oncken, William Jr. **Managing Manasgement Time: Who's Got the Monkey?** Prentice Hall, 1986. ISBN 0-13-550690-5.

One Hundred Fifty-Five Office Shortcuts And Time Savers For The Secretary. Englewood Cliffs, NJ: Parker Publishing, 1973.

Parikh, Girish. **The One Minute Organizing Secret: Finding Electronic Files, Papers, Books & Almost Everything Fast!** Shetal Enterprises, 1985.

Parkinson, C. Northcote. **Parkinson's Law.** Boston: Houghton Mifflin, 1957.

Pearson, Barrie. **Common-Sense Time Management.** 1991. Slawson Communications, Incorporated. ISBN 1-85251-046-3.

Phillips, Mike. **Getting More Done In Less Time.** Minneapolis: Bethany House Publishers, 1982.

Portner, Hal & Pauker, Robert. **How to Study Less and Accomplish More: Time Management for Students.** Portner Publishing. 1983. ISBN 0-913149-00-4.

Randall, John C. **How to Save Time...And Worry Less.** Hotline-Multi Enterprises, 1980.

Ravage, John. **Time Out: Time Management Strategies for the Real Estate Professional.** Dearborn Financial Publishing. 1991. ISBN 0-7931-0210-3.

Reynolds, Helen. **Executive Time Management: Getting 12 Hours Work out of an 8-Hour Day.** Ingrahm Data. 1983.

Ross, Joel E. **Managing Productivity.** West Nyack, NY: Management Books Institute, 1977.

Rothery, Brian. **How To Organize Your Time And Resources.** New York: Beekman, 1972.

Saaty, Thomas L. **Multicriteria Decision Making—The Analytic Heirarch Process: Planning, Priority Setting, Resource Allocation.** Reproduction of edited paper. ISBN 0-9620317-2-0. RWS Publications. 1990.

Schaill, William S. **Seven Days To Faster Reading.** Hollywood: Wilshire Book Company, n.d.

Schenck, Becky R. **How To Understand & Manage Your Time.** Chicago: Science Research Associates, 1986.

Schlenger, Sunny and Roesch, Roberta. **Organizing In Style—A Creative Approach To Managing Your Time & Space.** New York: NAL Penguin Incorporated, 1988.

Schofield, Deniece. **Springing the Time Trap: Time Management for Today's Busy Homemaker.** Deserst Book Company, 1987. ISBN 0-87579-100-x.

Schneiderjans, Marc J. **Topics in Just-in-Time Management.** 400p. 1992. Allyn & Bacon Publishers., 1992., ISBN 0-8120-4792-3.

Scirocco, Frank E. **How to Make Great Use of Your Precious Moments: A Guide to Successful Time Management.** FES Publications, ISBN 0-9623089-1-9.

Scollard, Jeanette R. **No-Nonsense Management Tips For Women.** New York: Simon & Schuster, Incorporated, 1983.

Scott, Dru. **How To Put More Time In Your Life.** New York: NAL Penguin Incorporated, 1981.

Scott, Dru; Crisp, Michael G. and Mapson, Ralph. **Time Management On The Telephone.** Los Altos, CA: Crisp Publications, Incorporated, 1988.

Seidenstricker, Marianne P., **Managing Motherhood: Support and Survival Techniques for Mothers of Very Young Children,** KMS Products, 1991. ISBN 0-9627437-0-4

Seiwert, Lothar J. **Time is Money...Save It.** Dow Jones Irwin, 1989.

Sharp, C. **The Economics Of Time.** New York: Halsted Press, 1981.

Shipman, Neil J. & Martin, Jack. **Effective Time Management Techniques for School Administrators.** Prentice-Hall, 1983. ISBN 0-13-246488-8.

Short, Mark. **Time Management for Ministers.** Broadmen Press. 1987. ISBN 0-8054-3114-4.

Skopec, Eric W. and Kiely, Laree. **Taking Charge: Time Management for Personal and Professional Productivity.** Addison-Wesley Publishing Company, 1991. ISBN 0-201-55039-3.

Sloma, Richard S. **No-Nonsense Management.** New York: Macmilliam, 1977.

Smith, Allan H. **Time Management for Business People.** Success Publishing, 1988.

Smith, Manuel J. **When I Say No I Feel Guilty.** New York: Dial, 1975.

Stein, Mark L. **The T Factor.** New York: Playboy, 1977.

Stretton, Barbara. **BLR Handbook Of Practical Time Management.** Madison, CT: Business & Legal Reports, 1986.

Sundin, Hakan. **More Effective Workdays.** New York: Vantage Press Incorporated, 1987.

Tanner, Ogden. **et al. Stress.** Alexandria, VA: Time-Life, 1976.

Taylor, Harold. **Making Time Work For You—A Guidebook To Effective & Productive Time Management.** New York: Beaufort Books, Publishers, 1982.

Timpe, A. Dale. **Management of Time.** Facts on File Inc., 1986. ISBN 0-9169-1461-2.

The Time Management Workbook. Grandville, MI: Time Management Center, 1980

Thomas, Philip R. & Martin, Kenneth R. **Getting Competitive: Middle Managers and the Cycle Time Ethic.** McGraw, New York, 1991.

using time management

Thomass, P.R. & Martin, K.R. **Competitiveness Through Total Cycle Time: an Overview for CEOs.** McGraw-Hill Incorporated. 1990. ISBN 0-07- 064273-7.

Timpe, A. Dale. **Management Of Time.** New York: Facts On File, Incorporated, 1986.

Turla, Peter and Hawkins, Kathleen. **Time Management Made Easy.** New York: E. P. Dutton, 1984. ISBN 0-525-48247-4.

Uris, Auren. **The Efficient Executive.** New York: McGraw-Hill, 1957.

Van Fleet, James. **Twenty-Two Biggest Mistakes Managers Make And How To Correct Them.** Englewood Cliffs, NJ: Prentice-Hall, 1973.

Vizza, Robert F. **Time And Territory Management For The Salesman.** New York: Sales Executive Club, 1971.

Waldo, Kay C. **About Time!-A Woman's Guide To Time Management.** New York: McGraw-Hill, 1981.

Walters, Raymond Jr., **Harvest Time: Wayus to Plan for and Enjoy Your Life After Fifty.** 1991. Ten Speed Press., ISBN 0-89815-375-1.

Webber, Ross A. **The Procrastinator's Guide to Getting Things Done.** Free Pr.

Webber, Ross A. **Time Is Money! Tested Tactics That Conserve Time for Top Executives,** Free Pr., 1980.

Webber, A. Ross. **Time And Management.** New York: Van Nostrand Reinhold, 1977.

Weiss, W. H. **Decision Making for First-time Managers.** AMACOM Books. 1986. ISBN 0-8144-5958-2.

Whiteman, Gilbert L. Bruce, Stephen D., Editor. **Managing Time and Stress. Business and Legal Reports.** Paper. 1985. ISBN 1-55545-554-2.

Whisenhurt, Donald W. **Administrative Time Management—Tips For Administrators & Aspiring Administrators.** Lanham, MD: University Press of America, 1987.

Whysler, R. O. **Get Going!–Tips On Managing Your Time & Increasing Your Effectiveness.** Tustin, CA: International Business & Management Institute, 1982.

Wilson, Howard. **Utilizing Time Effectively Through Better Management Processes.** Administrative Research Associates. 1972. ISBN 0-910022-   23-23.

Wing, Ralph. **Just Do It: Time Management.** Pangaea Press. 1990. ISBN 0-671-72601-3.

Wilson, Howard. **Utilizing Time Effectively Through Better Management Processes.** Irvine, CA: Administrative Research Associates, Inc. 1973.

Winston, Stephanie. **Getting Organized: Storage.** Warner Books, 1981.

Yohn, Rick. **Finding Time.** Waco, TX: Word, Incorporated, 1986.

Young, Helen & Silvey, Billie. **Time Management for Christian Women.** Zondervan Publishing Co., 1990. ISBN 09-310-51851-2.

using time management

index

Notes

About the Smith Collins Company

THE SMITH COLLINS COMPANY offers speaking and consulting services for industry and government. Seminars and workshops are offered on a contractual basis in a variety of areas, including ethical decision making.

OTHER SMITH COLLINS TITLES of interest to readers of this book are *Tough-Minded Management of Problem Employees: Don't Be a Gutless Nice Guy?* by Gareth S. Gardiner ($10.95), *In Pursuit of Ethics: Tough Choices in the World of Work,* by O.C. Ferrell and Gareth S. Gardiner ($12.95) and *Winning The Hiring Game* by Edward C. Andler ($12.95).

Our 24-hour order fulfillment and
telemarketing number is
1-800-345-0096

Notes

Notes